IRISH
TROUT AND SALMON
FLIES

These, my design to lay before his eyes,
In due succession, and the killing flies;
The less approv'd I mean to set aside,
And name but those by long experience tried;
To imitate their structure with due care,
Beasts must contribute and the birds of air,
Cock, partridge, grouse, the fox and timid hare.
THOMAS ETTINGSALL

IRISH
TROUT AND SALMON
FLIES

E. J. MALONE

COCH-Y-BONDDU BOOKS

ISBN 0 9533648 01

First published in 1984 by Colin Smythe Ltd.
Revised second edition published in a limited edition in 1993 by
The Flyfisher's Classic Library.

This paperback edition published in 1998 by Coch-y-Bonddu Books.

Text © E. J. Malone 1984, 1993.
Typesetting, photographs and design © 1993 The Flyfisher's Classic Library.
Cover design by Jon Ward-Allen.
Flies tied for cover by Frankie McPhillips.

We would like to thank Justin Knowles of
The Flyfisher's Classic Library for his permission
to reprint this book from the F.C.L. edition of 1993.

Published and distibuted by

COCH-Y-BONDDU BOOKS
MACHYNLLETH, WALES, SY20 8DJ
TEL 01654 702837
FAX 01654 702857

Printed and bound in Great Britain by
Biddles Limited, Guildford and King's Lynn

To my Wife
Judy

without whose understanding, patience,
and encouragement, this book would not
have been written.

CONTENTS

ILLUSTRATIONS

Colour section between pages 128 and 129

FOREWORD

THIS MANUSCRIPT is available at a time when the Governments of Northern Ireland and Southern Ireland are becoming increasingly aware of the great tourist potential to be found in angling in Irish waters and there is much useful information presented on fishing in Ireland which the tourist will find invaluable.

The angling public in Northern Ireland owes a tremendous debt to 'Ted' as he is affectionately known to his friends, in that he was responsible for and inspired much of the development work in Northern Ireland over the past twenty-five years. The Honorary Life Memberships he has been accorded show the esteem in which he is held by the angling fraternity.

He is a former Director of the Ulster Angling Federation and an active member of the Downpatrick and District Anglers Association. The development work carried out by the latter Association emanated, to a considerable extent, from his enthusiasm. With others he helped to establish the very successful rearing ponds which that Association operated and has, in addition, acted as Consultant to, and organised the development work of, many of the smaller Angling Clubs in the Province.

The main part of his book is devoted to fly dressings and the collection of the material has been a monumental task, spread over half a life-time during which he has devoted many years to fly-tying and has been responsible for teaching this art to a considerable number of the present generation of Irish fly-tyers, and, in particular, was instrumental in introducing the craft to physically handicapped persons who have found fulfilment in this field.

The dressings cover a wide range of artificial flies which have been used by Irish anglers since fly-tying became firmly established in Ireland. This most comprehensive collection will become one of the great standard references for the fly-tyer and in future years will be found on the bookshelves of all those anglers who have deep interest in, not merely the catching of fish, but in the whole philosophy of angling.

Robert G. Weaver
Chief Executive,
Fisheries Conservancy Board for Northern Ireland

PREFACE

MAY I FORESTALL CRITICISM of the title *Irish Trout and Salmon Flies* by saying that a full title of 'Trout & Salmon Flies as used in Ireland' would be awkward and cumbersome, and while many universally known patterns are recorded, many Irish patterns appear in print for the first time. Very many patterns that are unknown outside Ireland join company with others that were recommended many years ago for Irish angling.

I have confined myself to traditional flies and have not included the modern lures, such as the Black Lure and other streamer type dressings, although they too are now being used successfully, particularly for rainbow trout.

I am indebted to the following and wish to express my sincere thanks to:–

The former Inland Fisheries Trust, Dublin, for their permission to use various maps.

The *Impartial Reporter*, Enniskillen, for their permission to reproduce Sam Anderson's poem.

The late Doctor B. Deeney, Strabane, and his friend Mr John Doherty, for patterns and dressings supplied.

Mr Robert Weaver OBE, Former Chief Executive, Northern Ireland Fisheries Conservancy Board.

Mrs Dorothy Biscombe, for her continuing patience in typing the much revised manuscript – her assistance has been invaluable.

My thanks also to David Burnett and many friends for all their advice and assistance.

This special limited edition has been revised and corrected, and has given me the opportunity to include a few dressings which had previously eluded me. In particular my thanks to Kevin McKenna of Glenageary Co. Dublin for the Costello Blue dressing, and to Donald McClearn of Dromore, Co. Down whose nickname 'The Dabbler' will always be associated with a new style of dressing. There is not a fly called 'The Dabbler', but a new style of old traditional Irish trout flies dressed 'Dabbler fashion', which has proved successful.

To the sportsman who has his doubts about visiting Ireland in her present unhappy and troubled state, I would assure him of a hundred thousand welcomes, giving but one word of advice – talk of fishing, horses, dogs or whiskey, but avoid like the plague any discourse on religion or politics.

E.J. Malone

PART I

PART I

CHAPTER ONE

IRISH FLIES AND FLY-MAKERS

FOR MANY YEARS Ireland has been a Mecca for anglers, some intent on fishing the famous salmon rivers of the West, others seeking the solitude of the innumerable brown trout lakes of the mountains, or, more recently, sampling the now established rainbow fisheries.

Despite the pressures of modern civilization – poaching, drainage, and agricultural pollution – the visiting sportsman will still find all the ingredients that continue to make Ireland the 'Land of a Hundred Thousand Welcomes': hospitable people, unspoiled countryside and a wealth of angling.

The famous salmon and sea-trout stretches are mainly hotel-controlled waters, but the brown and rainbow trout fisheries must surely provide some of the cheapest fishing in the world. Those who prefer the silence of the mountains and their brown trout lakes fare even better, in that, in the Irish Republic, they may be fished without a licence or permit – lakes full of small but hard-fighting trout that may not have seen an angler's fly in their life-time. I say *fly* advisedly, for there is nothing to equal a light rod and line in savouring the delight of hill-fishing. The larger rivers and lakes will require heavier tackle, especially at May-fly time when two- or three- pounders are common, and the heart-stopping experience of stalking trout of five or six pounds may be expected.

The early history of Irish fly-fishing and fly-making is unknown prior to 1790 and even this date can only be established by the colour plate of flies, circa 1789–1797, with tyings by Thomas Cummess, Corny Gorman and Hynes of Gort, reproduced in *An Angler's Entomology* by J.R. Harris. It may be assumed that fly-fishing was introduced to Ireland by the English officers who manned the early garrisons, and was further promoted by the sporting gentlemen of the leisured class at the invitation of the Irish landlords, but this new method certainly found favour with the sporting Irish, who progressed from attendant to ghillie, and from ghillie to fly-maker and brother angler.

There is little recorded of Irish interest prior to the *Angling*

Excursions of Gregory Greendrake Esq., commenced in 1824 as Part I and completed in 1832 (known as the fourth edition, but in fact the first edition containing Parts I,II and III) with an addition by Geoffrey Greydrake Esq.

This little book deals with angling excursions in the counties of Wicklow, Meath, Westmeath, Longford and Cavan, it also contains one important element which has been forgotten, or overlooked, by generations of anglers – Thomas Ettingsall's 'Rythmical Table' – a calendar of fly-selection, month by month, with a wealth of angling and fly-dressing lore in its verses. Possibly because it is in verse form many anglers do not take the trouble to read it closely, and their lives and skills are the poorer as a result.

Let us look, and take the time to appreciate, a few short extracts:

> *'The hare is wanted only for his ears*
> *The fur of which the greatest value bears –*
> *This, mixed with orange, yellow , black, or green,*
> *On lake, or river, better ne'er was seen,*
> *With mallard fork, and silver-ribbed or tipt,*
> *The wings from starling or from mallard stript.'*

What a wealth of information for the fly-dresser in six simple lines. True, earlier writers have recorded dressings with a pinch of added colour, but none has ever written in such a precise manner.

> *'How he may read upon the varying skies,*
> *From thence to judge the order of his flies;*
> *How he may place them on his trailing link,*
> *Know which should float, or which should partly sink.'*

Here Ettingsall expresses quite clearly the need for the angler to take note of weather conditions, not only to choose the likely fly, but also to decide the best position on his cast.

I have, on occasions, read the correspondence between readers of angling journals, and their arguments as to which of the earlier generations of anglers were aware of, and used, the floating fly, but there is no doubt about this positive statement by Ettingsall, and it must surely award him the honour, pre-dating Pulman and Ogden by some twenty years.

I cannot recall any earlier record of the partly-submerged fly, and wonder if Ettingsall had personal knowledge of the pupae, or the hatching nymph, or was it merely to imitate a drowned fly? Certainly Irish May-fly anglers have long used a pattern designed to be fished in the surface film – the straddle-bug, a versatile dressing which, depending upon the particular dressing, can imitate the hatching nymph, the drowned May-fly, or the spinner. His awareness also of the changing colour of a natural fly, is vividly illustrated in his description of the Mayfly:

> *'Emerging from the deep recesses of the lake,*
> *Up-shoots the pebble-cradled soft green-drake;*
> *No sooner does it meet the atmosphere,*
> *Than with its lustrous wings it courts the air.*
> *Its morn of life is gilt by its own ray,*
> *But soon its bright embroidery wears away*
> *To sickly green, deep buff, and last to grey.'*

Thomas Ettingsall, Dublin tackle-dealer, fly-maker, angler, and writer, must emerge from obscurity and take his rightful place as one of the great names in Irish angling history, and as the book in which his Table appears is now a valuable and scarce collectors' item, I have included the verses in full at the end of this chapter.

W.H. Maxwell's *Wild Sports of the West* was published in the same year, and these two volumes I have read over and over again and still enjoy the fascinating accounts of angling, hunting, potheen-making, and the lively accounts of life amongst a community which enjoyed sporting life to the full. There is little of interest to the fly-tyer, apart from praise for the hooks made by O'Shaughnessy of Limerick, and complaints regarding the poor quality of London-made hooks.

The Angler in Ireland by Wm. Bilton appeared in 1834, but in his introduction he admits that his visit to Ireland was primarily to study the country, the people and their habits, and his writing shows a greater interest in churches, work-houses and gentlemen's residences than it does in angling. He writes of the abundance of fish which he encounters during his short forays with an exaggerated enthusiasm. For example, when writing of the Connemara fishing he states:

I was astonished at the extraordinary number of fish I everywhere rose. They were all white trout, varying in weight from half a pound to one pound and a half. Of these small white trout I am confident that in less than six hours I rose nearer two thousand than one thousand! I must have hooked two or three hundred at the very least, and actually basketed seventy-six, which weighed between fifty and sixty pounds.

He states that the flies which proved most successful were the local tyings, a dark green, or blue, or black-bodied fly, with silver twist and guinea-fowl wing, as the stretcher, and a bright claret-bodied fly, with mixed and very showy wings, as the dropper.

With regard to salmon flies – 'The Limerick flies are almost always very gaudy and have silk bodies; whereas those tied in Dublin are usually of mohair and fur, and much more sober in their colours, although infinitely more showy than the Scotch salmon flies.' He praises the hooks and flies made by O'Shaughnessy, and one fly he found successful in all districts he describes as – 'a deep orange silk body, with broad gold tinsel, rich mixed wings and macaw horns.'

A letter by him, written later in life, and now in my possession, apologises for the title of the book which he says was the choice of Mr Bentley, the publisher, and 'not from any ambitious egotism claimed for myself'.

The Sportsman in Ireland by 'Cosmopolite' (Robert Allen) appeared in 1840, and while there are many chapters of angling expeditions, there is little to interest fly-makers, and the two volumes are again chiefly a history of the state of the country and its inhabitants. Both Bilton and Allen are appalled at the poverty they encountered, and write of the continual approach by groups of ragged people begging for alms. At that time most of the rural population existed in their miserable half-acre of land, rearing a pig (to pay the rent), and growing their staple food – the potato. Those who lived in small towns depended upon the shop-keeper and tradesmen for employment, but there was never enough to go round and provide food for all.

Hunger was a familiar companion, and when the potato crop failed in 1845, thousands died of starvation; despite all hopes, the following year proved no better, and the potato blight persisted until 1849. In these four years over one million people died, and another million emigrated, mainly to America. Thousands more died on their journey to the 'land of opportunity', from malnutrition, cholera, or were drowned when many of the unseaworthy vessels sank. Those who survived and obtained work, assisted their relatives at home, and in succeeding years the emigration of young people became a common occurrence along the West coast of Ireland. In my own life-time I recall many aged couples who were supported by regular monthly remittances from sons, or daughters, who had made a new life in America. Today's strong Irish-American links were forged through Ireland's worst calamity – 'The Famine'.

In 1842, William Blacker, whose ancestral home was Newry, County Down, but domiciled in London, wrote *The Art of Angling (and complete system of Fly-making and Dyeing of colours)*, a little book of 38 pages with a wealth of information. In his list of trout flies there is nothing that has not been earlier recorded, and the bodies are mainly composed of mohair. His instructions in fly-making are detailed, but it is his record of salmon flies that is important, in that many call for a body of pig's wool. Of the Shannon flies he writes, 'they are of different jointed bodies of pig-hair and dyed hackle, red, purple, orange, wine-purple, blue, claret, brown, black and dark green successively – wings very large and gaudy'. His 'receipts' for dyeing are given in Chapter 7.

A further edition of his book was published in 1843, but it is the final, revised and re-written edition of 1855 which is the most important, particularly those copies which contain the beautifully executed hand-coloured plates of flies and materials. His list of trout flies is comprehensive but I would pick out five which were probably original:

1. *The Ash Fox* – Body formed from the light dun coloured hair of the fox cub's neck or face. (Variation of earlier fox dressings.)

2. *The Blue Fox* – Body fur from fox cub's neck which has a darker blue shade.

3. *Caperer* – This is my earliest recollection of the sedge being so named.

4. *The Winged Larva* – Present day anglers take for granted the trout and salmon casts which they can purchase in single lengths, or spools of monofilament, hundreds of yards in a continuous length! Whilst there was 'drawngut' which could produce a trout cast, salmon casts were made up of number of links of silk worm gut, knotted together to form the cast. These links, approximately fifteen inches in length, were sold in bundles, or hanks, and were priced according to the quality and thickness (or strength) required. Blacker found that, on occasions, silk worm larval cases would still be clinging to some links, and he used these empty cases in two ways. First, in his small larva pattern he tied the larval case close to the already formed body of the fly but hanging separately from it. Here surely we have the first ever pattern simulating a fly just emerging from its nymphal case. Secondly, he used the larval case, tied on top of the hook shank to simulate the upturned body of a dun.

5. *India-Rubber Green Drake* – A dressing given includes the final covering of the body by a length of tapered India-rubber. Whether or not Blacker found this an improvement on his earlier instructions to use gold-beater's skin for this purpose is not clear.

This dressing is unique for two reasons: the first recording of the use of India-rubber to cover the body, and the first detached body dressing.

Blacker gives a lengthy list of salmon fly dressings, not only for Irish waters, but also for the English, Welsh, and Scottish fisheries. These are given in full detail, as are the instructions in forming the fly, but overall there appears to be little difference in the style of dressings, i.e., mainly all with mohair or pig's wool bodies with full gaudy wings. Parrot feathers were a regular material for this type of wing, and certainly parrot wing feathers have a luminosity absent in most other birds.

The Practice of Angling, particularly as regards Ireland, by O'Gorman (1845) provided two volumes of great all-round Irish interest, in that, not only are the angling chapters enjoyable, but you feel you are sharing his wanderings in the wildest parts of Ireland, with nothing else to do but fish. His fly-dressings are given in an old style which, although full in detail, require some concentration. The fishing is described as superb, as indeed the Shannon fishery must have been before the hydro-electric scheme destroyed it forever. His fly-dressings, and his description of hook-making are given later in this text but it would be important to record his usage of glass beads, red or black, to represent eyes on his Rush fly, Westmeath fly, Moth fly, and on his Caterpillar dressing. He advises on the stripping of one side of the blue jay barred feather, or alternatively of carefully cutting down the centre of the stem. In the use of mohair or pig's wool for bodies, he emphasises the need to tease out long and straggly. He writes of a new method of covering bodies with India-rubber but confesses his ignorance of the method. In his choice of hooks he accepts no other but Limerick, and states his recommendation of Ettingsall, 12 Merchants Quay, Dublin, 'he having adopted my plan of making hooks filed from bars of German steel. Other Dublin hook-makers use rounded wire, often bearded and carelessly pointed.' His 'plan' was of course the method he had observed in Limerick. He describes a newly-invented hook, with an eye in the shank, as a Scottish invention and totally unsuited for fly-tying or fishing. The fly-tyer supreme for the Shannon at this time was Cornelius (Corny) Gorman, who enjoyed a wide reputation for his skill, but unfortunately was over-fond of whiskey. He died of cholera during the famine years.

On a lighter note he gives a method of preventing cold on the stomach – 'In case of sudden cold or wet, if you have, or can procure a raw onion or two, eat it by all means; nothing will keep the cold more effectually from your stomach' – and in the matter of personal comforts he differs little from any today – have with you 'besides a supply of cigars, a well-covered, well-size dram bottle, tolerably full'.

'*The Erne, its Legends and its Fly-fishing*' (1851) by Rev. Henry Newland is a wonderful tale of the country and its customs, but its main object is to extol the glories of the River Erne, Co. Donegal, and its wonderful fishing before it too became the victim of a further hydro-electric scheme. We are taken on a fishing tour of the famous throws from Kathleen's Falls at Ballyshannon, to the upstream village of Belleek, sampling the delights of Cos na Wonna, the Sod Ditch, the Cursed throw, the Captain's throw, the Earl's throw, the Bank of Ireland, and many others. He writes that in a single season about one hundred tons of salmon were taken from this five-mile stretch of water. The salmon flies which form the frontispiece of his book, hand-coloured, are six in number, but only one, called The Parson, still survives the passage of time. The others, Killmany, Killmore, the Butterfly, Jack the Giant-killer, and Foul-weather Jack, would never have been heard of without his recording, nor would his title-page illustration of the Butterfly. 'The Butterfly is distinguished readily from all others by its under wings, which, being made of the tippet feather of the golden pheasant tied on whole, gives it the appearance of a copper-coloured butterfly.' There are six body colours given; Red, Yellow, Green, Blue, Fiery-brown and Claret. Kill-many, Kill-more and Jack the Giant-killer are variations of the Parson, tails golden pheasant crest and wings composed of six or eight golden pheasant crest feathers. Newland writes 'The whole of this tribe of flies is expensive, and that is their principal draw-back; but the material of which they are almost entirely composed, the crest of the golden pheasant, is rare and difficult to procure.'

From the fly-maker's point of view, the chapter on fly-tying gives a historical record of the provision made by a visiting angler to replenish his stock of flies and shows his scepticism of the skill of local dressers. This is somewhat surprising in that Michael Rogan would have been about seventeen years of age, and was believed to have achieved local fame for his fly-tying skill. But let us proceed to the four characters who form the fishing party for the purposes of Newland's tale – they are four, the Parson, the Squire, the Captain, and the Scholar, and as we return to the apartment where preparations are afoot, I quote:

The ponderous folio, which the Parson had so designated, was a cross between a book and a small portmanteau . . . The first leaf contained six rows of parchment pockets, twelve in each row; these were filled with every variety of hook, from A to C C C, of genuine Limerick manufacture, for the Parson had imported them himself; and from 1 to 12 of their London imitations, together with lip hooks, long-shanked hooks, midge hooks, and numerous other varieties; swivels for pike and trout litches, spare rings for the rods; all duly labelled on the outside. Then came full thirty shades of pig's wood, by far the best material for the rough-bodied flies of the larger sort, as it is the only substance, besides fur, which completely withstands the water.

The edges of all these pockets had been carefully painted in water-colours, so as to match and indicate their contents. Then came as many shades of floss silk, each wound on its separate card; then the tying-silks of every degree of fineness. The next pockets contained the furs – the water-rat, the brown spaniel, the chinchilli, the sable, the bear and the beaver. Then came the smaller feathers – the blue jay, the green-blue kingfisher, the yellow topping, the orange cock-of-the-rock, the crimson toucan, the copper-coloured golden pheasant, beautifully barred with black and hundreds of other varieties; then large flannel leaves, extending across the whole book, for the larger feathers – the wing and tail feathers of the argus, the tails of common and golden pheasants, the black-cock, the cock-of-the-wood, the grey mallard and barred teal, landrails and starlings wings, hackles natural and stained, of every dye the nature or art could devise. On the end leaves, the pockets were of good stout morocco leather and contained silkworm gut of every quality and hue, gimp for pike, a coil or brass wire, barbers silk, Chinese twist, a spare reel line or two, and a case of instruments consisting of pen-knives, scissors, files, pliers, and such-like, with a flat box for cobbler's wax, leaders, and India-rubber.

This formidable collection of materials would suggest a difficulty in obtaining flies and materials locally, and show a necessity to arrive at their angling venue fully prepared for any eventuality.

The four friends are portrayed in this chapter discussing flies, materials, etc., and from their conversation we learn that they favour flies tied in England, accusing the Dublin fly-makers of using inferior materials, and of careless workmanship. They are concerned at the high cost of flies – 1/6d to 2/6d each – a considerable sum, one hundred and thirty years ago, when the weekly wage for a boatman/attendant was 3/6d per week!

Their comparison of fly-lines shows a strong preference for those made in Limerick, '*oiled, elastic and strong*'. The Dublin fly-lines were cheap but clung to the rods in wet weather, whilst the London lines were so bad they were given to the local grocer to tie up his parcels!

A remarkable book, not only for its record of the once famous Erne fishery, but also for its historical tales of the people and their customs and the legends of the area.

The Book of the Salmon, by 'Ephemera' (1850) contains not only dressings for the Irish waters, but for all waters in the British Isles. There is an abundance of dressings but in the Irish section the influence of Blacker is apparent, and the author thanks him for his assistance in tying most of the patterns displayed on the hand-coloured plates, and for the supply of the North of Ireland dressings. In comparing the winging materials used, it could be assumed that the Irish dressings contain less materials, and were, therefore, less bulky and less complicated to tie in comparison to their Scottish counterparts. 'Ephemera' records also the use of seal's fur and jungle-cock feathers as necessary materials for a salmon fly.

In 1867 appeared *A Book on Angling* by Francis Francis and this mighty compendium of angling, methods, flies and dressings, is a treasure house of information. For the purpose of historical facts, however, I will confine myself mainly to the section on Ireland, and to extract his notes on Irish flies and fly-makers.

If you were to ask present-day fly-fishermen to quote you the names of famous Irish fly-makers of the 19th century, I would guess that, unhesitatingly, they would reply – 'Rogan' – but would have great difficulty in naming any others. Francis Francis can be regarded as the historian of famous fly-makers, and in his opening chapter grieves on the passing of 'Pat McKay – no better artificer ever turned a fly out of hand'. We learn of his appreciation of the dressings of Pat Hearns of Ballina, whose Erris patterns were mainly jointed bodies, with manes of vari-coloured mohair protruding from the body joints at the upper side of the body. These manes are shown clearly in the Owenmore portrayed in one of the hand-coloured plates contained in the book. He also credits Hearns with being the originator of the Thunder and Lightning. He gives dressings obtained from Nicholson of Galway, 'who ties for the Galway and Connemara districts'. Stephen Ellis, of Killaloe, provides the Shannon patterns and, Hackett and Haynes of Cork, those for the Blackwater.

Most of the patterns are intriguing even today, and although the majority of dressings are recorded by numbers, there is beginning to emerge a more positive approach to naming flies, to some degree now necessary because of the variations of established patterns, viz., Parson, Orange Parson, Green Parson, etc.

He gives credit to O'Doherty of Bushmills for 'handwork neat and masterly, and the best authority on flies for the North of Ireland', and makes a mention of the new hook 'with a forged eye', but although impressed, is reserved in his judgement of it. He expresses great concern at the growing number of anglers – 'fifty salmon fishers to one of twenty years ago' – and he deplores some unsporting attitudes to each other.

Amongst the few advertisements enclosed at the end of his book is one from –

> *William Haynes, Fishing Tackle Manufacturer, Cork,*
> *'firmness and neatness (of flies), and durability of colour'.*
>
> *Salmon Flies from 6/-d per dozen*
> *Lake & Sea-trout flies from 2/6d per dozen*
> *Brown Trout flies from 1/6d per dozen.*

Of all the 19th century fly-makers, however, the one best remembered is Michael Rogan, esteemed not only for his dyeing of colours, but for his perfection in dressing. It was not uncommon for some of the fly-makers of his time to separate a few strands of the finished wing with a needle, but Rogan believed that individual fibre movement was so important that he combed the whole wing to separate each fibre.

Donald Overfield in his *Famous Flies and their Originators* (1972), gives a very vivid picture of Rogan, but does him an injustice in questioning the long acknowledged claim that he was the originator of the Fiery Brown fly. I believe he reaches this conclusion on the basis that many brown-bodied flies had already been recorded – *dark brown, light brown, bright brown, etc., and including fiery-brown;* but Rogan's skill was in the achieving of a shade of fiery-brown which, for many years after no one could imitate. This, combined with his dyed fiery-brown hackles and mallard wing, created a fly which Rogan christened with its present name. To question his creation on the grounds that the body colour had been used earlier would be tantamount to questioning the dressing of the Black Pennell for the same reason.

One of the great names in the angling and fly-making world is that of Major J. P. Traherne, who wrote, in 1885, – 'The Fiery Brown – Michael Rogan's ingenious off-spring , will very likely retrieve the situation . . . in pool, stream, or rapid. Rogan's mode of dyeing the seal's fur and hackles is most successful, and far superior to all others for securing the fierce flame-like tint desired.'

W. Peard takes us on a fishing tour of Ireland in *A Year of Liberty* (1867), and this volume is as interesting to read today as it was over a century ago. He, too, acclaims Pat Hearns as the uncrowned king of fly-makers, and his lavish praise concludes 'honest Pat Hearns . . . long may you remain and prosper'. We learn of Ned Ray, an extremely competent fly-maker, and two favourite flies are given in detail.

He makes a special mention of a method he discovered in the Killarney district, that of using a hook a size larger than the body dimension called for, and recognising the benefit of it, had adopted the method for his future dressings. Was this the beginning of the 'low-water' style of dressing? It is interesting to note that the wages of boatmen/attendants on the West coast had now increased to 1/6d per day.

Everywhere on his travels he finds an abundance of fish, and expresses the view that, without having seen it for himself, he would have found difficulty in believing it possible.

1886 saw the publication of the most comprehensive guide for those who contemplated angling in Ireland – *How and Where to Fish in Ireland* by 'Hi-Regan' (John J. Dunne). It is now obvious that the previous numbered flies of 'Ephemera', Blacker, and Francis Francis have now reached the stage of being named, and indeed we learn of many named imports by visiting anglers. There is reference to a full winging of mohair in the Nora Criena, and the Silver Canary, and he describes the Blackwater flies as having manes of mohair, green, deep blue, and red.

As a May-fly angler he prefers a cork-bodied fly, it being more buoyant than Blacker's pattern with a covering of gold-beater's skin. When using Blacker's dressing he discarded the skin and applied clear varnish to the finished body. We learn also that he has made a new use of the India-rubber strip, by using it to rib his bodies 'drawn very tight'.

In salmon fishing he favoured Rogan's Fiery Brown, the Spade Guinea, and the Ponsonby, and makes us aware of one peculiarity in the dressing of Grouse patterns – 'without which these flies fail' – the turns of grouse hackles which come down under the shank should be cut off square, so that, when pressed down, they just touch the point of the hook. He particularly names Hearns in Ballina, and Devanney and Tierney in Foxford, as fly-makers 'who dress beautiful flies . . . Hearns and Devanney work professionally, but Tierney only for the sportsmen he likes.' Patterns for the Erne are Rogan's Parson, Black and Claret, Pink and Orange, and Golden Olive; he stresses that he prefers Rogan's patterns to all others, and for Lough Melvin – still a first class salmon and trout fishery – he recommends The Gill, The O'Donaghue, The Robber, and The Fiery Brown as the best flies for salmon, with Rogan's Favourite for the Bundrowes River which flows from the lake.

Grimble's *Salmon Rivers of Ireland* (1913), contains many dressings but its main value is as a record of earlier fisheries that have today drastically changed, and its many photographs are a lasting record of the once famous Erne and Shannon. A similar photographic record is contained in *Salmon and Trout Angling* by Joseph Adams (1923) and in *Fifty Years of Angling* (1938).

The Anglers' Guide to the Irish Fisheries also by Joseph Adams (1924), provides a wealth of information on the rivers in North-West Ireland, particularly the County Donegal rivers which had received little or no attention from earlier writers. In his Donegal travels he writes of the Clady, the Owenea, the Owentocker, the Lackagh, the Gweebara, and the Finn rivers, with a special chapter on the Rosses Fishery, Dungloe, with its one hundred lakes. An absorbing book which should be in every fly-tyer's library, as the dressings are clear and detailed. As an angling adventure it rivals Peard's *Year of Liberty* and certainly excels it in the material recorded for the fly-maker.

The year 1933 saw the publication of T.J. Hanna's *Fly-fishing in Ireland* at a time of great controversy over nymph-fishing. Maybe it was because of the determination of the chalk-stream purists to resist this form of angling that the book never received the praise it deserves. Certainly there is evidence that Hanna and Skues had correspondence on its merits, which may have persuaded Skues to incorporate rubber strips in some of his patterns. A. Courtney-Williams in his *Dictionary of Trout Flies* places Skues in a class of his own, but Hanna he likens to that great man, but says that the Irishman had more imagination, and quotes Hanna's view that the angler who fished a Butcher when the Blue Dun was on the water had missed the whole point of angling: 'Fly-fishing is a riddle and he had confessed his inability to read it'. His book deals with wet and dry fly-fishing but it is his chapters on nymph fishing, and nymph dressings, that are most remarkable. His illustrations on the dressing of the nymph are excellent and easily followed; most of them incorporated rubber strip cut from yellow balloon rubber for bodies. He used balloon rubber also for covering the bodies of Mayflies and Spent Gnats, for wing cases, and to cover the cork body of his Blue bottle dressing. In Northern Ireland he will probably be best remembered for one particular pattern, the Ballinderry Black, and for his freshwater shrimp dressings, called 'Shell-backs' because of their semi-transparent sheathing from head to tail. A similar pattern, using raffeine for the bodycase, has emerged recently under the name of the Chomper. Hanna experimented also with dry flies, and his Blue Wickham is characteristic of him in that he did not claim to have evolved a new pattern, but had simply placed an additional pale smoke-blue head hackle on the Wickham.

Tommy Hanna of Moneymore, County Londonderry, was a professional fly-maker extraordinary, angler, and gentleman: may we hope for a re-publication of his book, as a tribute to his memory? He would have asked for no greater memorial.

Another publication of note this century was *Fly-fishing for Trout and Salmon on the Faughan* by E.C. Heaney who wrote the angling notes for his local paper, *The Londonderry Standard*, under the pseudonym 'Black Spider'. This wonderful little book, published in 1947, was a collection of his articles written during the previous year. The river Faughan flows into Lough Foyle not far from the city of Derry and has a very high reputation for its runs of sea trout and salmon.

E.C. Heaney takes us on a guided tour from source to the sea, carefully analysing each pool and run, and his great love for the river is obvious. His main contributions to history, however, are his dressings, particularly for the sea trout and salmon, and he is meticulous in his insistence on good materials, positive colours, and a well-tied fly.

So many of the older craftsmen have now gone and today a great many anglers tie their own flies and receive a great deal of satisfaction from their hobby, but there are a few, and very few, young professional fly-tyers of this generation. One who deserves the highest praise has given me the greatest assistance in tying 'The Grey Thunder' for the special edition of this book.

If Francis Francis were alive today I believe he would agree that here was another angler/fly-tyer who could equal Rogan in producing salmon flies 'that glow like jewels', and to Frankie McPhillips of Tempo Village, County Fermanagh, I commend my brother anglers. He can be seen tying every day, in his shop at the Old Buttermarket, Enniskillen, Co. Fermanagh and will readily advise any caller, (or sell them a framed fully dressed Salmon Fly!).

Two other North of Ireland fly-makers must not be omitted, one well-known outside Ireland for his dressing of the Shrimp fly, Curry's Red Shrimp. Pat Curry of Coleraine fully deserved this recognition for a salmon fly dressing which continues to catch its full quota of fish. There is a possibility that it might be even more successful if modern dressings of it were winged in accordance with the original, – Jungle-cock wings tied on in arrow-head fashion, roofing the front portion of the body, and the tips extending slightly over the centre hackle. His favourite river was the mighty Bann which flows from Lough Neagh through his hometown of Coleraine, and he tied flies for this river, the

27

Lough Neagh rivers, and for the North-East coastal rivers, as well as fulfilling requests further afield. Like Rogan's, the late Pat Curry's name will carry on in angling history.

The second was not known outside his native province, but to very many anglers, particularly those who fished the May-fly on Lough Erne, the late Sam Anderson of Maralin, County Down, was the doyen of fly-tyers. His love of Lough Erne and County Fermanagh is expressed in the lines of his poem contained in the text of this manuscript. Sam did not suffer fools gladly, and if he took any dislike to you, then you went away empty-handed . A man with a tremendous store of fun and wit, he generously gave of his time to instruct handicapped persons in the art of the fly-maker. Whilst he could tie a fully dressed salmon fly wing with perfection – building up the individual left and right bundles, then turning them inward to each other and tying on the bulky wing with as much ease as two single strips of feather – he believed in the traditional Irish style for salmon fly winging. This comprises a small bunch of golden pheasant tippets as an underwing, which served three useful purposes, one – it provides an underlying colour, two – it gives full support to the main wings, and three – the point at which it is tied in provides a good foundation which enables the main wings to be held in position without any danger of moving, or twisting, sideways. The main wings are double strips of dark bronze mallard, and, where required, jungle-cock sides were added.

To Sam Anderson I personally owe a great deal for the friendship he gave to me and my wife, for the number of hours, and indeed months, he tolerated us in his fly-tying room until he was satisfied that our skills were reasonable. A stickler in observing the rules of angling, woe betide any companion who transgressed, or even worse, his loud vocal condemnation of any boat that dared defy the unwritten law disturbing the water in front of another drifting boat. He is sadly missed.

I will finish with one of the classic angling books of the present generation, T.C. Kingmill Moore's *A Man May Fish*; his love of fishing for sea trout in the West of Ireland shines out from every page, and his love for angling, from every line. His death a short time ago, at an advanced age, robbed us of the hope that we might one day see a companion volume in print – but perhaps that would have been an impossible task. I am delighted to say that there has been a new edition of his book issued, and would urge all who have not yet enjoyed the experience, to add it to their collection. I would hope that the younger generation of anglers will take my advice, and learn much of the sportsmanship, etiquette and observation that combine to make a man an angler. His astute knowledge of sea trout fishing, flies, colourings, and dressing methods will give endless pleasure in the years ahead.

When I commenced this pleasurable task of compiling a short sketch of Irish angling history, I had, in common with many lovers of angling, read the books I have described many, many times, and yet in this simple research I have uncovered a number of important points previously overlooked, and I hope I have revealed some new and important information as to the originator of the Hare's Ear dressing, the use of rubber strips in fly-dressing, the first recording of a detached body dressing and possibly others, but the most important fact uncovered was Ettingsall's knowledge and use of the floating fly in the early 1820s, almost twenty years before any other known angler.

I have no doubt that this, and the other facts brought to your notice will cause great comment, and possibly some argument, from many who pursue the peaceful art of angling.

However that may be I end, as I earlier promised, with a copy of Ettingsall's *Rythmical Table.*

RYTHMICAL TABLE

Of the principal flies for angling, and the season in which they should be used; communicated to the Editor by the ingenious MR. THOMAS ETTINGSALL, proprietor of the sporting tackle establishment, Wood-quay, Dublin.

> '*Of various flies that sport upon the wing,*
> *Their angling seasons, and the names I sing.*'
> PETRUS PISCATOR.

> *From age to age the rural pastimes grew,*
> *Necessity first urged, then pleasures new*
> *From wants supplied arose, and none more pure*
> *Than from the deep the finny tribe to lure:*
> *The high, the low, the simple, and the wise,*
> *Make it a study how a trout to rise.*
> *The pale mechanic hails his holiday,*
> *And to the gurgling streamlet speeds his way;*
> *There, in the lonely vale, to praise his God,*
> *And seek contentment from his pliant rod;*
> *At eve returning with his basket's store,*
> *And health renew'd for six days' labour more.*

O! where on earth is pleasure so secure
From every ill to rich as well as poor,
As is the angler's free from harmful guile?
To take one sporting trout he'll trudge a mile,
Marking the flies that sail adown the brook,
Then try to match them from his fishing book.
Philosophers, with rod, may rove the stream,
To contemplate on nature's wondrous frame;
The monarch may forsake his cares and throne,
And seek the silent vale and brook alone.
One tumbling trout will give him more delight,
Than all the state which dazzles others' sight;
The youth will cheerfully his books resign
For health and pleasure with his rod and line,
From Greek and Roman lore awhile to rest,
And learn to tie the fly will please the best,
How he may read upon the varying skies,
From thence to judge the order of his flies;
How he may place them on his trailing link,
Know which should float, or which should partly sink;
And next to know the feeding hours that trout
Are most accustomed to, or frisk about;
And of the varying winds to know the best,
And at what side the brook his game may rest —
These, my design to lay before his eyes,
In due succession, and the killing flies;
The less approv'd I mean to set aside,
And name but those by long experience tried;
To imitate their structure with due care,
Beasts must contribute and the birds of air,
Cock, partridge, grouse, the fox, and timid hare,
Materials he from winter's sports shall find,
To furnish well his hooks, and cheer his mind;
The wren, itself, tho' smallest of his sort,
Contributes largely to the angler's sport,
His tail, as hackle, in all winds that blow,
A trout will take, for if the river's low,
A spider wren, a muscle's beard the frame,
Or dark brown olive mohair, much the same,
Will draw the scaly epicure from where he lies,
Sick with luke-warm stream or gorg'd with flies,
The hackles of the cock, red, black, or grey,
Form flies to kill from March to Lady-day;
The fox's skin will many shades produce,
Nor is his beard, for forking, without use;
The grouse is good, but that of deepest black;
Gives the best hackles from his dusky back'
The hare is wanted only for it's ears,

The fur of which the greatest value bears —
This, mixed with orange, yellow, black, or green,
On lake or river better ne'er was seen,
With mallard fork, and silver ribb'd or tipt,
The wings from starling or from mallard stript;
The hare's-ear tipt most excellent you'll find,
It forms a fly the best of all it's kind;
The sooty black will constant sport produce,
And, in the evening late, comes into use,
And now proceed we to recount the flies
That in their months will cause a trout to rise.

FROM 14th FEBRUARY TO 14th MARCH

The vernal breezes, with boreal blast,
Now struggle 'till the latter is out-cast,
The finny tribe make to the shallow streams,
From deeper water, to recruit their frames;
The genial spring new insects now create,
Their food to seek and be for others meat,
Hare's-ear and claret mohair, partridge wing
Mix'd with the stare, the vernal breezes bring;
The dark dun-fox is seen to cut the air,
And great brown coghlan called by some brown bear.
A dark-red hackle, orange body tied,
Will surely win the river's scaly pride;
A jet-black hackle on the foot-link's tail
With purple body tipt can never fail —
And mark, all flies that are of sombre hue,
In early spring more certain sport will show,
And the brown coghlan near to Patrick's day
Like modern statesmen, turns his coat to Grey.

FROM 14th MARCH TO 14th APRIL

The sun's increasing heat, and southern gales,
Still more and more against the cold prevails,
And kindly showers, mixing with the brook,
Dispel the chill — then on the waters look,
There you will see the grave hare's-ear, unmixt,
Floating the stream, or on the eddies fixt;
The brown rail too; the light and dark blow-fox,
And hackles from the grey and tawny cocks —
They end in March, but, if the month's severe,
They never show 'till April's softer air;
But let this rule be held by every man,
For ever hold the black cock, red, and wren,
As never-failing food — the common bread
On which the tribe of trout are fed;

You may adorn them round about with gold,
May change their wings reverse to nature's mould,
But the red hackle shows still at the breast,
And so it is with black wren, and the rest.

FROM 14th APRIL TO 14th MAY

'Tis an old saying, and 'tis truth they say,
That April showers bring forth the flowers of May;
And every flower that blows gives fragrant birth
To many creatures scarce perceiv'd on earth:
Each shrub and plant possesses in its kind,
The various beings that sport upon the wind.
No sooner does the cowslip burst its bell,
Then the cream camel leaves its golden cell;
The clover which the cow delights to taste,
When pass'd again, brings forth a tribe in haste,
The lady-cow is seen to flaunt about,
As any lady at a ball or rout;
But very soon she changes her green suit
To dusky yellow — orange — and at last
Hare's-ear and yellow is its destin'd cast;
The gosling fox, too, seems its nearest kin —
But hark! the cuckoo's note — sweet May comes in —
The yellow meads with cowslips studded o'er,
Send forth their natives to the pebbl'd shore.
The yellow May-fly wings o'er brook and lake,
The harbinger of the stone-prison'd drake,
The black-bank spider and the sooty black,
The golden olives show a wat'ry track,
With golden, sooty, and the meally grey,
Are all good flies throughout the month of May.

FROM 14th MAY TO 14th JUNE

Now Nature is accouch'd — each shrub and tree
Receives to nurse, her latest progeny —
The order of the insect world's complete,
As the sun's course attains meridian height.
Emerging from the deep recesses of the lake,
Upshoots the pebble-cradled soft green-drake;
No sooner does it meet the atmosphere,
Than with its lustrous wings it courts the air.
Its morn of life is gilt by its own ray,
But soon its bright embroid'ry wears away
To sickly green, deep buff, and last to grey.
Next look along the silver-pebbled strand,
The stone-fly skips, from stone to stone, to land,
As if (like cats) it fear'd to wet its feet,

It pauses ere it leaps, although its leaps are fleet.
The sun's meridian brings another feast
To tempt the epicure — the over haste
Of the industrious ant, returning home,
A rising wind drifts them amidst the foam
That dies away, a summer show'r takes place,
That o'er, a mist of midges strikes your face.
The blue-blows with their copper legs are seen,
The sooty midge, white gnat, and gosling green;
The orange cow-dung, olive camels too,
All fork'd none tipt, but every shade and hue,
On a good feeding spot if you cast out,
Will scarcely fail to rise a sporting trout.

FROM 14th JUNE to 14th JULY

Before Aurora opes her curtains wide,
Speed from your bed unto the river's side;
The flowers' wing'd inmates are confined with dew,
Seize on their absence, 'twill be best for you —
For when Sol's chariot tops the hill of noon,
The trout looks to his rays and promised boon,
The dew dries up, the fragrant prisons ope,
And all the captives from their cells elope;
Each whispering breeze will waft across the brooks,
The food for which the trout expectant looks,
As drifted to his mouth he basking lies,
So gorged he shuns your shade and scorns your flies
And all your art will fail to make him rise.
Then, take the morning as I've said before,
Doubt not your basket will contain a store —
'Tis then you may deceive him while his eyes
Are fix'd with hungry look upon the skies;
The flies to use are these I recommend,
A jet-black hackle at your foot-link's end,
The body, deepest blue, the tail, tipt gold,
The wings, light stare, next in esteem I hold
The golden ash and tied with yellow silk,
The wing the creamy tint of stripping milk;
The next, a spider wren with yellow fur,
Must move a trout if he's inclined to stir.
A hawthorn black, then, as the morn grows old,
Which how to tie I cheerfully unfold;
Pen-feathers of the jay the wings compose,
Black ostrich herl along the tail lay close,
Until you reach where you design the breast,
Which must be formed of the green plover's crest;
Then o'er the ostrich herl be closely laid

The blackest horse-hair, and the fly is made;
Nor e'er forget mixed hackles, black and red,
The Soldier-fly with dark and ominous head,
As suit it's name it is a slaught'ring fly,
Struck by it's barb full many a trout shall die.
Now breakfast o'er as it approaches nine,
Get out your dapping link both long and fine,
Your horn stock'd with blue-fly, and the oak
Called the down-looker – rest yourself and poke
Beneath some tree that over-hangs the pool
Where no breeze ripples, there a glutton fool,
Some bully trout, that scorns a puny fly,
May take your dap and like a glutton die.

FROM 14th JULY TO 14th AUGUST

The golden harvest wags it's yellow beard,
The twittering quail and corn-creak are heard;
The Naids quit the shallow sun-dried brook,
The trout exhausted seeks some hiding nook –
Some little pool beneath a rock or bank,
That scarce conceals his back within the tank –
He there lies pent, nor dare he rove for food,
But watchful nature in her care is good;
The caterpillar up the sedges crawls,
In spite of all his legs, he reels, he falls
Into the mouth that's waiting for his fall,
A sweet repast at angry hunger's call.
Now as the yellow corn moves to and fro,
Like ocean's waves, the water reeds also
Bend to the breeze and from the nodding blade
The flag-fly tumbles and a prey is made –
But let us now direct the angler's eyes,
Unto the order of the day and flies,
The orange palmer and the yellow too,
The flag-fly orange, and the slatish blue,
The shaggy caterpillars red and black,
The light cream camel and the soldier-hack,
These in the morning on the pools he'll find
To please the trout, provided there is wind.
When evening comes and clouds move o'er the skies,
The trout are seen on every pool to rise,
Prepare the foot-line, fine, and round, and clear,
And let it these three smaller midges bear –
Scare-crow, magpie, ostrich or white gnat,
With hackles black and red, and you'll find that
With these you'll rise, unless the sun sets bright,
Then look to moths and hoppers for the night.

FROM 14th AUGUST TO 14th SEPTEMBER

Now Iris bends her bow across the hills,
And looks with pity on the low sunk rills,
Betimes she weeps, then smiles, then weeps again,
Until her intermitting tears o'erflow the plain,
And, sudden rushing down it's ravine bed,
Swells stream and river to the sedges' head,
And as it drives along it brings such food
As worms, and snails, and all the creeping brood:
To cast a fly is useless – bait is best,
Altho' pot-fishing sportsmen should detest:
Yet, rather than return with sullen brow,
The brandling worm or black-head I allow
Are very good – but if the water clears,
The rising trout the angler's spirit cheers –
Put up a black and orange tipt with gold,
An orange palmer, altho' growing old;
Hare's-ear and yellow, hackled at the breast –
They are the killing flies if rightly drest;
But if with these you cannot stir a trout,
A good black-hackle silver'd round about,
Placed on your foot-link's end, and next to that
The fly called yellow mixt with fur of rat;
The next a fiery brown with partridge breast,
Or red or golden wren, as you think best,
Will kill from mid-day 'till the sun goes down,
When 'tis full time you turn your face to town.
But hark! what noise is that? 'tis from a gun,
The twentieth 'August calls to other fun –
A grouse is down, the trout too hears the noise,
And close among the rocks he torpid lies;
There let him rest until his fright is o'er,
Then try him with another cast once more.

FROM 14th SEPTEMBER TO 14th OCTOBER

Now autumn's hollow blast howls o'er the plain,
The farmer from the field draws home his grain;
The whist'ling winds the sickly trees now shake,
Down drop their yellow leaves on stream and lake,
Like rafts, they carry down the living freight,
The last repast to trout of insect meat.
The insect world is passing swift away,
The fly brown in the morn, at eve turns grey.
Look to the month of March, and recollect
The order of the flies you should select,
Two more 'twere well you add unto that list,
The grouse and woodcock ribb'd with golden twist;

But if the atmosphere continues light,
Throughout October trout at flies will bite;
For as the fly grows scarcer ev'ry day,
The fish more easily become your prey.
Some flies there are, which yet we have to name,
Tho' claiming less of gen'ral rank and fame –
The blue macaw, with purple body tipt,
The hackle black, or red without being elipt –
Some call it Wellington, some Waterloo,
For at that noted time it comes to view.
The snipe and partridge too, afford good flies,
And the grey-plover's hackle we should prize.
Angling now o'er, lay by your rod for good,
In vain you'd tempt the trout with insect food;
For Nature now provides what best agrees
With their soft pregnant state as fit she sees;
And would you Nature's kindly care assist,
Make the fell poacher from his arts desist.
The nets and faggot-lights, and spears by night,
Which devastate the spawning streams, and blight
The angler's hopes, when vernal airs return,
O'er river, lake, and primrose-bordered burn;
When past is winter's stern and frigid reign,
And grove and mead fresh clad, smile forth again;
When Nature's harmonists rejoicing sing
Their praise of Him who gives renewing spring.

NOTE:–As the pleasure and success of the angler depend principally on the goodness and unfading property of the colours composing the dubbing, or bodies, of his flies, the Editor has pleasure in acquainting his readers, that MR ETTINGSALL, to whom he is indebted for the foregoing excellent metrical instructions, has discovered a mode of dyeing colours, which, for sparkling brilliancy and retention of their hues, has not yet been equalled.

TABLES OF FLIES
MOST EFFECTIVE FOR ANGLING ON THE LAKES
OF WESTMEATH,
THROUGHOUT THE YEAR.

From the middle of March to the 21st May.

Cowdungs, he and she – Red hackle and rail's wing.
Green Dagh-a-dhu – Black hackle and stair's wing.
Brown　　　do.　　　　　　　　　　　Same.

Hare's ear and black spaniel's fur – Black hackle and mallard's wing.
Hedge-hog – Red or cuckoo hackle.   Do.
Hare's-ear and yellow.   Do.   Do.
——————————————————ribbed.   Do.   Do.
Dark olives – Ribbed, red hackle – mallard's wing.
Dark brown, tipped with orange – gold thread – red hackle and mallard's wing.
Hare's ear plain – Red hackle or cuckoo – mallard's wing.
    Do. ribbed – Do.   Do.   Do.
Clarets, of different shades, particularly dark – Red hackle and mallard's wing.

From about the 21st May to about the 10th June, on the large Lakes, particularly Derevaragh.

The green drake, or May fly, through all its shades, the first a dark ashy hue, then yellow, and terminating in a high buff, at the close of the season

The grey drake may be fished at the same time, although the general opinion is , that it should come after the green.

The green drake is best composed, when the fur of the green or Marmozet monkey can be had, with that and white mohair – Cuckoo hackle, dyed yellow, and mallard's wing, or widgeon's feather, dyed yellow, the speckles imitating the natural drake.

Hare's ear and olive, ribbed – cuckoo hackle and mallard's wing.

Hare's ear and yellow

Hare's ear and claret – Red hackle and mallard's wing.

Dark brown olive, ribbed – orange tip – red hackle wing of the tail feather of a red kite. This is a very killing fly.

Hedge-hog – Red hackle, light cinnamon tip – mallard's wing. This fly generally fished as a tail, or stretcher, and very killing on hazy wet days.

Cinnamons, in all their shades; some tied with mallard's and others with kite's wing – red hackle.

Crottle Do. being the best description, and tied with the same wing and hackle. The crottle is a moss, or lichen, growing on the rocks, the best being found in the neighbourhood of Ballina, county Cavan. While all other dyes, yielding to the influence of sun and water, fade, nothing affects the crottle dye. It is worthy of consideration, whether silk dyers might not use this material with great advantage in their business.

Olives, in all their shades, plain and ribbed – the golden and other lighter shades – red hackle and mallard's wing. It is to be remarked, that the golden olive, ribbed, is a very killing fly.

Clarets, in all their shades.

Mulberry, in all its shades – black and red hackle occasionally – plain and ribbed – mallard's wing.

Soldier fly – black and red hackles, mixed – gold thread body – wing, cock pheasant's tail.

The spirit, or Harry long-legs – red and black hackle, mixed – light kite's wing.

Hare's ear and green – red hackle and mallard's wing.

All the foregoing flies to be tied on single and double B hooks.

From 10th of June, or thereabouts, the great Lakes are down until autumn, when the following flies will be found most effective:–

Claret, of all shades, plain and ribbed, but the dark best – red hackle and mallard's wing.

Crimson fly, plain or ribbed – red hackle and crimson-dyed do. – mallard's wing.

Fiery brown, plain and ribbed – red hackle and, occasionally, dyed claret hackle – mallard's wing.

Orange fly – red hackle and mallard's wing, tipped with gold thread and light yellow.

Do. ribbed with gold tinsel – breasted with wren's hackle – red kite's wing.

Rat's fur, mixed with orange, gold tip, orange cuckoo hackle – light mallard's wing.

CHAPTER TWO

THE BEGINNING

OVER SIXTY YEARS AGO I was invited to accompany a school friend and his father on a fishing trip the following week-end. I shall never forget the interminable period of waiting – the fear that they might change their plans haunted me even in my sleep! But this promised excursion and my excitement had really very little to do with fishing – what really mattered was that I was to be a passenger in a motor car.

How often had I sat in the driver's seat of taxi-cabs parked near my home and twisted and turned the wheel and made all the appropriate engine noises. Often I was cursed by an irate driver for my over-zealous horn blowing, made possible by squeezing an immense bulb attached to what I can only describe as a bugle. The 'honk, honk' was music to my ears but distraction to passers-by. And now I was to share the privilege of looking out with a lordly air on those who walked to their destinations.

The day dawned at last and the journey gave me so much pleasure that, when we arrived at the river, I could scarcely tear myself away from the gleaming monster left lonely on the road.

Two metal rods and reels were produced for our use. (I can still remember my friend proudly announcing that they cost 6d apiece at a store of international repute.) A green flax line, on to which was tied directly a bait hook to gut, and we were given a supply of worms with strict instructions not to stray, and not to fall into the stream.

We found a placid pool below some rippling water and stripping some line from our reels commenced to fish the worm. Very soon I was in difficulties for as the flax line absorbed water it became a tenacious thing which insisted on clinging tightly to the rod and made casting almost impossible. When I did make a reasonable throw then my bait would surely snag on an obstruction and at times mighty efforts were required to free it. In general we splashed and moved and galloped around on the bank so much that no self-respecting trout would have stayed within a mile.

Most of my day was spent sitting under a tree dreaming of the homeward journey and wondering whether or not we would have to use those monster head-lamps to pierce the night's gloom. It was a wonderful thought. Idly I had withdrawn my line from the water from time to time and renewed the worm which forever was being nibbled away by tiny 'spricks'. I decided that this was a great waste of time and energy and covered the hook with every worm I had left in my tin. I can still see that writhing mass as I cast it – this time well across the pool as the added bait had given ample weight to overcome the drag of the wet line.

The rod was propped on its forked twig and I sank back into my dreams. Moments later I was brought back to reality by the furious movements of my rod tip. I sprang to my feet, my heart beating wildly as I realised that a fish had found my worms. Shouting for help at the top of my voice I seized the rod and the vibrations I felt as I tightened the line turned my legs to jelly. My vision became so constricted as to see only the spot where my line entered the water and the heaving thing which must be below it. The hurried arrival of my friend and his father helped my morale but did not improve my vision, nor indeed my hearing, for I was deaf to the shouts of 'give him line', let him run'! Holding onto the reel handle like a drowning man, I refused to give an inch and when my relentless pressure brought the fish to the surface I saw an enormous length of body and a huge powerful tail. A short burst of speed did nothing to make me relinquish my hold and the rod tip thrashed the top of the water. And then the pain! The surface of the stream seemed to explode as the fish hurled himself into the air to escape from his peril. My rod bowed more violently and then suddenly yards of wet line were entangled around my head as the gut parted! Trembling in every limb I sank to the ground as with an exhausted excitement I had never before experienced I became aware of my surroundings and friends, and bowed my head as I listened to the things I should have done.

On the homeward journey the car paled into insignificance with my adventure of the day and I desired more than anything that I should have been able to carry that huge fish home. For weeks afterwards I dreamed of that fish and the pool in which it swam – even today as I write these words I can see clearly the thrashing rod tip and the green flax line stretching away into the depths. At that moment I became a fisherman, and indeed, it would have been surprising had I not, for few boys get the opportunity of being initiated by such close contact with a fresh run salmon.

From then on I had no thought of any other pastime and I eagerly ran errands to the local tackle shop where I could, by virtue of being inside, get a closer look at the wonders of rods, reels, and nets. Oh! what an Aladdin's Cave it was to my young eyes and, indeed, that Aladdin's Cave draws me still.

But back to earlier years and memories of the first thread-line reel made of a cheap hand drill, butchered, and surmounted by an upturned bicycle bell.

The numbers of breakages I had with that contraption! With today's monofilament I might have managed but with gut which had to be looked after like a baby, carefully moistened some time before use and dried out afterwards, plus the fraying that occurred no matter how careful one was, caused endless heart-aches. When I first became the possessor of a well-worn but serviceable reel, my joy was boundless. Spinning with a Devon minnow now became my favourite occupation and I learned the new thrill of fishing at much greater distances.

Fly-fishing was still a delight awaiting discovery although I had made attempts to cast a fly with a bait rod which was fairly pliable but the green flax line, once it became wet, clung like glue to the rod and made fly fishing almost impossible. The War years came and afterwards I found myself affluent enough to purchase a fly rod and a proper fly line. Once I had caught my first trout on the fly I was lost for life! The delicacy I now experienced convinced me that this was the only way to fully enjoy my love. First class equipment became a priority and slowly but surely a wonderful new world opened.

My fishing days became a study not only of the fish but of the insects on which they fed and of the times when they were more inclined to feed on one or more of these, possibly in preference to all others: again I was merely following in the footsteps of many generations of lovers of the gentle art.

It was only natural that I should begin to query some of the fly dressings obtained from my local dealer, and I soon realised that if my new found critical eye was to be put to the test than I would have to do something about it.

My early efforts at fly-tying produced such crude specimens that I almost gave up in despair, but suddenly I found one day that I had managed to produce a fairly presentable dressing. Thank goodness the fish also thought well of my efforts and encouraged me to continue. For a considerable number of years I tied a few flies which probably did no better than those purchased over the counter but on the other hand they did no worse.

Some years later I made the acquaintance of Mr S.I Anderson, Maralin, Co. Down, a man who had then been a trout fisherman for

over half a century. Sam was well known in Mid and West Ulster
angling circles, wrote for local papers under the pseudonym of 'Grey
Quill', and although a Civil Servant, carried on a thriving part-time
occupation as a professional fly-tyer. He had learned the art as a boy in
his beloved Co. Fermanagh and his stories of his tutor, W. P. Hackett,
were glowing and delightful. He remembered him as an awe-inspiring
but kindly countryman, the possessor of a huge spade beard, a ready
and sometimes caustic wit, coupled with a natural manly dignity. He
was the local fly-tyer for the 'gentry', but if he did not care for their
looks, or their manner, then they would go away empty-handed.

He described his thatched cottage with its badly sited chimney
which continually smoked, so that the door had to be left open to help
take away the 'stour' from the fire when it was freshly stoked, and
spoke of the time when the local minister came visiting and had to
bend down in an endeavour to see through the waist-high fog and call
'Can I come in?'. 'Well', replied the cottage owner, 'the place is not
smaller and if you haven't swelled too much since your last visit, I'm
sure you'll manage'. And very shortly afterwards, tutor, apprentice and
minister were sitting on low stools, below smoke level, watching the
feathered jewels come to life.

At the beginning, Sam put up with me but realising from my
persistence that I really desired the fullest knowledge, he went out of
his way to show and explain to me his own particular way of working
and his reasons for using various colour and feather combinations. It is
thanks to him that this volume is now being written, for over the next
ten years, until he died, I regularly was expected in his home, both by
himself and his no less kindly wife, who made me feel most welcome.
Her love for Sam was great and when at times she would scold him for
keeping me in his fly-tying den when supper was getting cold on the
table I can still hear his cheerful retort 'Anderson's getting his character
read!'.

Thankfully I was very glad that I had carefully noted his dressings,
for when he died, (tying Mayflies for his yearly trip to Lough Erne), he
left very few of them recorded. Although many of these are fairly
standard, I have included them because they are in general use and in
some instances may show some variation from the normal pattern. I
have indicated the Mayflies, nymphs, spent gnats and sedges which he
himself used.

Later it was my good fortune to be introduced to the fly-dresser
Percy Quinn, whose skill and artistry was a revelation. He had dressed
flies from boyhood and was in every sense a perfectionist. His minute

smuts dressed on size 20 hooks show, under a powerful magnifying glass, the meticulous tying, which one can see with the naked eye in his pristine salmon flies. Not only in tying was he a perfectionist but also in his choice of materials and build-up. His love of the art is perhaps best expressed by the fact that in a season he tied, and presented to his friends, as many as a thousand flies. Patterns he has given to me will never be fished but will, I hope, in later years, be a yard-stick for a future generation. His stock of hackles was stored in cellophane envelopes and bundles, in colours, like pound notes in a bank! Do not think for one moment that these hackles were shaken into the packet unceremoniously! Oh no! his hackles were placed flat in each packet by means of tweezers – how often he scolded me for my careless storage and handling. Only the finest of hackles were retained by him and the second-best discarded. Each bundle was named and/or numbered and to see a bundle of say, 100 envelopes of natural black cock, Andalusian, or Barred Rock, was a sight in itself.

Before leaving I must not forget to mention his colour charts of dyed hackles. Dating from the 1920s he had a record of all his dyeings and the results of over-dyeing with various colours. This was a wonderful index and following his example I have now started to keep a colour chart record of failures of my own – remembering his advice on the subject.

A County Donegal Otter Board

CHAPTER THREE

REFLECTIONS

FOR YEARS WE HAVE HAD CULTS of all descriptions, from those of the 'purists' who demand exact imitation, to those of the 'immoral' who use nymphs made almost completely from wire.

The champions of each method have boldly proclaimed their reasons for such usage and few have escaped the castigation, or the praise, of their more learned, and also their more ignorant brethren.

Whilst all anglers avidly devour articles and books on fishing, the more experienced angler occasionally smiles, laughs, or scowls at dogmatic views expressed in them. And then one wonders is this really a laughing matter? What of the growing numbers of young anglers and novices who, hungry for advice, tend to accept the written word as being gospel truth. I have often been tempted to reply somewhat forcefully but did not and so must take part of the blame for not offering an antidote.

Having made that point I must clearly state that any views expressed in this volume are simply my personal opinions, some formed by associations with the older generation of fly-tyers and anglers, and the remainder, through sixty years of relaxed devotion to one of the most pleasant and gentle forms of recreation known to mankind.

Did I say gentle? What about the days spent pitching and tossing in a cockleshell of a boat when a sudden wind brought an almost impossible wave, and the blistered hands from rowing the mile that seemed like twenty in such conditions?

Sitting now in the comfort of my own hearth such an adventure was but one of the many thrilling episodes in half a life-time!

Think of the many, many pleasant waves which proclaimed the perfect fishing day, or the right height of water when the river had been low for weeks. Think of the glorious sight of a score of salmon in mid-air at the same moment in an ecstatic bid to conquer the obstacle that barred their instinctive journey from the sea.

What of the day when after only one drift, my companion glanced to the bottom of the boat and said 'We don't want any more?', not a statement but a question as she looked upon the five bars of molten glory which later proved to weight 15$^{1}/4$ Ibs. Or the days when the fishing was impossible and the hours that were spent watching the dipper as it walked into the rapids, or the wild ducks so tame that they fed industriously within feet of us. How pleasant to have all the time in the world to watch the spider spin her web or to lose oneself in the beauty of the lough and its sentinel mountains.

All these memories, and hundreds more, form part of the joys of angling, for above all it brings that wonderful peace of mind which is there, so freely available to all, rich or poor. There at the water-side you will find them all – statesmen, Church dignitaries, the professions and trades, tinkers, tailors, soldiers, sailors – all joined for a brief moment as one happy family.

Like most anglers, my early years were concerned only with the catching of trout and salmon and the methods varied from the humble worm to the glistening dry fly. The last forty years have been more leisurely, however, and I found myself absorbed in the wonderful study of how, when and why.

In this volume I have done little to explain how to tie flies simply because that is not my purpose and many authors have written and illustrated far more vividly than I could, how the fly is formed. Those who have, in my opinion, made a tremendous contribution in this respect I have noted in the list of recommended books, and whilst it would be impossible for me to put them in their order of precedence I know that the reference will be of importance to the amateur fly-dresser.

In recent times I have read the writings of two present day fly-dressers, in which both writers expounded their dogma regarding shape, colours, size and the mobility of flies and lures.

The first holds the view that in fly-fishing the most important thing is the movement given to the fly by the angler, enhanced by mobility of wings and hackle, yet within a breath of time he gives a 'killing' pattern of a salmon fly which is almost shorn of its pliable hackles – and then varnished! Not even in my wildest dreams can I imagine a shaving brush hackle stiffened with varnish being pliable and free moving!

Next he says size is largely to do with the depth at which a fly swims – and leaves us suspended in mid-water!

Third in order of merit he places colour and then discards it in one sentence as being the means by which 'light and shade affect the fly in the salmon's vision'. What a wonderful discovery that after all these years of theory and argument, the matter can be shrugged aside as being of little importance. Does he mean that he accepts the theory that fish see only in varying shades of muted intensity, i.e. that colours to them are simply greys and browns and blacks?

If we accept intensity rather than colour vision as the important factor then I wonder why two different colours with the same intensity produce entirely different results, even when fished on the same cast? Could colour be the determining factor after all, and not shade intensity? I do not know, and neither does anyone else, but my personal belief is that fish see 'colour' to some degree, and would point out the well-known liking amongst all fish for reddish tints. This applies to perch and pike as well as to trout and salmon, and here in Ireland this is taken advantage of in the most popular fly known – the Mallard and Claret.

The second writer believed that a solidly built lure attracted fish if it conveyed a reasonable impression of being a small fish. He conceded that colour and sparkle helped this illusion but life was given by the angler and this was all that was required. He did not believe that added life or mobility given by hackle feathers were of any importance! Indeed, he stated that such would create an artificiality to the lure in that fish have neither wings nor hackle – that fish do not 'flap' their fins – and that all the mobility necessary is given by the solid body.

Well, to be fair, many fish have been caught on solid bodied lures with very little inherent mobility but I would suggest that this generally happens in conditions of strict competition with other fish when it must necessarily be quick and thus have less time to examine its prey. Although I concede that there is something in what the writer says, could it not be that colour and sparkle are the real attractions? If this is so, then would it not be acceptable to believe that movement imparted by mobile feathers would help to strengthen the illusion of life? How often have I fished a lure right up to the side of the boat and watched a trout following behind – would it have simply followed a tiny live fish and then turned away. There is no doubt in my mind as to what the fate of the tiny fish, sparkling with points of light and colour combined with a sinuosity of movement, would have been.

It is my firm belief that colour, translucency, size and mobility combined with the skill of the fisherman in the presentation, or movement, of the fly are all equally important to success. Sparkling, translucent colour can be obtained by first-class cock hackles, or as in the majority of Irish flies, by the addition of dubbing, especially seal's fur, dressed in a rough fashion which allows individual fibres to transmit light and colour.

Although I personally believe in dressing my own wet flies for trout with henny-cock or hen hackles, I would not be too dogmatic. Occasionally it is necessary, say when fishing fast streams, to tie in two hackles – the inside one next to the body being stiff cock to give sparkle and to support the softer hen hackle tied in front. Thus the soft mobile fibres can move freely but the stiff hackle prevents the body from being covered. In such cases only the minimum amount of hackle turns are used and certainly in trout flies I believe this should not exceed a total of three turns, i.e. one turn cock and two turns of hen or alternatively not more than three turns of henny-cock.

In general appearance, Irish flies tend to look more full-bodied and shaggy compared with their English counterparts, but the shaggy body of seal's fur is deliberately created, not by a mass of fur, but by picking out the fibres after it is tied in. The general size of wet fly used is also large and I would imagine that more size eights (old size) are sold for lough fishing than any other. I would assess the Irish angler's wet fly box to contain the following sizes:–

Size 8	35%
Size 10	25%
Size 12	25%
'All others'	15%

'All others', in the case of lough fishers, may include a proportion of size sixes – quite a substantial iron! Nevertheless, the smaller sizes are used for patterns of pupae and midge.

Dry fly sizes are generally similar to those of Great Britain but in many patterns may be up to two sizes larger!

This book contains a great many lake patterns which do not have a natural living counterpart but, nevertheless, they do have something which continues to succeed in varying conditions.

Where two or more dressings are given for the same fly, I have ranked them in what I believe to be their proper order of merit.

Those who disagree with my choice are at liberty to promote or demote as they think fit.

CHAPTER FOUR

HOOKS

IRELAND HAS LEFT HER NAME firmly engraved on the world of hook-making by such names as Limerick, Dublin and O'Shaughnessy, but how many anglers today know the meaning behind the names? Let us look back to 1834 and *The Angler in Ireland* which describes the Limerick style of hook-making.

Every brother angler will at once guess that one of my first visits (in Limerick) was to O'Shaughnessy's shop. Its present occupier, I found, is a watch-maker, and no relation whatever to the old man who first made the Limerick hooks so deservedly famous. He is, however, as good fisherman, and keeps good tackle. He also employs a clever young man, who both makes hooks after the original pattern, and ties flies remarkably well.

After laying in a considerable stock of fishing implements and lore at this shop, I paid a visit to a person of the name of Glover, who now employs the identical O'Shaughnessy mentioned by Sir H. Davy; he is son to the old man above-mentioned, who has been dead fourteen or fifteen years. I had a long conversation with him, which was interesting, in as much as he may be considered a sort of piscatory character; but I was grieved to find that, with his father's skill in his business, he has also inherited the paternal fondness for whisky. He is, in fact, the best, or rather the worst, living example of a confirmed dram-drinker that I ever saw. Mind and memory seem almost entirely gone; although there are, at times, gleams of better things, which hint how far he has fallen below the character he ought to have maintained; indeed, as Mrs Glover said 'If he had only common prudence, he might have kept his carriage!' He mixes the colours &c. extremely well, and his hooks may be depended on for strength; but he does not, in general, now tie so neatly as he used. However, I frequently in my tour found his salmon flies much the most killing.

The Limerick flies are almost always very gaudy, and have silk bodies; whereas those tied in Dublin are usually of mohair or fur, and much more sober in their colours, though still infinitely more showy than the Scotch salmon flies.

At both shops I was shown the hooks in all their several stages of manufacture. They are at first small straight bars of the very best iron, and of the requisite length, with a rude kind of head at one end. They are first barbed, sharpened, and rounded by the file, and then bent with circular pincers to the proper degree of curvature: they are next steeled by the application of fire and charcoal, and then, after a little final polishing, are placed on a smoothing iron, heated to 580 degrees of Fahrenheit, which gives them the blue colour and temper; and are, lastly, immersed in grease, to prevent them from rust. In point of quality, I think there is little difference between them, and Kelly's of Dublin: but, in consequence of their forming a somewhat larger curve, and projecting more than his, they are more certain to strike the fish; while, for the same reason, they do not admit of equally neat tying. They are all of them, however, incomparably superior to the best London hooks, and are the only ones to be depended on for large fish; but they are dear.

It is interesting that at that time the price of ordinary Limerick hooks was around one shilling per dozen, but O'Shaughnessy's hooks were sold for as high as six shillings per dozen.

Let us move on another eleven years to 1845 and read O'Gorman's description of tempering hooks –

'As it is probable that many occasions may occur on which a knowledge of this very necessary process may be required, and as I do not judge it right to give any directions for making either them or rods, lest I should be thought to interfere with the tradesmen, I give the following directions which may be found of service in cases of emergency. If some of a parcel are soft, as will often happen in the temper, or that the points may have been broken, or that you are somewhere where you cannot procure any, or that you do not like the shape of those you have; in these latter cases, first soften the hooks, for doing which you will find directions by-and-bye, then sharpen the points which must be done with a very fine cut small, half-round file; have a cast iron small square ladle with a long handle, into which put your hooks; after which put them into a clear turf fire, that produces white ashes, and not yellow, and when you find that the hooks assume a blood-red appearance, dip them instantly into a bowl filled with cold water, and when you take them out of the ladle, try with a knife whether it scrapes them; and be careful how you handle them, for, if hard, they are as brittle as glass. If they scrape, they are not hard enough, and you must repeat the process until they are. You must next have a flat, even board, on which to put some sea sand, or pounded brick bat, and rub each hook carefully until it assumes a bright appearance, by doing which you will soon perceive the blue appearance in the temper. You must also have a long-handled square of iron, which should be at the large end about four inches in length, and three in breadth, and about half an inch in thickness: this you are to put into the fire, where it is to remain until sufficiently, but not too hot. This you will be able to judge of, by rubbing a bit of tallow to it, which, if it lights, it is too hot, except for very large hooks. You then put on the iron as many hooks as you can examine at a time, and when they turn to a light blue or sanguine colour, tip them with the tallow, or a small bit of candle, and as soon as it dries on the hooks throw them off, and let them cool before you try them. The flat part of the iron should be perfectly smooth, in this way if the iron cools too much, it can be easily re-heated, and before the hooks are put on, should always be rubbed clean to take off the ashes.

'It is unnecessary to state to an angler the different degrees of heat required for large or small hooks, or the absolute necessity of trying every hook before a fly is tied on it, which can best be done by sticking the point of a hook into a deal board or table, (but not in a mahogany or oak one, which are too hard timbers for the purpose, and may break the points of even good hooks). You will, by this means, judge whether sufficient permanence and elasticity has been attained.

The Limerick hook makers use the best German steel, and the hooks are filed from bars. The Dublin hooks are formed from wire, are often bearded and pointed carelessly, and rounded in the shank – a great inconvenience to fly-tiers.

'If you wish to change the shape of your hook, first put them into the ladle above described, and insert it into a clear turf fire until they assume a blood-red colour, take them up, and let them cool; they are then quite soft, you can shape them with plyers to any form you wish; after which again put them into the fire, and obey the directions given above.'

What a different story today when hooks are so easily obtainable in all sizes, shapes, and quality. Size is determined by the type and size of fish sought, the particular water being fished, or the condition of the water. Shape is largely a matter of personal preference – some anglers swear by Limerick bend hooks, other disagree and are only happy with Wide Gape, or Round Bend hooks. Here the answer is to use the type which gives you confidence and allows you to concentrate on your fishing.

Quality however, cannot be over-stressed and it is false economy to purchase cheap or inferior grade hooks which are invariably over–, or under–, tempered, and which generally commence rusting after use. What a waste it is to spend time and patience tying a selection of flies only to find later that they have rusted – and not only are they now suspect as regard strength, but the rust will also have stained the coloured silks of the body transforming your work into 'love's labour lost'!

Use only top quality hooks and whilst you may occasionally be unlucky enough to find a batch which is wrongly tempered, the manufacturer or tackle dealer will certainly replace any found faulty. Personally, I always use forged round bend hooks for my larger trout flies and wide gape for the smaller sizes. For pupae dressings I now use

Yorkshire Sedge hooks and for nymph / emerger hooks I find the longshank emerger / caddis hooks made by Partridge of Redditch superlative – they also manufacture the Yorkshire Sedge hook and the wide-gape Captain Hamilton.

There is a tendency today to dress dry flies on down-eyed hooks but I feel that this can lead to clumsy dressings.

Dry flies are generally imitating an insect which is fragile and delicate, so how then can you give of your best if the hook foundation is heavy and cumbersome?

The special up-eyed fine wire hooks assist the dresser and are no more difficult to use. A simple tip for those who find that the up-eye is difficult to finish off neatly is to reverse the hook in the vice before you commence your final whip finish. The up-eye is then in fact similar to a 'down-eye' and presents no problem.

The following four pages of hooks have been reproduced full size to enable the reader to examine the differences in shank length, gape, etc.

They form a small part of the many hooks made by Partridge of Redditch and from my own personal use I can give them the highest praise and recommendation.

WET FLY HOOKS

CAPTAIN HAMILTON SERIES

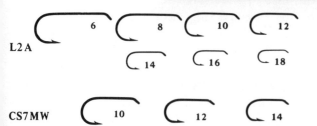

CAPTAIN HAMILTON WET FLY HOOK

The ideal hook for all types of wet flies (and nymphs). Forged Hamilton bend. Bronze finish. (Also in Grey Shadow finish as GRS2A - 10, 12, 14, 16)

CAPTAIN HAMILTON INTERNATIONAL MIDDLEWEIGHT HOOKS

An extra wide gape version of The Captain Hamilton hooks for all types of trout wet flies. Black finish.

TRADITIONAL WET FLY HOOKS

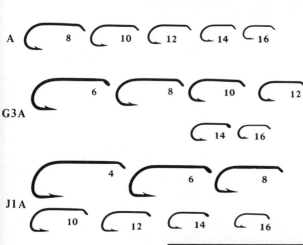

ALBERT PARTRIDGE WIDE GAPE DOWN EYE HOOKS

For wet flies (and shorter nymph patterns). Offset bend. Bronze finish.

SPROAT FORGED WET FLY HOOKS

Traditional strong wet fly (and nymph) hooks. Forged bend. Bronze finish.

PARTRIDGE LIMERICK WET FLY HOOKS

The traditional wet fly hooks with a limerick bend. Bronze finish.

SPECIAL WET FLY HOOKS

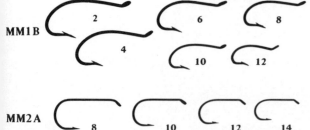

McHAFFIE MASTERS WET FLY HOOK

For traditional wet trout flies. Special Dublin point and up eye. Black finish.

BOB CHURCH GOLDHEAD HOOKS

Wide gape wet fly hooks which can take the gold (or silver) beads which are now popular as the heads on many wet fly patterns. Forged bend. Bronze finish.

GREY SHADOW WET FLY HOOKS

GREY SHADOW CAPTAIN HAMILTON WET FLY HOOKS

The L2A Captain Hamilton wet fly hooks but with a Grey Shadow finish.

LONG SHANK NYMPH HOOKS

PARTRIDGE STRAIGHT EYE STREAMER HOOKS

These were originally designed for attractor flies but have been used by many tyers in the smaller sizes for nymph patterns. Straight eye. Bronze finish.

HOOPER SERIES

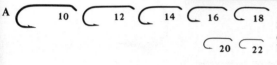

HOOPER L/S 4X FINE DRY FLY HOOKS

Slightly longer shank dry fly hooks. (Also excellent for buzzers.) Forged "Redditch" bend for extra strength. Bronze finish.

RITZ DRY FLY HOOKS

These offset bend dry fly hooks have always been popular in France. They hook very well. 4 X fine wire and forged. Bronze finish.

HOOPER 1X SHORT 4X FINE DRY FLY HOOKS

Shorter shank dry fly hooks. Forged "Redditch" bend. Bronze finish.

STRONGHOLD WET FLY HOOKS

STRONGHOLD WET FLY HOOKS

Made out of heavy wire. For very strong wet flies (and nymphs). Grey Shadow finish. (size 10 is within the limit for International competitions).

STRONGHOLD NYMPH HOOKS

STRONGHOLD NYMPH HOOKS

For most nymph patterns. Grey Shadow finish. (Size 12 is within the limit for International competitions).

STRONGHOLD LONG SHANK HOOKS

For longer flies - streamer and long nymphs. Grey Shadow finish. (Size 14 is within the limit for International competitions).

GREY SHADOW NYMPH HOOKS

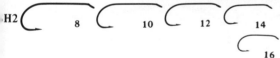

JARDINE LIVING NYMPH HOOKS

A graceful and effective hook for all curved body imitations. Turned up eye. Grey Shadow finish.

GREY SHADOW EMERGER/NYMPH HOOKS

The K12ST long shank Sedge/Caddis hooks with a Grey Shadow finish.

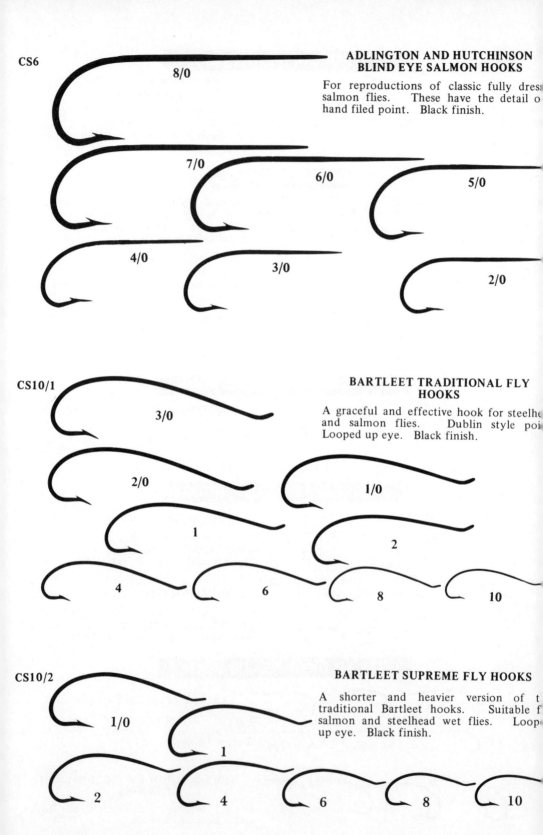

CS6

8/0

7/0

6/0

5/0

4/0

3/0

2/0

ADLINGTON AND HUTCHINSON BLIND EYE SALMON HOOKS

For reproductions of classic fully dres[ ]salmon flies. These have the detail o[ ]hand filed point. Black finish.

CS10/1

3/0

2/0

1/0

1

2

4

6

8

10

BARTLEET TRADITIONAL FLY HOOKS

A graceful and effective hook for steelh[ ]and salmon flies. Dublin style poi[ ]Looped up eye. Black finish.

CS10/2

1/0

1

2

4

6

8

10

BARTLEET SUPREME FLY HOOKS

A shorter and heavier version of t[ ]traditional Bartleet hooks. Suitable f[ ]salmon and steelhead wet flies. Loop[ ]up eye. Black finish.

P

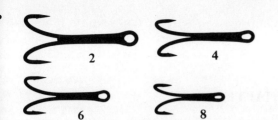

2

4

6

8

PARTRIDGE DOUBLE SALMON HOOKS

Double version of the single salmon irons. For heavyweight wet flies for salmon and steelhead. Up eye. Black finish.

10

12

CS12

2

A.E.M. 6X LONG SHANK SALMON FLY TREBLE HOOKS

An extra long shank treble hook for salmon flies. (Longer than X2B). Up eye. Black finish.

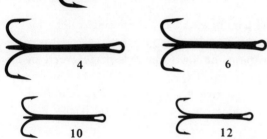

4

6

8

10

12

PARTRIDGE
OF
REDDITCH

CHAPTER FIVE

MATERIALS

FEATHERS, FURS, SILKS, AND TINSELS are materials which are easily identified, but the hackle feathers do cause difficulty until the colour terms become familiar.

Many amateur fly-dressers tend to interpret the dressings calling for a red hackle as being a dyed red hackle but, of course, the red is a natural red preferably from the game fowl. The reds range widely in colour and generally have a guiding prefix, e.g. blood, dark, medium or light. Game fowl are now so scarce that it is generally the bantam fowl which provides the natural colours, but a good Rhode Island Red should not be overlooked.

Care is also required with the colour blue, ranging from an iron blue to the soft misty blue-grey. With today's farming methods the old breeds of fowl are almost non-existent and, therefore, dyeing must be resorted to. With careful planning and dyeing even honey dun can be obtained.

Dun is a name given to the natural fly in its winged state, but dun when applied to hackles denotes a natural feather ranging in colour from chocolate brown to the lightest honey, and from dark slate to the lightest blue-grey, but all with a common factor in that they contain a smokey blue-grey centre which widens and strengthens in the lighter shades. This grey is very obvious at the butt and on the back of the hackles.

The present method of keeping poultry in confined pens – usually selected breeds for egg-laying or table birds – does not allow cross breeding and if we hope to find local supplies than one must seek out the smallholder who keeps a number of mixed fowl for domestic purposes, and, with a bit of luck, the unusual cape is sometimes seen. Such a cape, whether natural or freak, should be booked at once and the bird killed when the plumage is perfect. At this stage the old Irish dressers insisted on one thing – immediately the bird was killed the hackles had to be removed without wasting a second! They held the opinion that the feathers retained a more life-like sparkle if this was done. We have today a few people who rear specialised breeds for their

56

own use and these birds are not killed but the hackles are cut off as required. The only advice I can give to those who cannot keep or procure birds is to buy the best you can afford in cock hackles for dry-flies and to use commercial cock capes which are generally softish, (henny cock), for wet flies.

Use natural colours where you can, and dyed imitations only when no other avenue is open to you. Many other birds provide hackles for special dressings – the grouse, partridge, french partridge, snipe, starling and the jay are classic examples – and their wing, tail, and body feathers are an important part of the fly-dresser's store.

Furs have become more popular today with the introduction of hair wing flies, but great care must be taken to ensure that the resultant wing is light and mobile.

In Irish flies, seal's fur takes precedence over all for bodies, and it should be ensured that the fur has plenty of loose hairs mixed with the natural wool. The woolly addition greatly assists in holding these fine hairs and by its own tangled mass enables us to spin the dubbing on to the thread more easily. If you use undyed seal's fur in a dressing make sure that it has been thoroughly washed to remove the oily dirt which generally overshadows its brilliance. Where a full length fur body is called for, tie it on in a cigar or carrot shape and if it is too bushy in places pluck the surplus away before ribbing. After ribbing the dubbing needle is used to carefully pull out and gently break fibres so that they form a slight fuzz above the ribbing. This is most important in all seal's fur dressings as it is this fuzz which imparts a translucent aura to the body when viewed against the light. With other more opaque furs the pricked out fibres give a slight sinuosity and act in the manner of hackle fibres.

Floss silk still holds pride of place for smooth-bodied colours although many other materials are in my cabinet. In my opinion the hard outline of such bodies is their greatest disadvantage and a simple tip passed to me by a keen fly-tyer of many years experience is to slightly roughen the body before ribbing. This is done by means of a small fine wire brush which raises a very slight fuzz and gives the body the necessary translucent edge colour. Do not overdo the brushing or the fibres will break up.

New man-made fibres have brought a breath of fresh air to materials, but please be careful not to replace an old material with a new one just because it 'looks better'. It may not do so to the fish and you will be well advised to try both old and new equally before finally making any decisions.

Some nylon and terylene threads react violently to the aniline dyes so do not be surprised if the finished colour of these materials is of an entirely different shade to the dye! Some of these accidental colours are well worth experimenting with but be careful to take a note of which material was used and with what dye shade. I have occasionally relied on memory and found it faulty, causing me hours of further dye experiments.

Herls are single fibres obtained from ostrich feathers, peacock, turkey, condor and, indeed, from almost every bird. They are generally fibres from the wing feathers or tail feathers or, occasionally, as in the heron or swan, from long body feathers. They can be dyed in a similar fashion to the hackles. They are used either by winding around the hook shank so that the 'flues' (hairy appendages) stand up from the fibre, or they are, in some instances, used in multiple and in this instance are generally twisted around each other after the tip is tied and then wound toward the eye of the hook.

In the case of quill-bodied flies the flue is stripped off by drawing the herl between the thumb and forefinger at the same time using the thumb nail as a scraper. It may assist flue removal if the strand is moistened.

As it is now almost impossible to obtain seal's fur, fly-dressers have had to seek alternative body materials. Of these there is one outstanding substitute for seal's fur marketed by Davy Wotton, the internationally acclaimed fly-tyer, under the name of SLF (Synthetic Living Fibre) and obtainable from Partridge of Redditch in 48 colours.

CHAPTER SIX
DYEING

THE MOST IMPORTANT STEP towards successful dyeing is in ensuring that the materials to be dyed are carefully washed to remove all traces of dirt and grease, but even at this stage there are some considerations: first, when washing hackles do *not* use boiling water as this will have an adverse effect on the quills and inner pith, resulting in a hackle which will break, or cut when being tied in. Nothing is more exasperating if, like me, you tie palmered bodies from the tail forward, to have completed a body perfectly and then lose the hackle as soon as winding commences! Therefore always wash in hand-hot water using washing-up liquid.

Duck feathers for hackling are by nature more greasy, but I use the majority of these for Mayflies or Straddlebugs and therefore wish to retain as much natural grease as possible. A compromise has therefore to be made, and possibly a stronger dye bath may be required to penetrate the more greasy fibres to get the shade needed. If you do wish to remove the natural grease, then washing soda, a tablespoonful to a quart of hot water, will greatly assist you.

The second most important step is to ensure that *all* traces of soap or detergent are removed from the washed materials – irrespective of whether they are feathers, fur or threads – preparatory to dyeing. With furs (or threads) the water can be as hot as you like in that little if any damage can be caused here and the need to remove greasy dirt is probably more important.

Use old nylon stockings as bags for washing and dyeing the furs. One stocking makes about four bags and is cut thus:

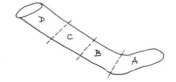

A. The foot is thus a natural bag

B. C. & D. are converted to bags simply by tying a knot at one end

Some of the fur will adhere to the nylon bag but this will come off readily when dry. Unless you intend to use the bag again for its original

59

dye colour, you should discard it as it could affect your dyeing of a different colour.

When dyeing feathers I use a small round tin which holds comfortably half a pint of water leaving about two inches of space between the dye surface and the lip. The feathers to be dyed are thoroughly washed and rinsed and then placed in a small fine wire kitchen sieve which fits neatly inside the tin and makes removal of material very easy.

For those who wish only to dye a few feathers at any one time I would suggest the use of a two-ounce tobacco tin which is shallow and so will permit the quick and easy removal of feathers with tweezers. A tiny pinch of dye will suffice for this small receptacle, say about match head size. Strengthen as desired.

For those seeking advice on dyeing, I can only recommend that they use the excellent dyes marketed by Veniards and follow the instructions given. One important point to remember is that if the shade is too delicate or pale, then it can be deepened by longer immersion or by strengthening the dye content. If the dye is too strong at the start it is much more difficult to control and indeed does not give the best result. If the colour required is a delicate one then use less dye, carefully examine the material and stop at the required shade by removing the sieve and immediately rinsing with tap water. A useful tip: use rain water in the dye bath for best results.

Do not, under any circumstances, allow feathers that are being dyed to reach boiling point. If by accident you do, it would be a wise course to discard them and start again.

At times when trying to obtain a very dark shade you will find that, despite the quantity of dye used and the time immersed, it cannot be reached. This is normal, as any material will only take up the optimum amount of the colour and having reached that stage cannot and will not darken further. How then is this achieved? By using for the darker colours of claret, brown, blue, black, etc., a naturally dark feather to start with. Try it with Rhode Island Red hackles and see the difference. You have to experiment here as the clear sparkling colour required for salmon flies is usually only obtained by using pure white or brassy white cock hackles.

With regard to body colours, the blending of various colours of pig's wools, seal's fur, and indeed chopped floss, can overcome some of your dyeing problems. The furs must be thoroughly teased out and mixed again and again to obtain a good result. If after mixing you still have not been fully successful, you can if you wish boil them gently for a few minutes and then sieve through a fine cloth. This will give a definite even mix. Many colours and colour variations can be obtained by experiment and patient perseverance. Here too you should take careful note of the exact proportions of each colour blended in, so that a successful experiment can be repeated. As I remarked earlier, with regard to experimental hackle dyeing, failures too should be noted so that unnecessary waste of material and time is avoided.

The blending of seal's fur or pig's wool meant a different thing to the old Irish fly-dressers. As an example, in a golden olive body you would find a pinch of yellow (at tail) then golden olive, then golden olive and med. olive (mixed), then golden olive and med. olive and green (mixed). Or alternatively also for golden olive, (1) yellow, (2) golden olive, (3) golden olive and brown olive, (4) golden olive and brown olive and claret. These colours were not put on in separate bands but skilfully inter-mixed so that they gave a graduated body colour.

If you decide to experiment with fluorescent dyes then my advice would be to keep your colours pale; do not use a strong dye bath, and use the dyed material very sparingly in any dressing. For instance, use a small tag of fluorescent silk on the Iron Blue but *do not* use fluorescent tying silk throughout the dressing.

Too strong an effect can actually repel fish.

CHAPTER SEVEN

NATURAL DYES
Animal, Vegetable and Mineral

THE USE OF NATURAL DYES was an essential part of the early fly-makers' craft, and even with the advent of chemical dyes, many persisted with a method which was more time-consuming, more laborious and, indeed, more expensive.

They did so, not because they were averse to change, but because they were aware that chemical dyes could not reproduce the subtle shades and tones obtained from the natural dye-stuffs.

The present-day range of chemical dyes adequately meets the needs of the average fly-tyer, but there are many who still seek colour perfection, and have a love of angling so great that they would follow the old traditionalists, if only they had the basic knowledge. To those who would persist and are not dismayed by the strange sounding names of ingredients given in old recipes – Logwood, Cudbear, Weld, Fustic, Copperas, etc. – this chapter is dedicated.

The first step is to tabulate the information necessary towards successful dyeing:–

Lists of local plants (flowers, leaves, stems and roots)
Classify the colours given
Foreign Plants and Dyestuffs
Classify the colours given
Sources of supply (purchasing)
Mordanting
Dyeing – Equipment – Preparation
Modern Recipes
Old Recipes

LOCAL PLANTS

There are many plants growing wild, and cultivated, which can be collected as dye materials, and many can be dried and stored for future use. Roots are best collected in the autumn, the tips of heather and ling, and the curled tips of young bracken in early summer, and the flower heads in full bloom. In general, flower heads are used immediately; leaves, stems and roots can be stored for later use but require to be dried in the sun, or a warm oven, to prevent mould and subsequent rotting.

Make out a colour card similar to the following and attach samples for future reference.

PLANT	PORTION	MORDANT	COLOUR	SAMPLE
BRACKEN	Tips	Alum	Yellowish Green	
BRACKEN	Roots	Alum	Deep Yellow	
BEDSTRAW	Flowers	Alum	Yellow	
BEDSTRAW	Roots	Alum	Yellowish Red	
BEDSTRAW	Roots	Chrome	Crimson	
ELDER	Leaves	Alum	Pale Green	
ELDER	Berries	Alum	Violet	
GOLDEN ROD	Whole Plant	Alum	Lemon	
GOLDEN ROD	Whole Plant	Chrome	Golden Yellow	
WELD	Whole Plant	Alum	Lemon	
WELD	Whole Plant	Chrome	Green Yellow	
WELD	Whole Plant	Tin	Orange	
WELD	Whole Plant	Iron	Olive	
MARIGOLD	Flowers	Alum	Yellow	

I will endeavour to explain the full process from preparation to the actual dyeing, but for more detailed information I would advise you to obtain a book dealing in full with natural dyes. One which I would recommend, detailed but inexpensive, is *The Use of Vegetable Dyes* by Violetta Thurstan, published by The Dryad Press, Leicester – this can be obtained from most craft shops. I am indebted to the late Mrs Thurstan's son and The Dryad Press for their permission to reproduce the following two pages:–

BRITISH DYE PLANTS
(Roots – Stems – Flowers – Berries)

FOREIGN
DYESTUFFS

YELLOWS

			YELLOWS
Apple	Dog's Mercury	Marigold	Flavine
Ash	Dyer's Greenwood	Pear	Fustic
Barberry	Golden Rod	Pine Cones	Kutch
Bedstraw	Gorse	Privet	Persian Berries
Birch Bark	Heather	Ragwort	Quercitron Bark
Bracken	St John's Wort	Weld	Weld
Broom	Lichen	Yellowwort	
Camomile	Ling		

GREENS

			GREENS
Bracken	Elder	Privet	Fustic
Buckthorn	Ling	Reeds	Indigo, etc.

BROWNS			BROWNS
Birch Bark	Juniper	Onion Skins	Fustic
Bird Cherry	Larch	Pine Cones	Kutch
Blackberry	Lichen	Sloe	Logwood
Buckthorn	Oak	Walnut	Madder
			Sumach

BLACK			BLACK
Blackberry	Iris	Walnut	Logwood
Elder	Meadow Sweet		

REDS			REDS
Bedstraw	St John's Wort	Madder	Cochineal
Blackberry	Lichen		Madder

BLUES			BLUES AND GREYS
Blackberry	Dog's Mercury	Whortleberry	Indigo
Buckthorn	Sloe		Logwood

ORANGE			ORANGE
Lichen	Onion Skins	Weld	Flavine
			Fustic
			Madder
			Turmeric

PURPLES			PURPLES
Birch Bark	Elderberries		Cochineal
			Cudbear
			Logwood
			Orchil

Recipes for all the plants listed will be found and although these are for larger dye-baths (1 lb wool), by reducing the quantities to the proportions I will give later, the recipes can be utilized for capes and furs.

FOREIGN DYE-STUFFS

MATERIAL	TYPE	MORDANT	COLOUR
Cochineal	Dried Insects	Alum	Magenta
Cochineal		Alum + Cream of Tartar	Crimson
Cochineal		Chrome + Alum	Deep Purple
Cochineal		Tin + Cream of Tartar	Scarlet
Cochineal		Iron	Purple/Grey
Flavine	Quercitron Bark	Tin + Cream of Tartar	Yellow/Orange
Fustic Chips	Dyer's Mulberry	Alum	Lemon Yellow
Fustic Chips		Chrome + Cream of Tartar	Old Gold
Fustic Chips		Tin + Cream of Tartar	Deep Yellow
Fustic Chips		Iron	Olive

Logwood	Wood Chips	Alum	Slate Blue
Logwood		Tin + Cream of Tartar	Purple
Logwood		Iron	Black
Logwood		Chrome + Cream of Tartar	Dark Grey
Madder	Dried Root	Alum + Cream of Tartar	Brownish Red
Madder		Tin + Cream of Tartar	Bright Red
Madder		Chrome	Red Brown

These constitute the main dye materials with one exception, Indigo for blue. This is purchased as Indigo Extract and is sprinkled into hot water to form the dye-bath – a liberal amount of vinegar is added to fix the colour. Oil of Vitriol was, and still is, used to extract the colour from Cake Indigo, but as the process is lengthy, and dangerous, it should be disregarded.

Where dye-materials are bought in powder form then the colour is immediately available without long boiling, indeed, over-boiling may destroy the colour.

SOURCE OF SUPPLY

FIBRECRAFTS, Style Cottage, Lower Eashing,
Godalming, Surrey, GU7 2QD.
Enclose stamped addressed envelope for catalogue

Will supply foreign dye-stuffs and mordants in small quantities. It is important to remember that some of these materials are poisonous and should be handled with care. It is particularly important that they are stored in a dry place and well out of reach of young children.

It would also be profitable to enquire, in your own area, if there are craft shops or weaving suppliers who could supply you with dried British plants.

MORDANTING

Most vegetable dyes are fugitive, that is, the dye is not fast, and so requires a chemical or mineral additive to act as a fixative. These are known as mordants, and not only do they make the colour fast, they also affect the shade and even the colour of the actual dye.

The most common are alum, chrome, tin, iron and copper sulphate, but a more full list including the other names used in old recipes is as follows:–

MORDANT	OTHER NAMES		
Alum	Potassium Aluminium Sulphate		
Chrome	Potassium Dichromate, Bichromate of Potash		
Tin	Crystals of Tin, Muriate of Tin or Stannous Chloride		
Iron	Ferrous Sulphate, Copperas, Green Vitriol		
Copper Sulphate	Bluestone, Blue Copperas, Blue Vitriol		
Verdigris	Acetate of Copper	⎧	Dyeing
Vinegar	Acetic Acid	⎨	Assistants –
Glauber Salts	Sodium Sulphate	⎪	Not True
Cream of Tartar	Acid Potassium Tartrate, Tartaric Acid	⎩	Mordants

Early weavers and dyers in Scotland and Ireland also used stale urine, i.e. urine allowed to stand for at least 14 days.

Copper Sulphate is generally used as a secondary mordant, i.e. after obtaining a yellow shade, to impart a greenish tinge to the colour.
Iron (Copperas) is similarly used to darken, or sadden, a colour.
Tin is used to brighten a colour but must be stored in an airtight container and any space filled with cotton wool or foam rubber to prevent oxygen absorbtion.
Chrome is light sensitive and must be stored in a dark bottle, and when the mordant bath is prepared this must also be covered by a lid to exclude light.

EQUIPMENT – The Ideal

For the dye-pot:– A cast-iron pot, preferably with enamelled interior, with at least a two-pint capacity. This will allow bulky stems, and roots, to be covered with water and will withstand long boiling.

For the dye-bath:– A stainless steel, or enamelled pot, of a one-pint capacity. This would be sufficient to contain the reduced liquid from the dye-pot, i.e. approximately 1/2 pint.

For the mordant-baths:– Ideally a separate pot of a one-pint capacity should be kept for each individual mordant, but in practical terms one container, well cleaned after each usage, will suffice.

A Plastic Vegetable Collander:– for the removal of debris between the dye-pot stage and the dye-bath.
A glass rod, or individual wooden dowel rods, for stirring and examining the material in the dye-bath.
A small hammer for pounding stems and roots, and an old potato

masher is useful for pressing and pulping stems etc., while they are being boiled.

In practical terms most amateurs will have to make do with less sophisticated vessels and use old aluminium pots or tins, but the disadvantages are that mordants are metal corrosive and may leach unwanted metal salts into the solution.

Preparation of Dye-bath

The plant material from which the dye is to be extracted should, as a minium, be sufficient to pack firmly into a half-pint measure. This is placed in the dye-pot and covered by approximately one pint of water. Stems and roots should be well bruised beforehand. When the material is tender in nature viz. flowers, leaves etc. boil for half an hour. Roots and stems may require up to two hours' boiling and if the evaporation reduces the liquid too rapidly, cold water should be added. Bark and wood chips should be soaked for 24 hours before boiling.

After boiling, the liquid is allowed to cool and then strained into the dye-bath ready to receive the mordanted fur or feathers.

Preparation of Material to be Dyed

All material must be clean and grease free, and the first step is a washing in hand-hot water to which some liquid detergent has been added. If the material is very dirty this may mean that the washing water will require one or more changes. Natural seal's fur and duck feathers are by nature greasy, and will probably require the addition of some washing soda in the cleaning process. Cock hackles will also benefit from this as it does tend to overcome their hardness.

I find that bleached seal's fur is more amenable to the dye and generally requires only a normal washing to remove dirt. Most suppliers of fly-tying materials will sell this by the ounce.

After cleansing, the materials must be well rinsed in warm water to remove all traces of detergent.

MORDANTING

The mordanting medium having been selected, is then dissolved in a small quantity of hot water and added to a half-pint of cold water in the mordanting pot. (Again I would remind you that chrome must immediately be covered to exclude light.)

The feathers, or material to be dyed, having been thoroughly rinsed, are then placed in the mordanting liquid and a gentle heat applied to bring the liquid up to just below boiling point. This should be maintained for 20/30 minutes and then removed to cool overnight.

DYEING

Both the mordant pot, containing the material to be dyed, and the dye-bath, should be brought up to just below boiling point. Then the material is transferred direct from the mordant to the dye-bath. The mordant is then discarded. The dye-bath is maintained at the hot temperature for approximately 30 minutes, or when visual examination of the material reveals that the desired colour has been reached. It is important to remember that the colour or shade reached will appear to be deeper when wet than when dry.

The material should now be gently rinsed in soapy water unless a secondary mordanting is to be done.

The liquid left in the dye-bath is now known as the "exhaust" i.e. the full dye-strength has been used but this remainder can be used again to produce a lighter, or weaker, shade. If it is to be kept for future use it should be stored in a dark bottle, prominently labelled such as, for example 'DANGER – Dye Exhaust' – with details of the dye in it.

All natural dyes and exhausts will ferment in a few days and if they are to be kept for up to two or three months then a strong pinch of sodium benzoate should be added to each bottle to retard the fermentation. Storage should be in a cool dark place. The dye-colours can be mixed in the one bath, viz. a mixture of yellow plus a moderate amount of green to give a greenish yellow.

A final word of warning, if you want to live in peace with your spouse, do not use the work-tops in the kitchen, the kitchen sink, or the kitchen stove! Splashes are unavoidable and you are advised to work in the garage or outside-shed where the fumes will be well ventilated and any colour spillages will pass unnoticed.

What you have read so far is a condensed detail of the dyeing process, and to apply it practically, the following recipes and procedure will be your guide to the dyeing of small quantities.

Colour Required – Pale yellow to olive yellow
Plant Material – Half-pint measure of onion skins
Mordant Bath – One level teaspoon alum & $^{1}/_{4}$ level eggspoon cream of tartar
Dye-Bath – One half level teaspoon Glauber Salts

a) The onion skins are put into the dye-pot, covered with $^{3}/_{4}$ to 1 pint of cold water, brought to the boil and allowed to boil for 30-45 minutes. During the boiling the material should be stirred regularly to assist in the dye extraction. Remove from the heat and allow to stand overnight before straining the liquid into the dye-bath.

b) The mordanting medium should also be prepared by dissolving the cream of tartar in a cup of hot water, then add the alum and stir until dissolved. This mixture is then added to $1/2$ pint of cold water in the mordanting pot, the rinsed feathers or fur immersed, and the liquid then brought up to just below boiling point. Remove to the side of the heat and maintain the temperature for 20–30 minutes. Then place aside to cool and soak overnight.

c) The following day both the dye-bath and the mordant are brought up to just *below* boiling point, the Glauber Salts dissolved in hot water and added to the dye-bath, and the material transferred from the mordant to the dye. Maintain the temperature for approximately twenty minutes when the material can be tested for colour – if it is too light in shade, re-immerse for a further ten minutes or until a satisfactory shade is obtained. Then remove from the dye-bath and wash in warm soapy water.

If a stronger shade of yellow is required, say deep yellow, then use chrome instead of alum but reduce the quantities of chrome and cream of tartar by half.

A source of onion skins is your local greengrocer – when a bag of onions is emptied for sale, there will be a fair quantity of loose skins dislodged during transit which are discarded as rubbish and these are what you need.

The green foliage of carrots may be used to give a good yellow and a secondary mordanting in a solution containing copper sulphate will change the yellow to olive.

A further recipe using dahlia flower heads ($1/2$ pint):–

1. *Mordant* – 1 eggspoon alum and cream of tartar – old gold
2. *Mordant* – $1/2$ eggspoon chrome and cream of tartar – rich tan
3. *Mordant* – $1/2$ level teaspoon copper sulphate and cream of tartar – brown olive

   Glauber Salts as before added to dye-bath.

Tin crystals may also be used for brighter colours, and the quantity is similar to chrome. The steps are exactly the same as before. Marigold flowers will give similar colours. Young nettle stems and leaves will give varying degrees of olive with different mordants.

The mordant or mineral salt content in these recipes is so small that you may be required to experiment by increasing or decreasing the amount slightly in order to overcome local factors such as water hardness, etc.

Glauber Salts, a modern additive to the dye-bath, are believed to give a greater degree of colour penetration and colour fastness.

OLD RECIPES AND INSTRUCTIONS

Having obtained a basic insight into natural dyeing methods, you may ask yourself how do they compare with the methods used in the last century?

For the answer to this question let us look at the following instructions given by William Blacker, fly-maker and dyer of colours, born in County Wicklow, but at the time of his writing his *Art of Flymaking* in 1855, carrying on his business at 54 Dean Street, Soho, London.

I will leave you to enjoy his advice but with a final warning – disregard his instructions to bring feathers to the boil! – 'Feathers boiled are feathers spoiled!' – and while furs will withstand a light boiling, over-boiling may destroy the natural 'spring'.

THE ART OF
DYEING FISHING COLOURS,

WHICH ARE
PIG'S HAIR, MOHAIR, FUR, & HACKLES,
COMMONLY CALLED DUBBING

The great advantage the fly fisher must derive from a knowledge of dyeing his colours and hackles is obvious. It affords amusement to the enthusiastic fisher to be acquainted with the various shades required for making his flies to suit the rivers, and the flies become valuable when made of good colours and hackles. Every hackle and colour that is used for making a salmon fly must be of the richest dye imaginable, that they may show brilliant and good to the fish's eye at the bottom of the water, and entice them to rise and take it at the top. The hackles must be taken from old cocks, both the neck and saddle ones, as they hold the dye best. Wool is not good for the fly, as it soaks the water, and is dull and heavy. Pig hair, that next the skin, with the stiff and coarse bristles picked and cleared away , and mohair, which is Spanish goat hair, a most beautiful brilliant substance for flymkaing when dyed well; white seal's fur, and furs of different kinds of a white colour. White hackles are best for yellows, oranges, bold colours, blues, greens &c.; red hackles do best to dye claret, red, or fiery browns, olives, and cinnamon browns, &c., and black hackles for sooty olives, and tawny colours. When the angler sees a white old cock he should buy him to procure his hackles, or a black cock, a grey cock, and old red cock of every hue, all of which are good for dyeing. These also must be washed in soap and hot water before being dyed, and the flue stripped off, tied in bunches (see the bunch of white hackles in the Plate of Feathers, ready for the dye) of proper sizes, and when about to be put into the dye-pot wet them and the hair in hot water.

Provide a small crucible or earthen pot, glazed inside, with an earthen handle, to hold a quart of soft water, and before you put in your hackles or hair, wash them well, as I said before, in soap and hot water. The five principal colours to work upon are blue, red, yellow, brown and black. From the combination of two or more of these may be produced every shade required, from the lightest to the darkest, so that it only requires some practice, to know the different ingredients to use, to become a Dyer of Fishing Colours.

TO DYE YELLOW

I will begin with yellow, the most useful colour in general for the gentle craft. Put your crucible on a slow fire nearly full of water, or say half full, for the first trial. Take a tea cup, and into it put a table-spoonful of the best turmeric, pour over it some warm water, and stir it well with a clean piece of fire wood; when the water begins to simmer in the pot, put in the ingredient out of the cup, and stir it well with a piece of stick; have a second crucible about half full of soft water, and boil it, into this put two table-spoonfuls of ground alum and one tea-spoonful of crystal of tartar, while these are boiling and perfectly dissolved, put into it your hackles or hair, and boil gently for an hour or half an hour; take off your pots and enter the hackles into the yellow dye out of the liquor into which you put the alum and tartar, and boil them very slowly for an hour, taking them out at intervals to see the shade you require; if too pale you must put more turmeric in, and if too heavy in shade the next trial, put in less, and do the same with all colours till you please your own eye. When they are the proper colour, take them out and wash them in soap and hot water. Draw them evenly through your fingers in the bunch, and let them dry, as this keeps them in shape.

There are three or four ways to dye yellow by changing the stuff. Fill your pots nearly full of soft water, and put into one the tartar and alum, and into the other two or three handfuls of yellow wood, which must be boiled slowly for three or four hours; when it is well boiled, strain off the liquor from the wood into a basin, and throw the wood away, put the dyeing liquor into the pot again, and when boiling take out the hackles from the mordant of tartar and alum and put them into the yellow dye, let them boil gently for some time till the yellow colour has entered the hackles or hair, then take them out and wash them in soap and water, straighten them between the fingers, and let them dry; take them in the right hand and strike them on the forefinger of the left till they are quite dry.

By boiling two handfuls of fustic and a table-spoonful of turmeric together, and repeating the above process, there will be produced a golden yellow, which is very good for fly making. There must not be too much alum used, neither must the ingredients be boiled too long. Persian berries, bruised and boiled slowly, with a spoonful of turmeric, produces a good yellow; and an ingredient called weld, boiled as before, and adding the alum, is a good dye for yellow – indeed, the weld is the best dye, if care is taken with it.

TO DYE BROWN

Put into your dye pot about two handfuls of walnut rinds, or as much as it will hold nicely to boil; simmer this slowly over the fire for three or four hours, and add a little water to it as it boils away. When all the juice of the dye is taken out of the rinds, strain the liquor off, put it into the basin, and throw away the rinds; you take two handfuls more and boil them in the same way, and add the stuff together in the pot; the rinds being thrown away, put your hackles, &c., previously washed, into the dye, and simmer them on the fire for four or five hours, till you have the proper colour struck on the hackles. The alum and tartar need not be added to this dye.

Take out the feathers and wash them well; the walnut roots, cut small, dye in the same way.

TO DYE A YELLOW BROWN

The Saunders' Wood, brought from the Indies, and sold in powder or ground mixed with sumach is good, it takes long to boil, adding the alum.

A Cinnamon Brown or Fiery Brown may be struck on the hackles or colours (pig hair or mohair) by first dyeing them yellow, the same as explained in the yellow dye; put the hackles, previously dyed yellow, into the liquor of walnut rinds, and simmer them over the fire slowly for three or four hours, and leave them in all night, if a dark fiery brown is required; the less of the rinds produce cinnamon or yellow brown, the roots and rinds of the walnut are the best for the various shades; the rind of the alder dyed with alum and tartar is also good.

TO DYE BLUE

Fill your crucible three parts full of soft water, and put it on a slow fire, at the same time put in your blue ingredients, previously prepared, (this is done by dissolving the powdered blue in oil of vitroil and water in a stopper bottle for twenty-four hours). If there is a very light shade of blue required, put in a couple of table-spoonfuls of the blue ingredient, and add to it as the shade may be varied at will according to the quantity of the stuff; boil the hackles in tartar and alum, say a table-spoonful of each, or rather less of the tartar, simmer it on the fire for two or three hours according to the process mentioned before; and when the proper colour is produced take out he hackles, hair, or fur, and wash them well in soap and hot water.

There is a paste blue prepared at the dry-salters all ready for the dye pot, take a table-spoonful of it and stir it well up in your pot nearly full of soft water, and boil it gently for about an hour (or less), then put in your hackles or hair, previously washed and wet going in, boil for two hours very slowly and wash off the dye; any shade of blue may be had in a very short time by this process; there are two or three dry-salters in Long Acre where this paste blue is sold, and any of the other ingredients may be purchased at their shops, or at chymists.

TO DYE RED

Prepare your dye pot by nearly filling it with soft water; and keep it at a scalding heat when the dye stuff is put in, as it must not boil, if it is allowed to boil it becomes dull in colour; put into the dye pot a handful of finest grape madder, and simmer it slowly over the fire, stir well, and prepare the hackles or hair in the alum and red tartar liquor; after having boiled an hour slowly, take out a bunch and look at them between your eyes and the sun or light to see how they take the dye, if too pale there must be more madder added, and allow them to remain in the dye all night, simmer them slowly, next day take them out, rinse and wash them well, and allow them to dry in the air; mix a table-spoonful of cochineal with the madder.

TO DYE ORANGE

When orange is desired take a handful of best madder and mix it with a spoonful of cochineal, boil it for an hour or two, add too a little ground red wood which requires more boiling than the madder itself; dye your hackles or stuff yellow first, and dip them into the red dye a short time, take them out and look at the shade you have; if too light allow them to remain in longer, and you will have darker shades of colour, put a little red tartar and ground alum into the dye to assist the red wood to strike on the materials, take them out and wash them in soap and hot water, and afterwards rinse them in urine which gives a lustre and softness to the stuff.

TO DYE PURPLE OR VIOLET

First dye the hackles or stuffs blue, and lay them to dry; then, fill the dye-pot more than half with soft water, and in the other pot prepare the tartar and alum, dip your hackles into this for a little while, and lay them on the table till you prepare the red dye; bruise a couple of table-spoonfuls of cochineal, and put them into the pot of hot soft water, boil for an hour, and put in the blue hackles, and allow them to simmer over the fire very slowly to keep them from burning; when you have the proper shade, take them out and wash them well.

TO DYE CRIMSON

Boil your hackles or hair in a tea-spoonful of alum, and nearly as much pure tartar, for an hour; bruise two table-spoonfuls of cochineal, and boil them in your clean water; take out the hackles from the alum-water, and put them into the cochineal liquor, and boil for two or three hours slowly or less, according to the shade you require; then take out the feathers and wash them well, and you will have the colour desired.

TO DYE SCARLET

Boil your hackles, etc., in a little crystal of tartar; procure two table-spoonfuls of cochineal, bruise them a little and boil them gently over the fire for an hour or two; take the hackles you have just boiled in the tartar, and put them into the dye-pot, and simmer them slowly for some time, say half an hour; then take your 'spirits of grain,'* and put into the dye-pot a tea-spoonful or a little more; take them out occasionally, and look at them between your eyes and the light, and when the right shade is obtained, rinse them and dry.

If you are in a hurry for scarlet, you may drop the particles of block-tin into aqua-fortis till they are dissolved, and add a little to the scarlet dye; the other is best, as it gives a more brilliant shade; – boil slow.

If the extract of bismuth is added to the red liquor of the cochineal in a small quantity, it will change it to a purple or violet colour.

CRIMSON RED IN GRAIN

Boil your hackles or hair in a quarter of an ounce of alum, and the same quantity of pure tartar, an hour gently; wash them out of this, fill your dye-pot with clean water, or as much as will conveniently boil; put in an ounce of well-powered dye stuff they call 'grain', with one drachm of red arsenic, and one spoonful of burnt wine lees, this gives a lustre; wash and rinse well after boiling a short-time, and the colour is good.

TO DYE GREEN DRAKE, FEATHERS AND FUR

Boil your hackles, mohair, or fur, in alum and tartar, a quarter of an ounce of each; rinse them well, and put them into the dye-pot with an ounce of savory, and as much green-wood as the pot will contain; (it is best to boil off the savory and green-wood first, throw away the wood, and boil the feathers in the liquor;) boil gently, and look at the feathers occasionally to see if they are the right shade, these give the natural shades of yellow green. The quantity of tartar and alum, and of dye-stuff is given in this dye; and the preceding which will show what must be used in all shades of colour, according to the quality of your own taste.

---

* Spirits of grain for scarlet – a quarter pint of spirits of nitre, a quarter of an ounce of ammoniac, add half water in a bottle, and drop into it half an ounce of block-tin in grains till dissolved.

TO DYE CLARET

Boil two handfuls of red-wood, or ground Brazil-wood, for an hour, with a handful of log-wood; then take a table-spoonful of oil of vitriol, and put it into half a tea cup of cold water; and when the dye-pot is a little cold, add it to the liquor, stir it, and put it on with the hackles or hair, and boil it gently for two hours; take out your material, and put it into cold water; add to the dye it comes out of a little copperas, and a small quantity of pearlash, about the size of a nut of copperas, and a quarter that size of the ashes; put in your hackles or material again, and when the proper shade is obtained, rinse and wash well, and finish in urine, which brightens them, and your colour is good.

ANOTHER WAY TO DYE CLARET

Take a handful of nut galls and bruise them, put them into the crucible and boil them half an hour, add to the dye a table-spoonful of oil of vitriol in half a cup of water, put in the hackles and boil two hours; then add to the liquor a little pearlash, and a piece of copperas the size of a nut, boil gently for two hours or as long as required to suit the taste of the dyer, rinse and wash them well, the ashes need not be used in this dye, but if used a very small quantity will suffice.

Another way:– boil red wood powdered for two hours (two handfuls), and then put the hackles in, boil an hour longer, let the liquor cool, and put into a tea cup half full of water and nearly a table-spoonful of aqua-fortis and pour it into the dye, stir well occasionally and keep the hackles down, boil for two hours more and rinse off, finish in a little urine. If a very dark claret is required lay them in to boil for a day and night with a scalding heat.

TO DYE BLACK

Boil two good handfuls of log-wood with a little sumach and elder bark for an hour, put in the stuff or hackles (boil very gently), bruise a piece of copperas about the size of two Spanish nuts, put it in with a little argil and soda; take out the hackles and hold them in the open air a little, then put them in again and leave them all night gently heated, wash the dye well out of them and your black will be fine. The argil and soda soften the dye stuff of the copperas, but a small quantity must be put in.

TO DYE GREENS OF VARIOUS SHADES

The greatest nicety of all is in finding the exact quantity of ingredients to put in, so as to prevent the dye stuff from injuring the fibres of the hackles, &c., for the light shades add the smallest quantity, and augment it by degrees. Dye the hackles a very light shade of blue first, in prepared indigo,* as I said before, take a spoonful and put it into the dye pot and boil it softly for half an hour. Add a very small quantity of alum and tartar to the dye, put in your hackles, and boil for a short time; add to the dye a table-spoonful of the best turmeric, savoy, or green wood, a little of each would do best, boil slowly for an hour, take out the hackles, rinse them, and you will have a green: you may have any shade of green by dyeing the blues darker or lighter, and putting in more yellowing stuff and less blue when light yellow greens are required, boil gently, and look at the hackles often to see that they have taken the shade you want.

TO DYE LAVENDER OR SLATE DUN, &c. &c.

Boil ground logwood with bruised nut galls and a small quantity of copperas, according to judgment: you may have a pigeon dun, lead colour, or dark dun. The ingredients must be used in small quantities, according to taste. You may have raven grey, or duns of various shades, by boiling with the logwood a small quantity of alum and copperas.

BLUES

Dissolve some indigo in oil of vitriol for twenty-four hours, put a couple of spoonfuls in your pot, add a little crystal of tartar, put in your hackles and boil, or at least keep them at a scalding heat, or the vitriol will burn the feathers, furs, etc., take them out, rinse them well, and the colour will be lasting.

If to the above liquor some fustic chips, well boiled by themselves, and the juice added, you may have any shade of the best green.

A SILVER GREY

Boil some fenugreek and a little alum half an hour, put in the white hackles, &c., and add a little pearlash and Brazil-wood, boil them gently an hour, rinse them, and your colour will be lasting.

A COFFEE OR CHESTNUT

Boil the hackles, &c., that have been previously dyed brown, in some nut gall, sumach, and alder bark, then add a small quantity of green copperas to the liquor, allow it to remain a day and a night in water that you can bear the hand in, and all the stuff will enter the materials.

TO DYE OLIVES AND A MIXTURE OF COLOURS

Olives are dyed from blue, red, and brown, of every shade, according to fancy.

---

* Half a tea cupful of water, and the same quantity of oil of vitriol, put into a bottle, the indigo to remain in twenty-four hours to dissolve.

From yellow, blue and brown, are made olives of all kinds.

From brown, blue, and black, brown and green olives are made.

From red, yellow, and brown, are produced orange, gold colour, marigold, cinnamon, &c.

See Haigh's *Dyer's Assistant of Woollen Goods*, for larger quantities.

A CONCISE WAY OF DYEING COLOURS

I will now add the way to dye the colours, for pighair, mohair, hackles, &c., in a concise and summary manner, to avoid giving trouble in too many words, and the quantities of ingredients I have given before, which would be superfluous to mention over so often, and which the dyer must know by this time. The great art is in knowing the quantities that each dye requires to obtain the exact colour, and this may be known by a close observation to the rules I have given.

Fustic and alum water will dye yellow, the hackles dipped three times in fresh stuff. Weld, turmeric, and fenugreek, will give a yellow, boiled in alum water, and the hackles dipped often, till they are the proper colour.

These may be dyed without tartar at pleasure.

Brazil-wood, boiled till you have a strong decoction, strain off the juice, then add alum water, boil the hackles in it slowly for a day or two, and it will produce good reds. If the colour of the Brazil-wood be very strong, there may be reds obtained in an hour's boiling. This is a wood which is of a hard nature, and it is difficult to extract the colour from it, although a good dye.

A claret may be produced from Brazil-wood mixed with red archil, and boiled in the usual manner, dipped in potash liquor, or brilla will act in the same way to strike the colour; use hard water.

A fiery brown may be made from fustic and turmeric boiled together with alum and a little crystal of tartar, (soft water for this dye), and then dip in liquor of potash.

A cinnamon brown may be made with a little madder, or stone crottle, boiled with alum and tartar, with a little turmeric to finish it.

A good blue may be had by boiling the hackles with alum water, and add a spoonful of the liquid blue; this is done by putting some oil of vitriol into a bottle with a little water, and then the indigo, powdered, which will dissolve in twenty-four hours, and be ready for use. (I have mentioned this twice before, as I am very particular.)

For a purple, dye blue first, then add the red dye, and dip it in potash; when the hackles, &c., are left long in the red, it is more of a wine purple.

To have a good green, dye blue first, then boil in turmeric and fustic bark, with alum and tartar as usual. You may have any shade of green by noticing the process in the dye pot.

To dye an orange, first make it a turkey red with Brazil-wood and alum water, then finish with turmeric and fustic till the colour pleases you.

To dye a golden olive, boil sumach and turmeric with alum water, add a little potash and copperas, and finish with new turmeric and a little potash.

Green olive may be made with a little more copperas and verdigris.

Sooty olive is made by adding to the first a little alder or oak bark, and finishing with turmeric and alum water.

An amber may be made with red, and finished with yellow dye; the first with stone crottle or madder, and finish with turmeric bark; the yellow with alum water. All fishing colours should be dyed yellow first with alum and crystal of tartar, but claret.

Claret may be made from Brazil-wood, barked first in alum water, adding new Brazil three or four times fresh to the liquor, and simmer slowly for a day or two.

A fiery brown may be made from lima or pethwood, barked with turmeric and alum water.

A golden yellow may be had from citrine bark, boiled in new stuff three times slowly, bark with alum, and dip in potash or brilla.

All blues may be dipped in potash to sadden the colour.

A crottle or red orange, boil madder and stone crottle together, and bark with alum water; the madder will do if the crottle cannot be had. The crottle grows on stones in rocky places, like red moss.

An orange may be had by dyeing yellow in strong liquid three times fresh; bark with alum , and dip in potash.

A Green Drake may be made by dyeing a good yellow first, and adding a few drops of the blue decoction from the bottle of prepared blue dye, this comes to the green drake colour; add a little copperas to make a green dark or light, as you please.

A golden olive may be made by dyeing brown red hackles in fustic and a little copperas, and dipped in potashes, finished in turmeric and alum; you will have a sooty olive by adding but very little of the turmeric root.

A sooty olive may be made by dyeing black hackles in yellow first with alum water, add fresh yellow stuff three times to the dye pot, and dip them in potashes.

A wine purple may be made from light dyed blue hackles, put them in the red dye of madder, Brazil, or cochineal, and dip them twice in potashes.

Liver-coloured hackles may be had from brown red hackles, barked with alum, and boiled in Brazil-wood juice, dipped in liquor of potash.

A bright olive may be made from fustic and oak bark, adding a little turmeric and alum water.

A fiery cinnamon may be had from yellow dye, Brazil juice, and madder mixed, boil these well, and add a little turmeric with alum.

A golden crottle may be made from stone crottle and yellow dyes with turmeric and alum water. The stone crottle is best for all golden colours, but as it may not be easily got at, use madder instead; golden orange may be had from the above, adding a little potashes, and boil very slowly.

A pea green may be had by dyeing yellow first, and add a few drops out of the blue dye bottle, till it comes to the shade, it may be darkened to a leek or bottle green.

A stone blue, – bark the hackle with alum, and add to the alum water as much of the prepared dye out of the bottle as will make it dark enough, this may be easily seen from the appearance of the liquor in the dye pot.

A Prussian blue is done in the same way, keeping out the indigo, and adding the Prussian blue.

Dip a red into potashes and you have a light wine purple; blue and red dye is best.

Dip a good yellow in potashes, well boiled and stir, and you will have an orange. A little tartar is good for all colours but black.

Sumach, logwood, iron liquor, and copperas, will form a black. Boil a small quantity of copperas with logwood, and it will dye gut properly.

A tawny cinnamon may be dyed from stone crottle or madder, mixed with turmeric, alum,and a little tartar, these must be gently boiled in fresh stuff, adding a little copperas.

PART II

Abbreviations used:
D = Dark
G.P. = Golden Pheasant
L = Light
Secondary = Inner wing flight feathers
Sh. Hackle = Shoulder Hackle
Th. Hackle = Throat Hackle

TROUT FLY DRESSINGS

ALDER

A FLY OF MARSHY PLACES rather than being a true waterfly. The eggs are laid on grassy margins and after they have hatched the larvae make their way down into the water for their initial life stage. Just prior to pupation they return to the land area where they remain in pupal form until the emergence of the adult fly.

The Alder resembles a shortened sedge fly but with glossy dark-veined wings roofed over its back.

ALDER (1)

DRY	HOOK SIZE 10-12
BODY	Bronze Peacock Herl dyed Magenta
WINGS	Grouse Wing
HACKLE	Blue Dun Cock

ALDER (2)

DRY	HOOK SIZE 12
BODY	Bronze Peacock Herl
RIB	Magenta Floss Silk
WINGS	Dark Speckled Hen Wing
HACKLES	Two Black Cock

ALDER (3)

WET	HOOK SIZE 12
BODY	Dark Red Floss
RIB	Bronze Peacock Herl
HACKLE	Ginger Cock
WINGS	Woodcock Wing

ALDER (4)

WET	HOOK SIZE 10-12
BODY	Bronze Peacock Herl
RIB	Oval Gold
HACKLE	Black
WINGS	Grouse or Dark Speckled Hen Wing

ALDER (5)

NYMPH	HOOK SIZE 12 (L.S.)
TAIL	Two fibres Cock Pheasant Tail
BODY	Claret Floss with fine copper wire wound on very closely
BODY HACKLE	Ginger Cock – trimmed to leave side fibres only
THORAX	$2/3$ Hare's Ear Fur + $1/3$ Dark Claret Seal's Fur (well mixed)
HACKLE	1 $1/2$ turns Honey Badger

ALDER (6)

LARVA	*HOOK SIZE 12*
TAIL	Ginger Cock hackle tip
BODY	Copper Wire
RIB	Short Ginger Cock – trimmed top and bottom
HACKLE	One turn long Natural Red Hen
HEAD	Bronze Peacock Herl

All Alder dressings to be tied with crimson silk.

ALEXANDRA

WET	*HOOK SIZE 8-14*
TAIL	Red Ibis, (or Dyed Swan), and Peacock Sword Tips
BODY	Flat Silver
HACKLE	Black
WINGS	Green Peacock Sword
CHEEKS	Strips of Ibis or Red Swan

In larger sizes ribbed with silver wire.

APPLE GREEN (1)

DRY	*HOOK SIZE 14*
TAIL	Three fibres Ginger Cock
BODY	Apple Green Floss (slim)
WINGS	Pale Starling
HACKLE	Ginger Cock

APPLE GREEN (2)

WET	*HOOK SIZE 12-14*
TAIL	Three fibres Ginger Cock
BODY	Apple Green Floss
HACKLE	Two turns Ginger
WINGS	Grey Partridge

A very good pattern of the Green Midge.

AUGUST DUN (1)

DRY	*HOOK SIZE 14*
TAIL	Three fibres Barred Rock Cock
BUTT	Claret Floss
BODY	Black Seal's Fur (slim)
HACKLES	1) Black Cock 2) Barred Rock Cock

Both hackles to be wound on together.

AUGUST DUN (2)

DRY	*HOOK SIZE 14*
TAIL	Three fibres Honey Badger Cock
BODY	Orange & Red Seal's Fur (Mixed)
WINGS	Speckled Partridge Tail
HACKLE	Natural Red Cock

Also known as the Autumn Dun.

BADGER QUILL (1)

DRY	*HOOK SIZE 14–16*
TAIL	Three fibres Black Cock
BODY	Stripped Peacock Eye Quill
HACKLES	1) Badger Cock 2) Barred Rock Cock (wound on together)

BADGER QUILL (2)

DRY	*HOOK SIZE 14–16*
TAIL	Three fibres Badger Cock
BODY	Stripped Peacock Eye Quill
HACKLE	Badger Cock

No. 1 is a dressing used by the late Tommy Hanna of Moneymore, Co. Londonderry, a fly-dresser whose patterns and renown will always be written into the annals of the famous.

BADGER HACKLE

DRY   *HOOK SIZE 14–16*

TAIL   Three fibres Black Cock
BODY   Black Floss Silk (slim)
RIB   Silver or Gold Wire
HACKLE   Badger Cock

Another dressing by Tommy Hanna – on occasions he used the finest oval for ribbing.

BALLINDERRY BLACK

WET   *HOOK SIZE 8–12*

TAG   Old Gold Pig's Wool
            (or Floss)
TAIL   Golden Pheasant Tippets
BODY   Black Seal's Fur
RIB   Flat Gold
HACKLE   Black
WINGS   Bronze mallard over
            tippets

This is remembered as Tommy Hanna's famous fly. It is a very popular dressing for both lake and river. However, it should be noted that the original dressing had a body of darkest blue pig's wool – so dark that it appeared black until held to the light. I believe this colour to be more effective.

BALLINDERRY BROWN

WET   *HOOK SIZE 6–12*

TAG   Gold wire and Orange
            Floss
TAIL   Golden Pheasant Tippets
BODY   Fiery Brown and Yellow
            Seal's Fur (well-mixed)
RIB   Oval Gold
HACKLE   Dark Ginger (dyed
            yellow)
WINGS   Bronze Mallard

In the larger sizes an underwing of Golden Pheasant Tippets is added.

BALLINDERRY OLIVE

WET   *HOOK SIZE 6–12*

TAIL   Golden Pheasant Tippets
BODY   Golden Olive Seal's Fur
            (slim)
RIB   Flat Gold (closely ribbed)
HACKLE   Ginger or Honey Badger
WINGS   Red Swan slips with
            Bronze Mallard over

Another of Hanna's dressings and a most effective fly for lake and river.

BANN OLIVE

DRY   *HOOK SIZE 12–16*

TAIL   Fibres of Ginger Cock
BODY   Fiery Brown and Yellow
            Seal's Fur (mixed)
RIB   Gold Wire (or Oval)
WINGS   Mallard Secondary Quill
            strips stained Brown
            Olive
HACKLES   Natural Light Red stained
            Brown Olive
SIDES   Three married fibres of
            well-speckled Partridge
            Tail (or Hen Pheasant
            Tail.)

Wet dressing also as above but on Hook Sizes 10–14. This is the dressing of another well known fly-dresser, Dan O'Fee of Coleraine, Co. Londonderry. Dressing for the Lower River Bann (Lough Neagh System).

BIBIO

WET	*HOOK SIZE 8–12*
BODY	Black Seal's Fur with a middle joint of Maroon or Light Claret Fur
BODY HACKLE	Graduated Black Cock from tail to shoulder
RIB	Fine Oval Silver
HACKLE	Black (Long and Sparse)

A dressing for Loughs Corrib and Mask but will be found useful in all the lakes. Another dressing has four bands of body colour – Black-Red-Black-Red. A further dressing with middle joint of Hot Orange Seal's fur is used in the West of Ireland and Peter O'Reilly attributes this to Major Charles Roberts, Burrishole, Co. Mayo.

BLACK ANT

DRY	*HOOK SIZE L.S.15*
BUTT	Bronze Peacock Herl
BODY	Stripped Peacock Herl (dyed black)
THORAX	Bronze Peacock Herl
WINGS	Iron Blue Cock hackle tips
HACKLE	Black Cock

BLACK CLARET

WET	*HOOK SIZE 8–12*
TAIL	Golden Pheasant Tippets
BODY	Darkest Claret Seal's Fur
RIB	Oval Gold
HACKLE	Darkest Claret Cock
WINGS	Bronze Mallard

In this dressing the claret appears black until held up to the light. The hackle is a natural black (dyed dark claret). For lake fishing it must find a strong place in your box. It is often confused with the Black and Claret, or Mallard, Black and Claret.

BLACK AND CLARET (1)

WET	*HOOK SIZE 8–12*
TAG	Silver Wire
TAIL	Bronze Mallard Fibres
BODY	Black Floss
RIB	Oval Silver
HACKLE	Claret Cock
WINGS	Married strips of red and yellow Swan, Teal Flank over

A dressing for sea-trout sometimes called Teal, Black and Claret.

BLACK AND CLARET (2)

WET	*HOOK SIZE 8–12*
TAIL	Golden Pheasant Tippets
BODY	Rich Claret Floss or Seal's Fur
RIB	Oval Silver or Gold
HACKLE	Black
WINGS	Rook or Crow Secondary

BLACK DEVIL

WET	*HOOK SIZE 10–12*
TAIL	G.P. Tippets
BODY	Black Floss Silk
RIB	Flat Gold
HACKLE	Black Cock
WING	Grey Speckled Turkey (or Grouse)

Narrow slip of duck flight feather (dyed scarlet) doubled over upper wing edge. A Co. Sligo pattern.
See also Green and Purple Devils.

BLACK GNAT (1)

DRY	*HOOK SIZE 14*
BODY	Stripped Peacock Quill
THORAX	Bronze Peacock Herl
WINGS	Blue Dun hackle tips
HACKLE	Black Cock

BLACK GNAT (2)

DRY	*HOOK SIZE 16*
TAIL	Three fibres Black Cock
BODY	Black Floss (slim but tapered, thickening at the Throat)
WINGS	Dark Starling
HACKLE	Black Cock

BLACK GNAT (3)

WET	*HOOK SIZE 14*
TAIL	Fibres Black Cock
BODY	Black Floss (slim but tapered)
HACKLE	Starling Neck or Black Hen
WINGS	Light Starling

BLACK GNAT (4)

WET	*HOOK SIZE 14*
BODY	Black Quill or Horse Hair
HACKLE	Lapwing Topping
WINGS	Blackbird or Dark Starling

A very old dressing.

BLACK, GOLD, AND OLIVE

WET	*HOOK SIZE 8–12*
TAIL	Golden Pheasant Tippets
BODY	Flat Gold
HACKLE	Dark Olive
WINGS	Rook or Crow Secondary

In the larger sizes the body is ribbed with gold wire.

BLACK AND GREY

WET	*HOOK SIZE 8–12*
TAG	Flat Silver
TAIL	Golden Pheasant Crest
BODY	Grey Seal's Fur and Hare's Ear Fur (mixed)

RIB	Oval Silver
HACKLE	Black
WINGS	Tippets, married strips of blue, red, and yellow swan. Teal Flank Over

A sea trout fly.

BLACK HACKLE

There were many combinations of body colours viz.,

Black Hackle/Blue Body
Black Hackle/Black Body
Black Hackle/Green Body
Black Hackle/Red Body
Black Hackle/Yellow Body

These were also known by their body colours – see Blue Body (2). The Black Hackle/Blue Body was no doubt the ancestor of the Donegal Blue. Dressed as a simple hackled fly or with light starling wings. Ribbed or unribbed body.

BLACK MIDGE (1)

DRY	*HOOK SIZE 14–16*
BODY	Black Floss (tied short and thick)
WINGS	Light Starling
HACKLE	Black Cock

BLACK MIDGE (2)

DRY	*HOOK SIZE 16*
TAG	Flat Silver
BODY	Bronze Peacock Herl
HACKLE	Black Cock

BLACK MIDGE (3)

WET	*HOOK SIZE 14*
TAG	Flat Silver
TAIL	Fibres of Black Cock
BODY	Bronze Peacock Herl
HACKLE	Black Hen (short)
WING	Light starling

BLACK MIDGE (4)

WET	*HOOK SIZE 14–16*
TAG	Flat Silver
TAIL	Three short fibres Hen Pheasant Tail
BODY	Black Floss (tapered)
HACKLE	Smallest Starling neck hackle

BLACK MOTH

DRY	*HOOK SIZE 10–12*
BODY	Deep Bright Maroon Floss
HACKLE	Dark purple-black from Cock Grouse
WINGS	Brown Owl or Woodcock

An old dressing recorded by 'Hi-Regan' in his book *How and Where to Fish in Ireland*.

BLACK OLIVE (1)

WET	*HOOK SIZE 8–12*
TAIL	Golden Pheasant Tippets
BODY	Black Floss
RIB	Oval Gold
HACKLE	Golden Olive Cock
WINGS	Bronze Mallard

A capital lake fly. The body silk should be tapered cigar-wise.

BLACK OLIVE (2)

TAIL	3 fibres Dark Bronze Mallard
BODY	Equal quantities of Golden Olive Seal's Fur and Dark Hare's Ear Fur – (well-mixed)
RIB	Oval Gold Tinsel
HACKLE	Black Henny-cock
WINGS	Darkest Bronze Mallard

BLACK OLIVE (3)

TAIL	Black Cock Hackle Fibres
BODY	Dark Olive Seal's Fur
RIB	Oval Silver
HACKLE	Black Hen
WINGS	Rook or Crow (or Blue Mallard Speculum)

When dressed with the Blue Mallard Speculum as a wing, I have heard this pattern described as the Butcher Olive or Olive Butcher, but this causes needless confusion.

BLACK AND ORANGE

WET	*HOOK SIZE 8–12*
TAIL	Golden Pheasant Tippets
BODY	Red-Orange Floss or Seal's Fur
RIB	Gold wire or Oval Gold
HACKLE	Black
WINGS	Crow

Known in some districts as the Orange and Black.

BLACK AND ORANGE SPIDER

WET	*HOOK SIZE 8–10*
BODY	Orange Seal's Fur
RIB	Oval Gold
HACKLE	Long Black Hen

Also known as the Black and Orange and in other districts as the Orange Pennell.

BLACK AND PEACOCK SPIDER

WET	*HOOK SIZE 10–14*
TAG	Flat Gold (or Silver)
BODY	Bronze Peacock Herl (Plump)
HACKLE	Long Black Hen (1 1/2 turns)

Also known as the Peacock Spider, and Peacock and Black. This dressing differs from that made widely known by T.C. Ivens in that it has a tinsel tag and a short pea-shaped body. Probably taken from the Black Hackle of Francis Francis who contributed in many ways to Irish Patterns. Ivens' pattern is also widely used.

BLACK PENNELL (1)

WET	*HOOK SIZE 8–12*
TAIL	Golden Pheasant Topping
BODY	Black Floss or Pig's Wool
RIB	Fine Oval Silver
HACKLE	Long Black Cock

This is extremely close to Cholmondeley Pennell's original dressing. The body is thickened at head so that the hackle fibres are flared outward.

BLACK PENNELL (2)

WET	*HOOK SIZE 8–12*
TAG	Black Floss
TAIL	Fibres of Black Cock
BODY	Black Seal's Fur
RIB	Oval Silver
BODY HACKLE	Shortest fibred Black Cock
SH. HACKLE	Black Hen (two turns)

This was the dressing used by Sam Anderson, Maralin, Co. Down, who was extremely well-known in Mid and West Ulster both for his fly-tying and his great wealth of local knowledge. He wrote very many articles under the pseudonym of 'Grey Quill'.

BLACK PRINCE

WET	*HOOK SIZE 10–12*
TAIL	Golden Pheasant Tippets
BODY	Flat Gold
HACKLE	Black
WINGS	Cock Blackbird

This is a western Ireland sea trout pattern.

BLACK QUILL

WET OR DRY	*HOOK SIZE 12–16*
TAIL	Three fibres Black Cock
BODY	Black Quill or Dark Peacock Quill
HACKLE	Black
WINGS	Starling

For the Dry dressing the hackle should be of best natural black cock and the wings double split.

BLACK AND SILVER (1)

DRY	*HOOK SIZE 12–16*
WET	*8–14*
TAIL	Three fibres Black Cock
BODY	Flat Silver
RIB	Silver Wire
WINGS	Cock Blackbird
HACKLE	Natural Black Cock

Black and Gold as above but with flat gold body and rib.

BLACK AND SILVER (2)

DRY	*HOOK SIZE 12–16*
REAR HACKLE	Black Cock
BODY	Flat Silver
RIB	Silver Wire
HACKLE	Black Cock

A Fore and Aft dressing.

BLACK AND SILVER (3)

WET	*HOOK SIZE 8–14*
TAIL	Golden Pheasant Tippets
BODY	Flat Silver
RIB	Silver Wire
HACKLE	Black
WINGS	Light Starling

A simple but popular dressing occasionally varied by using rook or crow wing.

BLACK AND SILVER (4)

WET	*HOOK SIZE 8–12*
TAIL	Golden Pheasant Tippets & Red Swan
BODY	Flat Silver
HACKLE	Black
WINGS	Grey Duck
CHEEKS	Jungle Cock

This is the sea trout dressing.

BLACK AND SILVER (5)

WET	*HOOK SIZE 8–12*
TAIL	Golden Pheasant Tippets
BODY	1/2 Flat Silver
	1/2 Black Floss or Seal's Fur
RIB	Fine Oval Silver or Wire
HACKLE	Black
WING	G.P. Tippets – Married Red & Yellow Swan, Bronze mallard over

Except for colour the dressing closely resembles the Peter Ross. A popular sea trout dressing which is also known as the Jointed Black and Silver, or the Magpie.

BLACK AND SILVER (6)

WET	*HOOK SIZE 10–12*
TAIL	Red Ibis or Swan
BODY	Flat Silver
THORAX	Black Ostrich Herl (or Peacock Herl)
HACKLE	Black
WINGS	Light Starling

A sea trout dressing for the North-West which is also know as the Peacock, Black and Silver. The Black and Silver patterns also prove most effective for rainbow trout.

BLACK AND SILVER SPIDER

WET	*HOOK SIZE 12–14*
BODY	Flat Silver
HACKLE	Long Black Hen (1 1/2 turns)

The body is thickened by floss under the silver and appears plump and tapered. The long flowing mobile hackle makes it attractive.

BLACK SPIDER (1)

WET	*HOOK SIZE 12–14*
BODY	Dark Brown Floss or Fur (short and plump)
HACKLE	Dark Greenish Starling Neck feather

The dry version uses floss body.

BLACK SPIDER (2)

WET	*HOOK SIZE 12–14*
TAG	Flat Silver
BODY	Black Seal's Fur
HACKLE	Long Black Hen (1 1/2 turns)

BLACK TURKEY

WET	*HOOK SIZE 6–12*
TAIL	Golden Pheasant Tippets
BODY	Black Floss
RIB	Flat Gold or Silver
HACKLE	Rich Claret
WINGS	White-tipped Turkey

Also known as the Turkey and Black.

BLACK WIDOW

WET	HOOK SIZE 8–12
TAIL	Golden Pheasant Topping
BODY	Black Floss
RIB	Fine Oval Silver
HACKLE	Natural Black or Dark furnace
WINGS	Bronze Mallard

The body is closely ribbed and tied slim.

BLAE AND BLACK (1)

WET	HOOK SIZE 8–14
TAIL	Fibres Black Cock
BODY	Black Floss
RIB	Flat Silver
HACKLE	Black Hen
WINGS	Light Starling or Jay

BLAE AND BLACK (2)

WET	HOOK SIZE 8–14
TAIL	Golden Pheasant Tippets
BODY	Black Seal's Fur or Floss Silk
RIB	Oval Silver
HACKLE	Black
WINGS	Grey Duck or Starling

The Blae and Black is a good pattern to represent the Duck Fly.

BLAE, BLACK AND GOLD

WET	HOOK SIZE 8–14
TAIL	Fibres Black Cock
BODY	Black Floss
RIB	Flat Gold
HACKLE	Natural Red
WINGS	Light Starling

BLAE AND BLUE

WET	HOOK SIZE 8–12
TAIL	Golden Pheasant Tippets
BODY	Light Blue Pig's Wool or Seal's Fur
RIB	Oval Silver
HACKLE	Light Blue Cock
WINGS	Jay Quill

A sea trout pattern for Western Ireland.

BLAE AND GOLD

WET	HOOK SIZE 8–14
TAIL	Fibres Dark Grizzle Cock
BODY	Flat Gold
HACKLE	Dark Red Grizzle
WINGS	Mallard Quill Slips (tied very slim)

BLAE AND GREY

WET	HOOK SIZE 8–12
TAIL	Golden Pheasant Topping
BODY	Grey Monkey or Pig's Wool
RIB	Oval Silver
HACKLE	Black
WINGS	Jay Quill

BLAE AND SILVER

WET	HOOK SIZE 8–14
TAIL	Golden Pheasant Tippets
BODY	Flat Silver
HACKLE	Badger or Barred Rock Cock
WINGS	Mallard Quill Slips (tied very slim)

BLAE, ORANGE AND BLUE

WET   *HOOK SIZE 10–14*

Tail	Golden Pheasant Tippets
Body	Orange Seal's Fur
Rib	Oval Gold
Hackle	Light Blue Cock (dyed)
Wings	Starling or Grey Duck

BLUE BADGER

DRY   *HOOK SIZE 14–16*

Tag	Flat Silver
Tail	Three fibres Badger Cock
Body	Light Blue Floss (slim)
Rib	Silver Wire
Hackle	Badger Cock

BLUE BLOW

Tag	Yellow Floss
Tail	Black Human Hair
Body	Mole Fur
Wings	Tom-tit

A pattern given by O'Gorman in his book *The Practice of Angling* (Ireland) 1845. He recommended its use during April and May.

BLUE BODY (1)

WET   *HOOK SIZE 8–12*

Tag	Flat Silver
Tail	Golden Pheasant Topping
Body	Blue Floss
Rib	Flat Silver
Body Hackle	Black Cock

BLUE BODY (2)

WET   *HOOK SIZE 8–12*

Tail	Golden Pheasant Topping or Black Cock
Body	Dark Blue Floss
Rib	Flat Silver
Hackle	Black
Wings	Starling

Also known as Blue Body Black Hackle or simply as the Blue & Black. The earliest recorded dressing (Irish) appears in Ettingsall's *Rythmical Table* (1832) – 'A jet-black hackle at your footlinks end, The body deepest blue, the tail, tip't gold, The wings, light stare [starling]'.

BLUE BOTTLE (1)

DRY   *HOOK SIZE 12*

Body	Medium Blue Chenille (covered by clear rubber)
Wings	Blue Dun hackle tips (tied flat over body)
Hackles	Two Black Cock (short & thick)

A dressing by Hanna.

BLUE BOTTLE (2)

DRY   *HOOK SIZE 12*

Body	Medium Blue Floss
Body Hackle	Blue Dun Cock (short-fibred)
Wings	Blue Dun hackle tips (tied flat over body)
Hackles	Two Black Cock

A dressing by Sam Anderson.

BLUE BOTTLE (3)

DRY   *HOOK SIZE 12*

Tag	Flat Silver
Tail	Rats whiskers
Body	Royal Blue Floss
Rib	Flat Silver
Wings	Light Starling
Hackle	Black Cock

This is a very old dressing recorded by 'Hi-Regan' in *How and Where to Fish in Ireland* (1886).

BLUE BOTTLE (4)

DRY   *HOOK SIZE 12*

BODY	Medium Blue Floss
BODY HACKLE	Clipped Iron Blue Dun Cock
WINGS	Ginger Grizzle hackle tips (tied flat over body)
HACKLE	Short-fibred Iron Blue Dun

BLUE BOTTLE (5)

DRY   *HOOK SIZE 12*

BODY	Bright Blue Floss
BODY HACKLE	Clipped Black Cock
WINGS	Dark Red Grizzle hackle tips (tied flat over body)
HACKLE	Short-fibred Black Cock
HEAD	Large – Varnished Red

BLUE BOTTLE (6)

WET OR DRY   *HOOK SIZE 12*

BODY	Dark Blue Seal's Fur
RIB	Fine Oval Silver
WINGS	Light Starling
HACKLE	Black Cock or Hen

The wet dressing has very short wings with hen hackle (tied in front).

BLUE BOTTLE (7)

WET   *HOOK SIZE 12*

BODY	Medium Blue or Purple Chenille
HACKLE	Long Black Cock

This is a Donegal dressing.

BLUE DUN (1)

DRY   *HOOK SIZE 16*

TAIL	Three fibres Blue Dun Cock
BODY	Mole Fur or Water Rat Fur
RIB	Silver Wire
WINGS	Dark Starling
HACKLE	Pale Blue Dun Cock or Steel Blue Cock

BLUE DUN (2)

DRY   *HOOK SIZE 14*

TAG	Flat Gold
TAIL	Two fibres Bronze Mallard
BODY	Mole Fur with an added pinch of Golden Olive Seal's Fur
WINGS	Snipe
HACKLE	Blue Dun Cock

Tied without wings it becomes the Hackle Blue Dun.

BLUE DUN (3)

NYMPH   *HOOK SIZE L.S. 14*

TAIL	Three short fibres Dark Olive Cock
BODY	Grey Seal's Fur
RIB	Gold Wire
WING CASES	Dark Starling
THORAX	Dark Olive Seal's Fur
HACKLE	Short Dark Olive Hen (one turn)
HEAD	Wing cases tied down

The Blue Dun is a representation of the Early Olive Dun.

BLUE AND MIXED

WET	HOOK SIZE 8–12
TAG	Silver Wire
TAIL	Tippets and Indian Crow (or Red Swan)
BODY	Dark Blue Seal's Fur
RIB	Oval Silver
BODY HACKLE	Light Blue Cock (Wound from tail to throat)
WINGS	Tippets and Ibis (or Red Swan)
	Teal
	Bronze Mallard over

A West of Ireland sea trout fly. In larger sizes suitable for salmon.

BLUE PENNELL

WET	HOOK SIZE 10–12
TAIL	Golden Pheasant Topping
BODY	Dark Blue Seal's Fur
RIB	Fine Oval Silver
HACKLE	Black or Dark Furnace Cock (long)

BLUE QUILL

DRY	HOOK SIZE 14–16
TAIL	Three fibres Blue Dun Cock
BODY	Stripped Peacock Eye Quill (can be dyed slate)
HACKLES	Two Blue Dun Cock

BLUE UPRIGHT

DRY	HOOK SIZE 14–16
TAIL	Three fibres Blue Dun Cock
BODY	Stripped Peacock Quill
WINGS	Light Starling
HACKLES	Two Andalusian or Dark Steel Blue Cock

The quill is taken from the long tail and has a pale root. The pale portion should occupy the first two turns at the tail.

BLUE WICKHAM

DRY	HOOK SIZE 12–14
TAIL	Fibres Dark Ginger Cock
BODY	Flat Gold
RIB	Gold wire
BODY HACKLE	Ginger or Light Red Cock
HACKLES	1) Dark Ginger Cock
	2) Andalusian Cock

A dressing by T. J. Hanna. The two shoulder hackles to be wound on together finishing with a turn of Andalusian. Can also be fished wet – Hook Sizes 10–14.

BLUE WINGED OLIVE (1)

DRY	HOOK SIZE 14–16
TAIL	Three fibres Blue Dun Cock
BODY	Peacock Eye Quill (stripped and tapered)
WINGS	Light Teal Wing Quill (dyed Inky-Blue)
HACKLE	Medium Olive Cock

The wings are to be tied double-split.

BLUE WINGED OLIVE (2)

DRY	HOOK SIZE 14–16
TAIL	Three fibres Blue Dun Cock
BODY	Peacock Eye Quill (Stripped and tapered)
WINGS	Cock Blackbird
HACKLE	Dark Green Olive Cock

These were the dressings used by the late Sam Anderson, Maralin, Co. Down. The natural fly has large sooty blue wings.

BLUE WINGED OLIVE (3)

NYMPH	*HOOK SIZE L.S. 14*
TAIL	Three Dark Grey Cock fibres
BODY	Medium Olive Floss
RIB	Clipped Greenish-Olive Cock
WING CASES	Fibres of Cock Pheasant tail
THORAX	Dark Olive Seal's Fur
LEGS	Olive-stained Grey Hen hackle
HEAD	Wing cases tied down

This is a dressing by T. J. Hanna.

BLUE WINGED OLIVE SPINNER

DRY	*HOOK SIZE 14–16*
TAIL	Three fibres Blue Dun Cock
BODY	Stripped Peacock Eye Quill (dyed Orange)
WINGS	Coot tied spent fashion
HACKLE	Dark Green Olive Cock (tied half-circle)

See also Sherry Spinner, Orange Quill, Red Quill, and Pheasant Tail. All spinner patterns.

BLUE WITCH

DRY	*HOOK SIZE 14–16*
TAIL	Fibres Speckled Mallard
BODY	Light Hare's Ear Fur and Blue Body Undercoat (mixed)
RIB	Fine Gold
HACKLE	Steel Blue Cock

BLUE, YELLOW AND JAY

WET	*HOOK SIZE 8–12*
TAIL	Golden Pheasant Topping
BODY	Rear – Yellow Pig's Wool or Seal's Fur
	Front – Light Blue Pig's Wool or Seal's Fur
HACKLE	Blue Jay
WINGS	Tippets with Hen Pheasant over
SIDES	Yellow Macaw

An old sea trout dressing. Also known as Jay and Mixed and Pheasant and Mixed.

BLUE ZULU

WET	*HOOK SIZE 8–12*
TAIL	Red Wool
BODY	Black Seal's Fur
RIB	Fine Oval Silver
BODY HACKLE	Short-fibred Black Cock
SH. HACKLE	Long Light Blue Cock

A universal sea trout fly. Some commercial dressings leave out the body hackle and indeed sometimes use light blue seal's fur. In the correct dressing only the shoulder hackle is blue.

BOG FLY (1)

WET	*HOOK SIZE 8–12*
TAIL	Golden Pheasant Tippets
BODY	Black Ostrich Herl
RIB	Fine Oval Silver
HACKLE	Bright Red (dyed) Hen
WINGS	Swan strips, dyed Scarlet, with Crow over

This is the normal dressing but in my opinion the following dressing is much more effective and greatly superior.

BOG FLY (2)

TAIL	None
BODY	Black Ostrich Herl
RIB	Silver Wire (close-ribbed)
SH. HACKLE	Black Henny-cock (dyed Dark Claret)
WINGS	Swan strips, dyed Darkest Claret, with Rook or Crow over, which should extend the full length of the hook

BROWN MIDGE

DRY   *HOOK SIZE 16–18*

TAIL	Three fibres Brown Grizzle Cock
BODY	Clipped Dark Grizzle Cock (Plump)
HACKLES	Two Dark Grizzle Cock

BROWN OWL

WET   *HOOK SIZE 10–12*

BODY	Cinnamon Cream Seal's Fur (mixed)
HACKLE	Badger Hen (or Cock)
WINGS	Brown Owl

For the Bumbles, see pages 126-127

BUSTARD AND ORANGE

WET   *HOOK SIZE 8–12*

TAIL	Golden Pheasant Tippets
BODY	Orange Mohair or Seal's Fur (tied plump)
RIB	Oval Gold
HACKLE	Light Red Cock
WINGS	Well-marked Bustard

BUSTARD AND YELLOW

WET   *HOOK SIZE 8–12*

TAIL	Golden Pheasant Tippets
BODY	Yellow Mohair or Seal's Fur
RIB	Oval Gold
HACKLE	Ginger Cock
WINGS	Well-marked Bustard

The Bustard dressings are very old and are principally used as an evening or night fly for sea trout. A sedge or moth representation. Bustard and Orange – Orange body.

BUTCHER

WET   *HOOK SIZE 8–14*

TAIL	Red Ibis or Swan
BODY	Flat Silver
RIB	Silver Wire (in larger sizes)
HACKLE	Black Hen
WINGS	Mallard Speculum or Crow

This fly is found in most fly-boxes whether the quarry be brown trout, rainbow, or sea trout.

BLOODY BUTCHER

As Butcher but with scarlet hackle.

CANARY BUTCHER

As Butcher but with bright yellow hackle.

CLARET BUTCHER

As Butcher but with dark claret hackle.

See also Gold Butcher, Kingfisher Butcher and the Irish Butcher.

BLACKER'S FLIES

WILLIAM BLACKER was probably the first Irish Author by virtue of his writing, and publishing, *Art of Angling and Complete System of Fly-making*, in 1842, and this slim volume of thirty-eight pages is rightly recorded amongst the notable angling books of the 19th century. It gives a very clear description of fly-tying methods and contains a very short, but descriptive, passage on how to cast a fly with delicacy, and includes lists of flies and methods of dyeing.

He settled in London and traded at 54 Dean Street, Soho Square, advertising 'Flies, Irish Hooks and Tackle, and all kinds of materials for Fly-making, and Foreign Feather, of every description', and earned a worthy reputation both as an angler and fly-dresser. It is a great pity that I cannot advocate that you read his book as it is one of the very rare items in any collector's library, and I can only offer, for your information, some extracts of his recommended dressings.

The flies listed below are recommended for general use in the British Isles, but Blacker mentions three specifically as being most effective patterns for Irish Waters.

(1) WREN-TAIL

BODY	Amber Mohair
TAIL	Two fibres of the Drake feather (bronze Mallard)
HACKLE	Wren Tail
WINGS	Partridge Tail Feather

(2) HARE'S EAR AND YELLOW

BODY	Hare's Ear Fur and a little Yellow Mohair (mixed)
WINGS	Starling, Bunting, or Woodcock

(3) LITTLE SOLDIER FLY

BODY	Gold Coloured Mohair or Floss
LEGS	Small Black-red Hackle
WINGS	Starling & Partridge Tail (mixed)

Another fly of interest is his dressing of –

THE SOOTY OLIVE

BODY	Dark Olive Mohair
TAIL	Gold Tip
LEGS	Dark Olive at the Shoulders
WINGS	Woodcock or Starling

It would also be worthy to note –

THE LITTLE GOSLING

BODY	Yellow Green Mohair
LEGS	Red or Cinnamon Hackle
WINGS	Starling or Bunting Wing

as it will continue to kill trout especially around May-fly time.

To all Irish anglers or those who angle in Irish Waters, the Gilleruigh Fly (modern Gillaroo) no doubt dressed especially for the capture of the handsome Gillaroo Trout from Lough Melvin, Counties Fermanagh/Leitrim, is described as follows—

BODY	Yellow Silk and Silver Tinsel
LEGS	Black Hackle and Dun-Crow Back Feather at the Shoulder

He states that this is a particular favourite and I would assume it was a straddle-bug type of dressing, and the 'Dun-Crow' must surely be the Grey Crow.

He later re-issued his book under the title *A Catechism of Flymaking, Angling and Dyeing* and in 1855 produced *The Art of Flymaking* comprising angling and dyeing of colours. This edition was much enlarged – to 259 pages – and covered the principal rivers of England, Ireland, Scotland and Wales. The trout flies are given in a monthly sequence and most were in common use. Those which he particularly associates with Ireland are as follows–

THE DUN DRAKE

The body is made of Golden Olive mohair mixed with hare's ear fur (light and dark) and the tail is two short fibres of Bronze Mallard. The wings are land-rail and brown mallard mixed together. There is an Irish Dun Drake, called the Coughlan, made thus–

WINGS	Grey Partridge Tail
BODY	Light Brown Bear's Fur, Bright Yellow Mohair and Fur from the Hare's Face (well-mixed together)
TAIL	Two strips of Dark Mallard
HACKLE	Partridge

THE YELLOW SALLY

The Body is made of buff-coloured fur, and a small yellow hackle, for legs, at the head. The wings are made of the buff-coloured feather inside the wing of a thrush. This is the forerunner of the Green Drake of Mayfly.

THE GREEN DRAKE

The body of this beautiful fly is made of yellow-green mohair, the colour of a gosling newly come out of the shell, and ribbed with yellow-brown silk, a shade of light brown mohair at the tail, and a tuft of the same colour at the shoulder, picked out between the hackle. The whisks of the tail to be of three black hairs of the mane of a horse, about three-quarters of any inch long; the hackle to be a greenish-buff dyed (dye a silver dun hackle with bars across it, called a cuckoo) or a light ginger hackle bordering on a yellow.

The wings, which should be made full, and to stand upright, are made of dyed mallard feathers of a greenish-buff or yellowish shade: a brown head of peacock harl tied neatly above the wings. The wings may be made of the ends of two large dyed mallard feathers, with each side stripped off, and the beautiful long ends to form the wings, tie them on whole, back to back, a little longer than the bend of the hook – these feathers stand up well and appear very natural in the water. Large size will kill well on the lakes, with bright yellow mohair bodies and gold twist rolled up them. A long honey-dun palmer kills well on windy days, allowed to sink near the bottom, ribbed with gold twist.

THE GREY DRAKE

The body is made of pale yellow mohair, of floss, three fibres of dark mallard for tails, ribbed with brown silk, a grizzled dun-cocks hackle for legs (or silver-grey). Grey mallard for wings, and a peacock harl head.

The body should be made taper and full at the head — it is a capital fly on rough days in May and June, and used to advantage on warm evenings. The body may be also made of dun fox fur, grey at the ends, a silver grey hackle for legs, and forked with three hairs from a fitch's tail; the wings grey mallard and widgeon mixed. It is also made of straw body, grey cocks hackle, and mallard wings — these two methods are very good. They kill well in Scotland and Ireland (where they are called the Grey Cochlan).

THE ALDER FLY

The body is made of brown coloured peacock harl, a black-red hackle for legs, and the wings from a brown spotted hen's wing.

A second dressing — grey and red partridge tail mixed for wings, a copper-brown peacock harl body, and a dark brown red hackle off a cock neck for legs. The legs may be also made of the wren's tail, or woodcock hackle (this feather is found on the roots of the outside of the wings of the woodcock). Rib with gold for lakes.

THE LITTLE PEACOCK FLY
(River Bann)

BODY	Red-brown peacock
LEGS	Amber-brown
WINGS	Mottled light brown
TAIL	as wings

Blacker's Salmon fly dressings will be found in later pages.

CANARY ALEXANDRA

WET	*HOOK SIZE 8–12*
TAIL	Red Ibis or Swan, Peacock Sword Tips
BODY	Flat Silver
RIB	Silver Wire
HACKLE	Bright Yellow
WINGS	Green Peacock Sword Herls
CHEEKS	Strips of Red Ibis or Swan

The various patterns of Alexandra are used extensively for lake and sea trout. For river fishing the smaller sizes are used. Another variation is the Donegal Alexandra which has a magenta hackle replacing the yellow.

CINNAMON AND GOLD

WET	*HOOK SIZE 8–12*
TAIL	Golden Pheasant Tippets (or Dark Ginger Cock)
BODY	Flat Gold
HACKLE	Dark Ginger Cock
WINGS	Landrail or Cinnamon Hen Wing

CLARET DUN

DRY	*HOOK SIZE 14–16*
TAIL	Three fibres Dark Grizzle Cock
BODY	Dark Claret Seal's Fur
RIB	Gold Wire
WINGS	Darkest Starling or Jay
HACKLE	Dark Grizzle Cock

Hackled Claret as above but minus wings.

CLARET AND GOLD

WET	*HOOK SIZE 6–12*
TAIL	Golden Pheasant Tippets
BODY	Flat Gold
HACKLE	Dark Claret
WINGS	Grouse tail or Secondaries (dyed Claret)

Known also as the Gold Claret. Occasionally the wing is goose or swan (dyed dark claret).

CLARET AND GREY

WET	*HOOK SIZE 8–12*
TAIL	Golden Pheasant Crest and Tippets
BODY	Rear–1/3 Claret Seal's Fur
	Front–2/3 Grey Seal's Fur
RIB	Flat Gold (sometimes Oval)
HACKLE	Amber Cock
WINGS	Red, Blue and Yellow Swan Teal
	Bronze Mallard over

An excellent pattern for sea trout.

CLARET AND MIXED (1)

WET	*HOOK SIZE 6–12*
TAIL	Golden Pheasant Tippets
BODY	Dark Claret Seal's Fur
RIB	Oval Gold
BODY HACKLE	Dark Claret Cock
SH. HACKLE	Blue Jay
WINGS	Yellow, Blue and Green Swan
	Bronze Mallard Over

CLARET AND MIXED (2)

WET	*HOOK SIZE 6–12*
TAIL	Bronze Mallard Fibres
BODY	Claret Mohair or Pig's Wool
RIB	Gold
BODY HACKLE	Claret Cock (thickened at Throat)
WINGS	Ibis, Blue Peacock and Teal
	Bronze Mallard Over

A first class sea trout and salmon fly. The mallard wing should be narrow to show underwing strips. A West of Ireland pattern.

CLARET NYMPH

WET	*HOOK SIZE L.S. 12–14*
TAIL	Short fibres Bronze Mallard
BODY	Medium Claret Seal's Fur
RIB	Fine Oval Gold
THORAX	Dark Claret Seal's Fur (plump and unribbed)
HACKLE	Two turns of short-fibred Natural Red or Black Hen

CLARET OLIVE

WET	*HOOK SIZE 8–12*
TAIL	Golden Pheasant Tippets
BODY	Golden Olive Seal's Fur
RIB	Oval Gold
HACKLE	Dark Claret
WINGS	Mallard Wing Quill Slips

An old Golden Olive dressing which is little known today but which still remains an excellent lake or sea trout pattern.

CLARET PEACOCK

DRY   *HOOK SIZE 14*

BODY   Bronze Peacock Herl
BODY HACKLE Dark Claret Cock
SH. HACKLES   1) Two turns of Claret
               Cock
           2) Dark Grouse

A sea trout pattern.

CLARET PENNELL

WET   *HOOK SIZE 8–12*

TAIL   Golden Pheasant Topping
BODY   Light Claret Seal's Fur
RIB   Oval Silver
HACKLE   Furnace or Black Cock

The Wet version as above but has only the dark grouse at the shoulder, Hook Size 10–12. Also known as the Peacock and Claret.

CLARET TURKEY

WET   *HOOK SIZE 8–12*

TAG   Flat Gold
TAIL   Golden Pheasant Tippets
BODY   Dark Claret Seal's Fur
RIB   Oval Gold
HACKLE   Dark Claret Cock
WINGS   Oak Turkey

In this dressing the wing is very full and sedge-like. A sea trout dressing which is also excellent for the lakes. Also known as the Turkey Claret.

COACHMAN

DRY   *HOOK SIZE 12–16*

BODY   Bronze Peacock Herl (tied
             full and plump)
WINGS   Mallard Satins (from
             under Mallard wing)
HACKLE   Darkest Ginger or Red
             Cock

The wings are double split and divided by turns

of hackle. The Wet version as above but tied in the normal fashion, Hook Size 8–14.

COCH-Y-BONDHU

The standard pattern is popular but for an Irish variation Kingsmill Moore give the following–

BODY   Bronze Peacock Herl
HACKLE   Red Landrail

COCK ROBIN

WET   *HOOK SIZE 8–12*

TAIL   Bronze Mallard Fibres
BODY   Rear-^{1}/$_2$ Golden Olive
             Seal's Fur
             Front-^{1}/$_2$ Scarlet or Red
             Seal's Fur
RIB   Oval Gold
HACKLE   Natural Red
WINGS   Bronze Mallard

Also known as a 'Jointer' or Jointed Mallard or Mallard and Mixed.

CONNEMARA BLACK (1)

WET   *HOOK SIZE 6–12*

TAG   Silver Wire (or Oval
             Silver) and Yellow
             Floss
TAIL   Golden Pheasant Crest
BODY   Black Seal's Fur
RIB   Fine Oval Silver
HACKLES   1) Black
           2) Blue Jay
WINGS   Bronze Mallard

One of Ireland's favourite trout flies. The blue jay is generally not hackled but tied in at the throat, nevertheless some anglers demand a full hackle.

CONNEMARA BLACK (2)

WET	HOOK SIZE 6–12
TAIL	Golden Pheasant Tippets
BUTT	Yellow Orange Seal's Fur
BODY	Black Seal's Fur (unribbed)
HACKLES	1) Black Hen
	2) Blue Jay
WINGS	Bronze Mallard

A sea trout dressing from the Connemara district.

COSTELLO BLUE

WET	HOOK SIZE 10–12
TAIL	Red Ibis (or dyed Swan)
BODY	Raffia dyed Royal Blue
RIB	Oval Silver
HACKLE	Black Cock
WINGS	Paired Jungle Cock

A sea trout fly devised by the late Christy Deasy of international fame. I am indebted to Kevin McKenna angler/historian for his research and authentification.

COWDUNG (1)

DRY	HOOK SIZE 14
TAIL	Fibres Red Cock
BODY	Hare's Ear Fur and
	Golden Olive Seal's Fur
	(well mixed)
WINGS	Landrail
HACKLE	Four turns of short Ginger
	Cock.

The landrail wing is tied upright. Wet version as above. Hook Size 10–12 and with only two turns hackle.

COWDUNG (2)

WET	HOOK SIZE 10–12
BODY	Mustard Yellow Seal's Fur
HACKLE	Two turns Dark Red Cock
WINGS	Landrail

This is a very early Irish dressing.

COWDUNG (3)

DRY	HOOK SIZE 12
BODY	Chenille dyed Brownish-Yellow
RIB	Light Green Silk
HACKLE	Dark Honey Dun
WINGS	Dark Honey Dun hackle tips (tied flat on top of body)

This is a dressing by T. J. Hanna and is recorded in A. Courtney William's book *A Dictionary of Trout Flies*. He also records a precise build up of the method of tying.

COWDUNG (4)

WET	HOOK SIZE 8–12
TAIL	Golden Pheasant Tippets
BODY	Greenish Yellow Seal's Fur
RIB	Oval Gold
HACKLE	Red Cock
WINGS	Woodcock

Another of T. J. Hanna's dressings.

COW DUNG (5)

WET	HOOK SIZE 8–12
TAIL	Two fibres Fox Fur
BODY	Ginger Mohair
HACKLE	Ginger Cock
WINGS	Landrail (or Starling)

Another of Hi-Regan's dressings.

CROW'S WING

WET	HOOK SIZE 8–12
TAIL	Fibres of Crow Wing
BODY	Black Seal's Fur
RIB	Oval Silver
HACKLE	Black Hen or Crow
WINGS	Crow

THE DABBLER

For some considerable time I had heard of the Dabbler which was apparently proving very effective for trout and grilse, and I am indebted to Patsy Deery of Cootehill, Co. Cavan, who sent me a specimen he had been given at an International match but was unable to supply me with any history. Enquiries to local professional fly-tyers brought me six dressings - each supposed to be an authentic pattern! - and continuing research brought no success until an article by Verdon Edgar, a local angling writer/school-teacher, identified the originator as Donald McClearn of Dromore Anglers in County Down.

I spoke to Donald (whose schoolboy nickname of "Dabbler" had been a natural choice, by his friends, in naming the fly). Donald has helped his club to gain both national and international status and he, himself, won the Irish National, using a Golden Olive and a Claret version of the Dabbler.

Donald has not produced a new fly - what he has done is more fundamental in that his new style consists of dressing old established patterns with a bunch of tail fibres to represent a discarding shuck and a broken wing of straggly fibres which makes a perfect imitation of a hatching sedge.

His style of dressing will be forever known in fly-tying terminology as "tied Dabbler Fashion".

THE DABBLER

WET	*HOOK SIZE 8–10*
TAIL	8 Fibres Cock Pheasant Tail (³/4" long)
BODY	Golden Olive Seal's Fur
BODY HACKLE	Two Red Game Cock
RIB	Oval Gold
SH. HACKLE	Red Game Cock
WINGS	Bronze Mallard, tied in flat, long and straggly fibres around body

This is a Golden Olive Dabbler – Claret Dabbler has Claret body and hackle, Orange Dabbler has Orange body and hackle. It has also been dressed "bumble fashion" i.e. with the Bronze Mallard feather, stripped on one side, wound on as a hackle.

DADDY-LONG-LEGS (1)

DRY	*HOOK SIZE L.S. 8*
BODY	Natural Raffia
RIB	Strand of Cock Pheasant Tail
LEGS	Cock Pheasant Tail Fibres (Knotted) First Pair - $3/4$ long Second pair - $1/2$ long tied in pointing outwards and backwards
WINGS	Dark Grizzle hackle tips (tied spent)
HACKLE	Large Red Game Cock tied in by butt. One turn between paired legs, then one turn behind wings Figure of eight through wings and two turns in front
LEGS	Third Pair. Tied in facing forwards and outwards at 45° angle and balancing length of rear legs

This dressing calls for two fibres of Cock Pheasant Tail knotted together so that the knots form the knee joints of the natural fly. Varnish is then applied to each leg and the legs are left to dry before being tied in. For those who may feel that the double varnished fibres give too stiff an appearance to the dressing then they may use single fibres of Golden Pheasant Tail as an alternative. Knotted as before and varnished, or left natural. The body is lightly varnished and ribbed while tacky then left to dry.

DADDY-LONG-LEGS (2)

WET	*HOOK SIZE L.S. 10*
BODY	Natural Raffia
RIB	Strand of Cock Pheasant Tail
LEGS	Six, as for dry pattern, but this time the back four are tied in together on top of the hook and at the shoulder of the body. The remaining pair are tied in underneath the hook at the same position. This will cause them to flare away from the body
WINGS	Two henny-cock hackles back to back. These should be similar in colour to light speckled Partridge (Matuka) or alternatively Ginger Grizzle
HACKLE	Long Matuka or Ginger Grizzle henny-cock tied in behind wings. One turn behind wings and a maximum of two turns in front

DADDY-LONG-LEGS (3)

DAPPING	*HOOK SIZE 8*
BODY	Two Plastic or detached bodies tied in at 45° angle
WINGS	Four Ginger Cock hackle tips tied in singly at various angles and varying in lengths
HACKLE	Long Dark Well Speckled Grouse tied through wings and finishing in front

The Daddy-long-legs is also known as the 'Daddy' or the 'Harry'.

DARK FITZGERALD

DRY	*HOOK SIZE 14–16*
TAG	Orange Floss
BODY	Peacock herl (dyed Magenta)
WINGS	Grey Duck
HACKLE	Fiery Brown Cock

Wet version as above but Hook Size 12–14

DELPHI

WET	*HOOK SIZE 8–12*
TAIL	Two small Jungle Cock feathers
BODY	1/2 Flat Silver (ribbed silver wire)
CENTRE HACKLE	Short Black Cock
BODY	1/2 Flat Silver (ribbed silver wire)
SH. HACKLE	Long Black Hen

A West of Ireland sea trout pattern. I personally add a Teal Wing as I think it enhances the pattern for sea trout and salmon.

DESMOND

WET	*HOOK SIZE 8-10*
TAG	Orange Floss
TAIL	Golden Pheasant Crest
BUTT	Black Floss
BODY	Maroon Floss
RIB	Black or Gold Thread
HACKLE	Blood-Red, or Purple, or Black
WINGS	Bronze Mallard

An old sea trout, and salmon fly. When tied for salmon the butt is black ostrich. Occasionally was varied by wings of landrail and woodcock.

DIRTY OLIVE (1)

WET	*HOOK SIZE 8–12*
TAIL	Fibres Grey Mallard
BODY	Brown Olive and Light Olive Seal's Fur (well-mixed)
RIB	Oval Gold
HACKLE	Medium Olive
WINGS	Grey-brown Mallard

DIRTY OLIVE (2)

WET	*HOOK SIZE 8–12*
TAIL	Golden Pheasant Crest and Tippets
BODY	Dirty Olive Seal's Fur
RIB	Oval Gold or Silver
SH. HACKLES	1) Blood Red Cock 2) Blue Jay
WINGS	Tippets and Blue Peacock Bronze Mallard over

The Dirty Olive body is a mixture of golden olive, medium olive, green olive and fiery brown seal's fur. These patterns are used extensively in the North, North-West, and West of Ireland.

DONEGAL BLUE

WET	*HOOK SIZE 8–12*
BODY	Dark Blue Seal's Fur
RIB	Flat or Embossed Silver
HACKLE	Black (Long and Sparse)

The body should be short and plump. A local Donegal angler who swears by this pattern for sea trout ribs it with broad flat silver – two turns only. Rogan's pattern has plump light blue chenille body without rib. The original name of this fly was the Blue Spider. A descendant of the Blue Body/Black Hackle.

See also Arran Blue, the salmon fly version of this highly successful sea trout and grilse fly.

DONEGAL BUMBLE

WET	*HOOK SIZE 10–12*
TAIL	Bronze Mallard Fibres
BODY	Dark Blue Seal's Fur
RIB	Oval Silver
BODY HACKLE	Light Blue Cock
SH. HACKLE	Black Hen (long and sparse)

DONEGAL OLIVE (1)

WET	*HOOK SIZE 8–12*
TAIL	Red Swan Fibres
BODY	Hare's Ear Fur
RIB	Flat Gold Tinsel
HACKLE	Yellow Cock
WINGS	Speckled Grouse

Stephen Gwynn's pattern

DONEGAL OLIVE (2)

WET	*HOOK SIZE 8–12*
TAIL	Grey Mallard Fibres
BODY	Mixed Seal's Fur
RIB	Oval Gold
HACKLE	Dark Claret
WINGS	Bronze Mallard

A sea trout pattern for the North-West. The body mixture comprises equal parts of emerald green, bright yellow, scarlet, light blue, golden olive, and deep orange seal's fur (well-mixed).

DUCK FLY (Black)

WET	*HOOK SIZE 12–14*
BODY	Black Floss or Crow Herl
HACKLE	Short-fibred Black
WINGS	Short Light Starling

Sometimes ribbed with fine Gold or Silver.

DUCK FLY (Olive)

WET	*HOOK SIZE 12–14*
BODY	Medium Olive Floss or Swan Herl
HACKLE	Short-fibred Furnace
WINGS	Short Starling

DUCK FLY (Brown)

WET	*HOOK SIZE 12–14*
BODY	Ash Floss or Oak Turkey Herl
RIB	Claret Silk
HACKLE	Dark Grizzle
WINGS	Short Light Starling

The Duck Fly is a representation of the Chironomid as are Blae and Black, Black Pennell, etc.

DUCK FLY (Nymph)

WET	*HOOK SIZE L.S. 14*
TAIL	Fibres Black Cock
BODY	Black Seal's Fur (slim)
RIB	Gold Wire
WING CASES	Cock Pheasant Tail fibres
THORAX	Black Seal's Fur (plump)
LEGS	Dark Partridge
HEAD	Wing Cases tied down

A dressing by T. J. Hanna.

Mr Michael Kennedy, Ph.D., in his book *Trout Flies of Irish Waters* issued by the Inland Fisheries Trust, says—

'When Chironomids are ovipositing, a wet fly fished just under the surface will sometimes be successful. The bodies are best tied with a single feather fibre on tying silk of similar colour, ribbed with fine silver wire and thickened at thorax. The wings should be short and thin, sloping backwards. The hackle should be sparse. The most useful patterns are—

1) Black Silk herled with rook feather fibre. Starling Wing. Hook Size No. 2 This is the Spring Duck Fly or Black and Blae.

2) Olive Silk herled with heron fibre dyed yellow or yellow seals fur (slim). Woodcock wing Hook Size No 3–4. (May – June, evenings; also later in season).

DUNKELD (1)

WET	*HOOK SIZE 8–12*
TAIL	Golden Pheasant Crest
BODY	Flat Gold
RIB	Gold Wire
HACKLE	Orange Cock from mid-body to shoulder
WINGS	Bronze Mallard
CHEEKS	Jungle Cock

DUNKELD (2)

WET	*HOOK SIZE 8–12*
TAIL	Golden Pheasant crest and Tippets
BODY	Flat Gold
RIB	Gold Wire
SH. HACKLES	1) Orange Cock
	2) Blue Jay
WINGS	Bronze Mallard
CHEEKS	Jungle Cock

A popular sea trout pattern for the North-West. T. J. Hanna used a deep golden olive hackle on his dressing but an older dressing had a hackle of red game cock from mid-body.

DUNKELD (3)

DRY	*HOOK SIZE 12–14*
TAIL	Fibres Ginger Cock
BODY	Flat Gold
WINGS	Grouse (tied upright)
HACKLES	1) Orange Cock behind wings
	2) Natural Dark Red in front of wings

This dressing sometimes saves a blank day during hot bright weather. Extremely good for rainbows and sea trout.

EXTRACTOR

WET	*HOOK SIZE 8*
TAIL	Bunch of red Golden Pheasant Body feather fibres
BODY	Flat Gold Tinsel
RIB	Gold Wire
SH. HACKLE	Long Lemon-Yellow Cock
TH. HACKLE	As Tail – Sweeping back to cover hook
WINGS	Bronze Mallard

A dressing by Michael Rogan of Ballyshannon also known as "Rogan's Extractor".

FENIAN (1)

WET	HOOK SIZE 8–12
TAG	Gold Wire
TAIL	Golden Pheasant Crest
BODY	Rear-$1/3$ Orange
	Front-$2/3$ Green Olive
	Floss or Seal's Fur
RIB	Oval Silver
SH. HACKLE	Golden Olive
WINGS	Bronze Mallard

FENIAN (2)

WET	HOOK SIZE 8–12
TAG	Silver Wire
TAIL	Golden Pheasant Crest
BODY	Rear-$1/3$ Yellow-Orange
	Floss
	Front-$2/3$ Emerald Green
	Floss or Seal's Fur
RIB	Oval Silver
BODY HACKLE	Natural Red Cock (to
	shoulder)
WINGS	Bronze Mallard

In the larger sizes there is an underwing of tippets and/or blue peacock.

FENIAN (3)

WET	HOOK SIZE 8–12
TAG	Silver Wire
TAIL	Golden Pheasant Crest &
	Tippets
BODY	Rear-$1/3$ Orange Floss
	Front-$2/3$ Emerald Green
	Seal's Fur
RIB	Gold or Silver Oval
BODY HACKLE	Yellow Cock
SH. HACKLE	Orange
WINGS	Bronze Mallard

FIERY BROWN (1)

WET	HOOK SIZE 6–12
TAG	Yellow Floss
TAIL	Golden Pheasant Tippets
BODY	Fiery Brown Seal's Fur
RIB	Oval Gold
HACKLE	Fiery Brown (or Natural
	Red)
WINGS	Bronze Mallard

One of the oldest of Irish patterns. Probably it is the best remembered dressing of Rogan of Ballyshannon, Co. Donegal, who had the secret of obtaining the shade necessary for success. One of the stories attributes this colour being achieved by the use of stale Jack-Ass urine and this could be quite possible as it is a fact that Scottish weavers even today use urine in the dyeing of tweeds. Fiery Brown is a colour akin to the fallen leaves in Autumn – a glowing flame-brown.

Too many commercial patterns have a red based brown fur which is completely wrong. The underlying tint has a warm yellow base.

FIERY BROWN (2)

WET	HOOK SIZE 6-12
TAIL	Golden Pheasant Crest,
	Tippets, and Green
	Peacock
BODY	Fiery Brown Seal's Fur
RIB	Oval or Flat Gold
HACKLE	Fiery Brown (or Blood-
	Red)
WINGS	Tippets, Red Ibis and
	Peacock Sword
	Bronze Mallard over

Occasionally this dressing is ribbed with flat silver. A dressing for sea trout.

FIERY BROWN (3)

DRY   *HOOK SIZE 12*

TAG	Silver wire
TAIL	Fibres Fiery Brown Cock
BODY	Fiery Brown Seal's Fur (slim)
WINGS	Starling (double split)
SIDES	Three fibres Light Speckled Partridge
HACKLE	Fiery Brown Cock

A dressing originally tied for the Lower Bann River by Dan O'Fee, Coleraine, Co. Londonderry.

FIERY BROWN AND BLUE

WET   *HOOK SIZE 8–12*

TAG	Light Blue Floss
TAIL	Golden Pheasant Tippets
BODY	Fiery Brown Seal's Fur
RIB	Oval Gold
HACKLE	Dark Blue
WINGS	Dark Starling Strips Bronze Mallard over

FIERY BROWN AND BLACK

As above but with Yellow Tag and a Black hackle.

FIERY BROWN AND CLARET

As above but with Claret Tag and a Dark Claret hackle.

All the dressings are capital lake and sea trout flies.

FIERY BROWN AND YELLOW

WET   *HOOK SIZE 6–12*

TAG	Silver Wire
BODY	Rear-^{1}/3 Golden Olive Pig's Wool Front-^{2}/3 Fiery Brown Pig's Wool

RIB	Flat Silver
HACKLE	Blood-Red Cock
WINGS	Tippets Bronze Mallard over

Most present day dressings use–

^{1}/3 Yellow Floss
^{2}/3 Fiery Brown Seal's Fur.

FIERY BROWN NYMPH

WET   *HOOK SIZE 12*

TAIL	Short Bronze Mallard fibres
BODY	Fiery Brown Seal's Fur
RIB	Fine Oval Gold
THORAX	Fiery Brown Seal's Fur (plump)
HACKLE	Short Black Hen

GALWAY BUTCHER

WET   *HOOK 10–12*

TAIL	G.P. Tippets
BODY	Bright Blue Floss
RIB	Silver Wire (or Oval)
HACKLE	Dark Claret Cock
WINGS	Blue Peacock Fibres

Light Claret hackle for coloured water.

GINGER QUILL

DRY   *HOOK SIZE 14–16*

TAIL	Three fibres Ginger Cock
BODY	Stripped Peacock Eye Quill
WINGS	Dark Starling (double-split)
HACKLE	Light Ginger Cock

Hackled version as above less wings.
Wet version as above but with wings tied back to back. Hook Sizes 10–12

GOLD ALEXANDRA

WET	*HOOK SIZE 8–12*
TAIL	Red Ibis (or Swan) and Peacock Sword Tips
BODY	Flat Gold
RIB	Gold Wire
HACKLE	Golden Olive (or Orange)
WINGS	Green Peacock Sword Herls
CHEEKS	Strips or Red Ibis (or Swan)

The wing should be kept long and light, and the cheek strips should lie at bottom edge of wing and measure three-quarters its full length. A capital sea trout pattern.

GOLD BUTCHER

WET	*HOOK SIZE 8–14*
TAIL	Red Ibis or Swan
BODY	Flat Gold
HACKLE	Golden Olive (or Black, or Claret)
WINGS	Mallard Speculum or Crow

Dry version as above but tied with upright split wings. Hook Size 12–14. A very good sea trout. Ribbed in large sizes with gold wire.

GOLD MARCH BROWN

WET	*HOOK SIZE 8–14*
TAIL	Fibres Dark Speckled Partridge
BODY	Flat Gold
RIB	Gold Wire
HACKLE	Dark Partridge (sparse)
WINGS	Hen Pheasant or Oak Turkey

GOLD MIDGE

DRY	*HOOK SIZE 16*
TAG	Flat Gold
TAIL	Three fibres Badger Cock
BODY	Old Gold Floss
HACKLE	Badger Cock

A dressing by T. J. Hanna.

GOLDEN DUN MIDGE

DRY	*HOOK SIZE 16*
TAIL	Three fibres Brown Olive Cock
BODY	Yellow Silk
RIB	Gold Wire
WINGS	Dark Starling
HACKLE	Brown Olive Cock

GOLDEN GROUSE (1)

WET	*HOOK SIZE 8–12*
TAG	Flat Silver
TAIL	Fibres of Dark Grouse
BODY	Rear-$2/3$ Golden Olive Pig's Wool Front-$1/3$ Orange Pig's Wool
RIB	Oval Gold
HACKLE	Ginger
WINGS	Dark Grouse

GOLDEN GROUSE (2)

WET	*HOOK SIZE 8–12*
TAG	Flat Gold
TAIL	Fibres of Dark Grouse
BODY	Rear-$1/2$ Flat Gold Front-$1/2$ Golden Olive Pig's Wool
HACKLE	Golden Olive
WINGS	Dark Grouse

GOLDEN OLIVE (1)

WET   *HOOK SIZE 6–12*

TAG	Orange Floss and Gold Wire
TAIL	Golden Pheasant Tippets and Crest
BODY	Golden Olive Seal's Fur
RIB	Oval Gold
HACKLE	Golden Olive or Natural Red
WINGS	Bronze Mallard

A famous Irish pattern. The above is the normal dressing but I prefer No. 2 which is an old pattern favoured by the late Sam Anderson. The body colour should be strengthened at the throat by the addition of a pinch of orange seal's fur.

GOLDEN OLIVE (2)

WET   *HOOK SIZE 6–12*

TAG	Orange Floss & Gold Wire
TAIL	Golden Pheasant Tippets
BODY	Golden Olive Seal's Fur
RIB	Oval Gold
HACKLE	Blood Red (or Ginger)
WINGS	Landrail

GOLDEN OLIVE (3)

WET   *HOOK SIZE 6–12*

TAIL	Golden Pheasant Tippets
BODY	Rear-$1/2$ Yellow Floss Front-$1/2$ Light Olive Seal's Fur
RIB	Oval Gold
BODY HACKLE	Golden Olive Cock
SH. HACKLE	Natural Red
WINGS	Tippets Bronze Mallard over

GOLDEN OLIVE (4)

WET   *HOOK SIZE 8–12*

TAIL	Golden Pheasant Tippets
BODY	Golden Olive Seal's Fur
RIB	Flat Silver
HACKLE	Natural Red
WINGS	Tippets, Blue & Yellow Swan Bronze Mallard over

A Co. Londonderry dressing for sea trout.

GOLDEN OLIVE (5)

WET   *HOOK SIZE 8–12*

TAIL	Golden Pheasant Tippets and Crest
BODY	Golden Olive Seal's Fur
RIB	Flat Gold
HACKLE	Teal
WINGS	Bronze Mallard

An old Co. Donegal dressing.

GOLDEN OLIVE (6)

WET   *HOOK SIZE 8–12*

TAIL	Golden Pheasant Tippets and Topping
BODY	Yellow Seal's Fur and pinch of Hare's Ear Fur
RIB	Oval Gold
HACKLE	Golden Olive (Greenish)
WINGS	Mallard Wing Quill Strips

GREER'S GOLDEN OLIVE

WET   *HOOK SIZE 8–12*

TAIL	Golden Pheasant Tippets
BODY	Light Olive and Green Olive Seal's Fur (well-mixed)
RIB	Fine Oval Silver
BODY HACKLE	Ginger Cock (stained Golden Olive)
WINGS	Bronze Mallard

GOLDEN PLOVER

WET   *HOOK SIZE 12*
Tag   Flat Gold
Body   Yellow Floss
Hackle   From the outside edge of
             a Golden Plover Wing

The hackle should be speckled with colour.

GRACE KELLY

WET   *HOOK SIZE 8–12*
Tail   Fibres of Cock Pheasant
             Tail
Body   Golden Olive Seal's Fur
Rib   Oval Gold
Hackle   Ginger Cock
Wings   Grey Mallard (dyed
             Golden Olive)

A dressing for the Midland lakes especially at
Mayfly time.

GRASSHOPPER (1)

WET   *HOOK SIZE 8*
Body   Well marked stripped
             Peacock quill
Underwing   Cock Pheasant Wing
             (Secondary)
Overwing   Mallard quill slips dyed
             light grass-green
             (These slips are from the
             inner flight quill)
Legs   Roughly stripped Peacock
             quill about twice body
             length. These are tied
             in after wings and lie
             along body. Leg joint
             (knot) about 3/4 way
             from head
Head Hackle Grass-Green

GRASSHOPPER (2)

WET   *HOOK SIZE 8*
Body   Golden Olive Seal's Fur
Rib   Fine Oval Gold
Body Hackle 1) Golden Olive Cock
             2) Crimson Cock in close
                turns
Wings   Married Strips Red,
             Yellow and Blue Swan
             covered by long slim
             mallard inner flight
             quill

GRASSHOPPER (3)

WET   *HOOK SIZE L.S. 8–10*
Tail   Grey Mallard fibres
             (stained pink)
Butt   Yellow Floss
Body   Black Seal's Fur (slim)
Rib   Flat Gold (close ribbed)
Hackle   Black Hen
Wings   Grey Mallard (stained
             pink)
Legs   Two long strands of
             Peacock Sword at
             bottom edge of wings

The wings are long and slim tied close to the
body. This is a pattern by the late Sam Anderson.

GREAT RED SPINNER

DRY   *HOOK SIZE 14*
Tail   Fibres Red Cock
Body   3/4 Red and 1/4 Fiery
             Brown Seal's Fur
             (mixed)
Rib   Gold Wire
Wings   Andalusian hackle tips
             (tied spent)
Hackle   Natural Red Cock

GREEN DEVIL

WET	HOOK SIZE 10–12
TAIL	G. P. Tippets
BODY	Emerald Green Floss Silk
RIB	Narrow Flat Gold
HACKLE	Black Cock
WING	Cock Pheasant

Narrow slip of duck flight feather (dyed Emerald Green) doubled over upper wing edge. A Co. Sligo pattern.
See also Black & Purple Devils.

GREEN MIDGE

DRY	HOOK SIZE 16
TAG	Flat Gold
TAIL	Three fibres Teal
BODY	Green Olive Seal's Fur
RIB	Gold Wire
WINGS	Woodcock
HACKLE	Black Cock

Hackled version minus wings and with light blue dun cock hackle.

GREEN MONKEY (1)

WET	HOOK SIZE 8–12
TAIL	Golden Pheasant Crest and Tippets
BODY	Rear-$1/3$ Green Monkey Fur
	Front-$2/3$ Grey Monkey Fur
RIB	Oval Gold
HACKLE	Dark Green Olive
WINGS	Starling

GREEN MONKEY (2)

WET	HOOK SIZE 8–12
TAG	Silver Wire and yellow Floss
TAIL	Topping fibres and Peacock Sword
BODY	Green Monkey Fur
RIB	Silver
BODY HACKLE	Green Cock
HACKLE	Teal breast
WINGS	Grey Duck

The original Green Monkey would appear to have been a Mayfly dressing. Gregory Greendrake wrote as follows, well over a century ago – 'The fur of the real green monkey is short, soft, and of a gosling green colour, approaching to yellow, and the belly has a dull white down which is mixed with the fur'. This monkey, he stated, was a native of Demerara and known as the Sacawinki. Other green monkey fur he regarded as being inferior.

GREEN OLIVE (1)

WET	HOOK SIZE 8–12
TAG	Flat Gold
TAIL	Golden Pheasant Crest and Tippets
BODY	Green-Olive Seal's Fur
RIB	Oval Gold
HACKLE	Black (or Dark Claret)
WINGS	Bronze Mallard

GREEN OLIVE (2)

DRY	HOOK SIZE 14
TAG	Flat Gold
TAIL	Three fibres Teal
BODY	Green-Olive Seal's Fur
RIB	Gold Wire
WINGS	Woodcock
HACKLE	Black Cock

GREEN OLIVE (3)

WET	HOOK SIZE 8–12
TAIL	Brown Olive Cock fibres
BODY	Grass Green Seal's Fur
RIB	Flat Gold
HACKLE	Dark Olive
WINGS	Light Starling

This is a dressing by T.J. Hanna.

GREEN PARSON (1)

WET	*HOOK SIZE 8–12*
TAIL	Golden Pheasant Tippets
BODY	Green Peacock Herl
RIB	Oval Gold
HACKLE	Teal Breast
WINGS	Red Swan Strips
	Bronze Mallard over

GREEN PARSON (2)

WET	*HOOK SIZE 8–12*
TAIL	Bronze Mallard fibres
BODY	Green Peacock Herl
RIB	Oval Gold
HACKLE	Golden Olive
WINGS	Ibis or Red Swan
	Teal
	Bronze Mallard over

An old Co. Donegal sea trout pattern.

GREEN PENNELL (1)

WET	*HOOK SIZE 8–14*
TAIL	Ibis or Red Swan
BODY	Apple Green Pig's Wool
RIB	Flat Gold
HACKLE	Long Black

GREEN PENNELL (2)

WET	*HOOK SIZE 8–12*
TAG	Gold Floss
TAIL	Light Olive Cock fibres
BODY	Mid-Green Floss
RIB	Oval Silver
HACKLE	Long Laurel Green

A dressing by Sam Anderson.

GREEN QUINN

WET	*HOOK SIZE 8–12*
TAIL	Golden Pheasant Tippets
BUTT	Green Peacock Herl
BODY	Emerald Green Floss
RIB	Oval Gold
BODY HACKLE	Emerald Green Cock
WINGS	Bronze Mallard

GREENTAIL (1)

WET	*HOOK SIZE 8–12*
TAIL	Three short fibres cock Pheasant Tail
BUTT	Green Peacock Herl
BODY	Light Hare's Fur
RIB	Oval Gold
HACKLE	Ginger Cock
WINGS	Hen Pheasant

GREENTAIL (2)

DRY	*HOOK SIZE 10–14*
TAG	Pea-green Floss
TAIL	Fibres Honey Cock
BODY	Grey Water Rat
WINGS	Woodcock
HACKLE	Dark Honey Cock

A dressing by T. J. Hanna.

GREENWELL'S GLORY (1)

DRY	*HOOK SIZE 14–16*
TAIL	Three fibres of G. P. Tippets
BODY	Primrose tying silk (waxed to a dirty Olive tone)
RIB	Gold Wire
WINGS	Light Starling (double split)
HACKLE	Light Furnace Cock

GREENWELL'S GLORY (2)

DRY   *HOOK SIZE 14–16*

TAIL	Three fibres Red cock
BODY	Lime-yellow floss
RIB	Gold Wire
WINGS	Dark Starling (double split)
HACKLE	Dark Red Cock

Wet version as above, Hook Size 12–14.

GREENWELL'S GLORY (3)

DRY   *HOOK SIZE 14–16*

TAIL	Fibres of badger Cock (dyed Blood-red)
BODY	Waxed Primrose Silk
RIB	Gold Wire
HACKLE	Badger Cock (dyed Blood-red)

This was T. J. Hanna's dressing of the Hackled Greenwell known also as the Dark Greenwell.

GREENWELL'S GLORY (4)

NYMPH   *HOOK SIZE L.S. 14*

TAIL	Three fibres Ginger Cock
BODY	Lime-yellow floss (slim)
RIB	Gold Wire
WING CASES	Landrail
THORAX	Fiery Brown Seal's Fur
HACKLE	Two turns short Furnace Hen

Tie down wing cases to cover thorax and hackle.

GREENWELL'S GLORY (5)

PUPAE   *HOOK SIZE L.S. 14*

TAIL	Three fibres Ginger Cock
BODY	Lime-yellow floss
RIB	Gold Wire
THORAX	Bronze Peacock Herl
HACKLE	Two turns Light Furnace (short)

The hackle should be tied dry-fly fashion, (undoubled), with inside of feather facing tail. Tied correctly the hackle resembles umbrella shape over the body.

GREY CLARET

WET   *HOOK SIZE 8–12*

TAG	Silver Wire
TAIL	Golden Pheasant Tippets or Grey Mallard Fibres
BODY	Claret Seal's Fur
RIB	Oval Silver
HACKLE	Dark Claret (or Black)
WINGS	Grey Duck

GREY DUSTER

DRY   *HOOK SIZE 12–16*

TAIL	Fibres Badger Cock
BODY	Light Blue Rabbit Fur
HACKLE	Badger Cock

Alternative body – Black Greyhound undercoat.

GREY MIDGE

DRY   *HOOK SIZE 16*

TAIL	Three short fibres Barred Rock Cock
BODY	Clipped Barred Rock cock
HACKLES	Two Barred Rock Cock (wound on together)

A dressing by Sam Anderson.

GREY MONKEY (1)

WET	*HOOK SIZE 8–12*
TAIL	Fibres Teal Breast
BODY	Rear-$^1/3$ Golden Olive Seal's Fur
	Front-$^2/3$ Grey Monkey or Seal's Fur
RIB	Oval Gold
HACKLE	Blue Dun or Barred Rock Hen
WINGS	Starling

On occasions tied with Jungle cock cheeks.

GREY MONKEY (2)

WET	*HOOK SIZE 8–12*
TAIL	Three fibres Bronze Mallard
BODY	Grey Monkey Fur
RIB	Oval Silver
HACKLE	Black
WINGS	Well-marked Widgeon

GREY OLIVE

WET	*HOOK SIZE 8–12*
TAG	Gold Wire
TAIL	Golden Pheasant Crest
BODY	Olive Mohair and Hare's Ear Fur (mixed)
RIB	Gold
HACKLE	Red or Lemon Game Cock
WINGS	Grey Coot or Grey Mallard

The body mixture was on occasion olive mohair & green monkey fur. Known also as the Gillaroo and stated, by 'Hi-Regan', to be exceptional for gillaroo trout.

GRIZZLY DUN

DRY	*HOOK SIZE 16*
TAIL	Three fibres Badger Cock (long)
BODY	Yellow Silk (covered by plastic sheath)
HACKLES	Two Badger Cock

On occasions Barred Rock replaces Badger.

GROUSE AND BLACK (1)

WET	*HOOK SIZE 8–12*
TAIL	Three fibres Dark Grouse
BODY	Black Pig's Wool or Seal's Fur
RIB	Flat or Oval Silver
HACKLE	Dark Grouse
WINGS	Grouse or Dark Speckled Hen

GROUSE AND BLACK (2)

WET	*HOOK SIZE 8–12*
TAG	Gold Wire
TAIL	Peewit Crests or Grouse fibres
BODY	Black Pig's Wool or Seal's Fur
RIB	Oval Silver
BODY HACKLE	Dark Grouse
WINGS	Bronze Mallard

For sea trout an underwing of Tippets, Red, Yellow and Blue Swan.

GROUSE AND BLUE

WET	*HOOK SIZE 8–12*
TAIL	Golden Pheasant Tippets
BODY	Dark Blue Pig's Wool
RIB	Flat Silver
HACKLE	Dark Blue
WINGS	Dark Grouse

GROUSE AND CLARET (1)

WET	HOOK SIZE 8–12
TAIL	Golden Pheasant Tippets
BODY	Claret Seal's Fur
RIB	Fine Oval Gold
HACKLE	Black
WINGS	Grouse

GROUSE AND CLARET (2)

WET	HOOK SIZE 8–12
TAIL	Grouse fibres
BODY	Dark Claret Pig's Wool
RIB	Flat Gold
HACKLE	Dark Grouse
WINGS	Grouse

GROUSE AND GOLD

WET	HOOK SIZE 8-12
TAIL	Grouse fibres
BODY	Flat Gold
RIB	Gold Wire
HACKLE	Dark Grouse
WINGS	Grouse

Grouse, Gold, and Claret as above but with Dark Claret Hackle.

GROUSE AND GREEN (1)

WET	HOOK SIZE 8–12
TAIL	Grouse fibres
BODY	Dark Green Pig's Wool
RIB	Flat Silver
HACKLE	Dark Ginger (or Grouse)
WINGS	Grouse

GROUSE AND GREEN (2)

WET	HOOK SIZE 8–12
TAIL	Golden Pheasant Tippets
BODY	Light Green Seal's Fur
RIB	Oval Silver
HACKLE	Light Red (or Black)
WINGS	Grouse

Where a mixed wing is required – Blue Peacock, Tippets, Red and Yellow Swan, Bronze Mallard over.

GROUSE AND JAY

WET	HOOK SIZE 8–12
TAIL	Golden Pheasant Tippets and Grouse fibres
BODY	Dark Olive Pig's Wool
RIB	Flat Silver
HACKLE	Blue Jay
WINGS	Dark Grouse

Also known as the Jay Grouse.

GROUSE AND OLIVE

WET	HOOK SIZE 8–12
TAG	Flat Gold
TAIL	Golden Pheasant Tippets
BODY	Olive Seal's Fur (L.D. or Medium)
RIB	Flat or Oval Silver
HACKLE	Claret
WINGS	Grouse

Known also as the Olive Grouse.

GROUSE AND ORANGE (1)

WET	HOOK SIZE 8–12
TAG	Gold Wire
TAIL	Grouse fibres
BODY	Red-Orange Pig's Wool
RIB	Oval Gold
BODY HACKLE	Dark Grouse
WINGS	Dark Grouse

GROUSE AND ORANGE (2)

WET	*HOOK SIZE 8–12*
TAIL	Golden Pheasant Tippets
BODY	Orange Seal's Fur
RIB	Oval or Flat Gold
HACKLE	Natural Red (or Grouse)
WINGS	Grouse

See also Orange Grouse.

GROUSE, ORANGE AND GREEN

WET	*HOOK SIZE 8–12*
TAIL	Grouse fibres
BODY	Rear-1/2 Yellow-Orange Pig's Wool
	Front-1/2 Pea-Green Pig's Wool
RIB	Oval Silver
HACKLE	Dark Grouse

Optional wing – Grouse or Bronze Mallard known also as the Grouse and Mixed or simply as a Grouse Jointer.

GROUSE, ORANGE AND BLACK

As above with Black replacing Green.

GROUSE AND PURPLE

WET	*HOOK SIZE 8–12*
TAIL	Grouse fibres
BODY	Bronze Peacock (dyed Purple) or Purple Floss or Seal's Fur
RIB	Oval Silver
HACKLE	Dark Grouse
WINGS	Grouse or Dark Speckled Hen

GROUSE AND SILVER

WET	*HOOK SIZE 8–12*
TAIL	Grouse Fibres
BODY	Flat Silver
RIB	Silver Wire
HACKLE	Dark Grouse
WINGS	Grouse (or Bronze Mallard)

GROUSE AND YELLOW

WET	*HOOK SIZE 8–12*
TAIL	Golden Pheasant Tippets or Toppings
BODY	Yellow Pig's Wool or Seal's Fur
RIB	Oval Gold
BODY HACKLE	Light Olive Cock
HACKLE	Darkest Grouse

Also known as the Grouse Hackle. All the grouse patterns may be tied as hackled, or spider, patterns by omitting the wing and using the Grouse feather as a shoulder hackle.

GUINEA WICKHAM

WET	*HOOK SIZE 6–12*
TAIL	Well Speckled Guinea-fowl
BODY	Flat Gold
RIB	Gold Wire
BODY HACKLE	Ginger Cock
HACKLE	Long Guinea-fowl (stained reddish-brown)

'The hare is wanted only for its ears,
The fur of which the greatest value bears –
This, mixed with Orange, Yellow, Black, or Green,
On lake or river better ne'er was seen'.

                –T. ETTINGSALL

HARE'S EAR (1)

WET	*HOOK SIZE 10–14*
TAIL	Three fibres Bronze Mallard
BODY	Dark Hare's Ear Fur with a pinch of Golden Olive Seal's Fur mixed in
HACKLE	Dark Dun (2 turns)
WINGS	Landrail

This is an old Irish dressing. The body mixture should be thickened at the thorax by a further addition of Golden Olive Seal's Fur.

HARE'S EAR (2)

WET	*HOOK SIZE 10–14*
DRY	*14–16*
TAG	Flat Gold
TAIL	Three fibres Grey Mallard
BODY	Hare's Ear Fur
HACKLE	Ginger
WINGS	Starling

The dry dressing has double-split wings.
May also be found ribbed with Yellow Floss.

HARE'S EAR (3)

WET	*HOOK SIZE 10–14*
TAIL	Three fibres Bronze Mallard
BODY	Hare's Ear Fur with pinch of Claret Seal's Fur added
WINGS	Starling

In this dressing the body is thickened at the thorax and picked out to form legs.

Gold Ribbed Hare's Ear as above – ribbed gold
Silver Ribbed Hare's Ear as above – ribbed silver

HARE'S EAR NYMPH (1)

WET	*HOOK SIZE L.S. 14*
TAIL	Three short fibres Bronze Mallard
BODY	Dark Hare's Ear Fur
RIB	Gold Wire
WING CASES	Dark Grouse
THORAX	Dark Hare's Ear Fur + Claret Seal's Fur (equal parts well mixed)
HACKLE	Two turns short Furnace

Wing Cases tied down at head.

HARE'S EAR NYMPH (2)

WET	*HOOK SIZE L.S. 14*
TAIL	Short fibres Hen Pheasant tail
BODY	Hare's Ear Fur
RIB	Flat Gold
WING CASES	Landrail (or Red Partridge Tail)
THORAX	Hare's Ear Fur + Dark Claret Seal's Fur (equal parts – well mixed)
HACKLE	Short Dark Partridge

Wing Cases tied down at head.

The following Hare's Ear dressings were given about 150 years ago by Thomas Ettingsall, the Dublin fly-dresser and tackle dealer, whose fame was widespread at that time. In his 'Rythmical Table of Flies' recorded in the *Angling Excursions* of Gregory Greendrake, he intermingles flies, dressings, colours, and seasons in a delightful manner.

HARE'S EAR AND BLACK

WET	HOOK SIZE 12–14
TAIL	Fibres Bronze Mallard
BODY	Hare's Ear Fur and Black Pig's Wool, (mixed)
RIB	Silver
HACKLE	Natural Red or Black Hen (short and sparse)
WINGS	Dark Starling or Brown Mallard

HARE'S EAR AND CLARET (1)

WET	HOOK SIZE 12–14
TAIL	Bronze Mallard
BODY	Hare's Ear Fur and Claret Mohair, (mixed)
RIB	Silver
HACKLE	Fieldstare Neck hackle or Natural Red
WINGS	Light Partridge

HARE'S EAR AND CLARET (2)

WET	HOOK SIZE 12–14
TAIL	Bronze Mallard
BODY	Hare's Ear Fur and Claret Pig's Wool, (mixed)
RIB	Gold
HACKLE	Black Hen
WINGS	Starling

HARE'S EAR AND GREEN

WET	HOOK SIZE 10–12
TAIL	Bronze Mallard
BODY	Hare's Ear Fur and Pea-green Pig's Wool, (mixed)
RIB	Silver
HACKLE	Wren Tail
WINGS	Starling

HARE'S EAR AND ORANGE

WET	HOOK SIZE 10–12
TAIL	Bronze Mallard fibres
	Hare's Ear Fur and Orange Pig's Wool, (mixed)
RIB	Gold
HACKLE	Natural Red Hen (short)
WINGS	Grey Duck

HARE'S EAR AND RED

WET	HOOK SIZE 10–12
TIP	Silver Wire
TAG	Claret Floss
BODY	Dark Hare's Ear Fur
RIB	Fine Oval Silver (or Wire)
HACKLE	Blood-red Cock (or Claret)
WINGS	Woodcock Wing Quill

HARE'S EAR AND YELLOW

WET	HOOK SIZE 10–12
TAIL	Bronze Mallard fibres
BODY	Hare's Ear Fur and Yellow Pig's Wool
RIB	Silver
HACKLE	Natural Red or Black Hen
WINGS	Starling or Grey Duck

HAWTHORN FLY (1)

DRY	HOOK SIZE 14
BODY	Clipped Black Cock hackle (plump)
RIB	Gold Wire
LEGS	Two tips Bronze Peacock (lying down and backward)
WINGS	Light Starling
HACKLE	Black Cock

HAWTHORN FLY (2)

WET	*HOOK SIZE 12*
BODY	Black Ostrich Herl
RIB	Black Horse Hair (close turns)
THORAX	Green Plover Crest
HACKLES	Natural Red and Black Cock (wound on together)
WINGS	Starling or Jay

HAWTHORN FLY (3)

WET	*HOOK SIZE 12*
TAG	Flat Gold
TAIL	Golden Pheasant Tippets
BODY	Slim Black Floss
THORAX	Black Ostrich
HACKLE	Black Hen
WINGS	Grey Duck

HAWTHORN FLY (4)

WET	*HOOK SIZE 12*
BODY	Rear–^{1}/2 Black Quill Front–^{1}/2 Black Ostrich Herl
LEGS	2 Fibres Bronze Mallard pointing downward and backwards from Herl
HACKLE	Black Hen
WINGS	Starling (short)

HAWTHORN FLY (5)

WET	*HOOK SIZE 12*
BODY	Slim Black Horse Hair
LEGS	Two fibres Brown Mallard (pointing down and backwards)
THORAX	Thick Black Horse Hair
HACKLE	Black Cock

WINGS	Light Starling
HORNS	Two short fibres Brown Mallard

A dressing given by O'Gorman.

HAWTHORN (6)

WET	*HOOK SIZE 8–12*
TAG	Flat Gold or Silver or Orange Floss
TAIL	Fibres Teal (or Topping)
BODY	Black Floss or Horse hair
HACKLE	Black or Port-wine Brown
WINGS	Brown Mallard (or Dark Coot and Woodcock)
OPTIONAL	Blue Jay Throat

An old sea trout pattern for Western Ireland.

HIDDEN DEATH

WET	*HOOK SIZE 10–12*
TAG	Red or Orange Floss
TAIL	Golden Pheasant Crest
BODY	Black Floss
HACKLE	Natural Red Cock
WINGS	Tippets & Bronze Mallard

A dressing by 'Hi-Regan'.

INVICTA (1)

WET	*HOOK SIZE 8–12*
TAIL	Golden Pheasant Crest
BODY	Yellow Seal's Fur
RIB	Fine Oval Gold
BODY HACKLE	Dark Ginger Cock (to shoulder)
THROAT	Blue Jay
WINGS	Hen Pheasant

Silver Invicta as above but with Flat Silver body ribbed fine Oval Silver.

INVICTA (2)

WET	*HOOK SIZE 8–10*
TAIL	Golden Pheasant Tippets
BODY	Dull Yellow Seal's Fur
RIB	Silver
HACKLE	Pale Yellow-Olive Hen
THROAT	Blue Jay
WINGS	Woodcock

A dressing by Michael Kennedy – (Inland Fisheries Trust).

IRISH BUTCHER (1)

WET	*HOOK SIZE 6–12*
TAIL	Red Swan
BODY	Flat Silver
RIB	Silver Wire
BODY HACKLE	Yellow-Orange Cock (from mid-body)
HACKLE	Black
WINGS	Crow

IRISH BUTCHER (2)

WET	*HOOK SIZE 6–12*
TAIL	Red Swan and Green Peacock
BODY	Flat Gold
RIB	Gold Wire
BODY HACKLE	Dark Grizzle Cock (from mid-body)
HACKLE	Natural Red
WINGS	Crow

Both patterns are excellent for sea trout and lake trout.

IRON BLUE

DRY	*HOOK SIZE 15–16*
TAIL	Blue-Grey fibres
BODY	Dull Purple Tying Silk (varnished) or lightly dubbed with mole's fur and ribbed with gold wire
HACKLE	2 or 3 Blue-Grey hackles from a Jackdaw's throat

This is Michael Kennedy's Hatching Iron Blue.

IRON BLUE DUN (1)

DRY	*HOOK SIZE 14–16*
TAIL	Three fibres Iron Blue Cock
BODY	Stripped Peacock Herl
HACKLES	Two Iron Blue Dun Cock

In all Iron Blue dressings the tying silk should be Crimson.

IRON BLUE DUN (2)

DRY	*HOOK SIZE 14–16*
TAIL	Three fibres Sooty Olive Cock
BODY	Stripped Peacock Eye Quill (dyed Dark Olive)
WINGS	Dark Starling (dyed Inky-Blue)
HACKLE	Iron Blue Cock

IRON BLUE DUN (3)

DRY	*HOOK SIZE 16*
TAIL	Three fibres Iron Blue Cock
BODY	Stripped Peacock Eye Quill (dyed Dark Claret)
WINGS	Starling (dyed Deep Blue)
HACKLE	Two Brown Olive Cock

IRON BLUE DUN (4)

WET	*HOOK SIZE 12–14*
TAIL	Fibres White Cock
BUTT	Crimson Silk
BODY	Iron Blue Seal's Fur
RIB	Oval Gold
HACKLE	Iron Blue
WINGS	Brown-Blue G.P. Wing

IRON BLUE DUN (5)

WET	*HOOK SIZE 12–14*
TAIL	Fibres Iron Blue Cock
BUTT	Crimson Silk
BODY	Mole Fur with pinch of Dark Claret Seal's Fur
HACKLE	Iron Blue
WINGS	Dark Starling

IRON BLUE NYMPH (1)

WET	*HOOK SIZE L.S. 14*
TAIL	Three fibres White Cock
BUTT	Crimson Silk
BODY	Mole's Fur
WING CASES	Water Hen Wing
THORAX	Mole's Fur (thick)
HACKLE	One turn Blue Dun Hen

Tie down Wing Cases at head.

IRON BLUE NYMPH (2)

WET	*HOOK SIZE L.S. 14*
TAIL	Three fibres Greenish-Grey Cock
BODY	Cinnamon Floss
RIB	Clipped Smoke-Blue Cock
WING CASES	Cock Pheasant Tail Strands
THORAX	Field-mouse Fur
LEGS	Blue Dun Hen

Tie down Wing Cases at head.

JACKDAW

WET	*HOOK SIZE 10–12*
BUTT	Red Silk
BODY	Mole Fur
HACKLE	Jackdaw Grey Neck Feather

JACOB'S LADDER (1)

WET	*HOOK SIZE 8–12*
TAIL	Golden Pheasant Tippets
BODY	1/2 Mid-Claret Seal's Fur 1/2 Magenta Seal's Fur (well mixed)
RIB	Flat Silver (or Gold) (close-ribbed)
HACKLE	Black
WINGS	Bronze Mallard or Dark Grouse

A dressing by Doherty, Donegal. A great believer in the colour Magenta for sea trout.

JACOB'S LADDER (2)

WET	*HOOK SIZE 8–12*
TAIL	Golden Pheasant Tippets
BODY	Magenta Seal's Fur
RIB	Oval Gold (close-ribbed)
HACKLE	Magenta (or Black)
WINGS	Bronze Mallard

A West of Ireland dressing.

JAY CLARET (1)

WET	*HOOK SIZE 8–12*
TAIL	Golden Pheasant Tippets
BODY	Dark Claret Seal's Fur
RIB	Oval Gold
HACKLE	Dark Claret (or Black)
WINGS	Blue-barred Jay Sides

JAY CLARET (2)

WET	*HOOK SIZE 8–12*
TAIL	Golden Pheasant Tippets
BODY	Mid-Claret Seal's Fur
RIB	Oval Gold
BODY HACKLE	Mid Claret cock
SH. HACKLE	Blue Jay

An effective sea trout fly.

JAY CLARET (3)

WET	*HOOK SIZE 8–12*
TAIL	Golden Pheasant Tippets
BODY	Rear– $1/3$ Flat Gold (tapered) Front–$2/3$ Purple-Claret Seal's Fur
RIB	Flat Gold
HACKLE	Blue Jay
WINGS	Bronze Mallard

JAY OLIVE (1)

WET	*HOOK SIZE 8–12*
TAG	Flat Silver or Wire
TAIL	Bronze Mallard fibres
BODY	Golden Olive Seal's Fur
RIB	Fine Oval Silver
HACKLE	Natural Red or Golden Olive
WINGS	Blue-barred Jay Sides

JAY OLIVE (2)

WET	*HOOK SIZE 8–12*
TAIL	Golden Pheasant Tippets
BODY	Greenish Olive Seal's Fur
RIB	Fine Oval Silver
HACKLE	Claret
THROAT	Blue Jay
WINGS	Bronze Mallard

A West of Ireland sea trout dressing.

JAY OLIVE (3)

WET	*HOOK SIZE 6–12*
TAIL	Golden Pheasant Crest and Tippets
BODY	Light Olive Seal's Fur
RIB	Oval Gold
BODY HACKLE	Golden Olive Cock
HACKLE	Blue Jay
WINGS	Tippets Bronze Mallard

JOHNSON'S FANCY

WET	*HOOK SIZE 8–12*
TAIL	Ginger Cock fibres
BODY	Flat Gold
RIB	Gold Wire
HACKLE	Barred Rock (dyed Orange) from mid-body to neck
WINGS	Hen Pheasant

A dressing for the Ballinderry River and the Moyola River, Co. Londonderry. (Tommy Hanna's dressing.)

JUDY'S BLACK SHRIMP

WET	*HOOK SIZE 8*
TAIL	Tips of Bronze Peacock
BUTT	Bright Red Floss
TAIL HACKLE	Long Black Hen (2 turns – Shrimp fashion)
REAR BODY	Green Lurex
CENTRAL HACKLE	Short Black Hen
FRONT BODY	Bronze Peacock Herl
HACKLE	Long Black Hen
HEAD	Bright Red Varnish

A dressing by a lady angler – Miss Judy Williams – consistently successfully for large lake trout and rainbow trout.

KILL-DEVIL SPIDER

WET	*HOOK SIZE 10–12*
TAIL	Furnace Cock fibres
BODY	Rear–$^1/3$ Fine Oval Silver or Wire
	Forward–$^2/3$ Plump Bronze Peacock Silver
RIB	Silver
HACKLE	Furnace Cock (long and sparse)

KINGFISHER BUTCHER (1)

WET	*HOOK SIZE 8–14*
TAIL	Blue Kingfisher fibres
BODY	Flat Gold
RIB	Gold Wire
HACKLE	Orange
WINGS	Mallard Speculum (Dark Blue)

Dry Version as above, Hook Size 12–14. The dry-fly dressing is sometimes most effective for sea trout on hot calm days.

This is a contrast to the Scottish dressing which has Coot, or slips from the inner side of a duck wing feather, for. wings. (Blae wing.) When a Blae wing is used in Ireland it is generally stained a faint Light Blue.

KINGFISHER BUTCHER (2)

WET	*HOOK SIZE 8–12*
TAIL	Blue Kingfisher fibres
BODY	Flat Gold
RIB	Gold Wire
BODY HACKLE	Dark Dun Cock from mid-body
HACKLE	Two turns Orange
WINGS	Blue Kingfisher Wing

THE KINGSMILL

TAIL	Golden pheasant topping
TAG	Blue Floss (R.H.S. Enamel Blue 48/1), tied rather broad and prominent
BODY	Black Ostrich Herl ribbed Oval Silver
HACKLE	Best quality Black Cock
WING	Rook secondary, closely rolled to keep solid, and tied long, low, and rather narrow
SIDES	Jungle Cock – small and not too white in enamel
TOPPING	A good Golden pheasant topping to lie along the top edge of the wing, and long enough to intersect the topping at the tail

Small size for sea trout, Large for salmon

Created by the late Chief Justice T.C. Kingsmill Moore ('Saracen'), author of *A Man May Fish*. He also developed the following patterns of Bumbles. His chapter on a choice of patterns is essential reading for every trout angler.

KINGSMILL MOORE'S BUMBLES

THE HOOK SIZES are generally 8 to 12 old numbers, and the two body hackles are wound on together. R.H.S. is a reference to the Royal Horticultural Society's two volume colour chart.

THE BRUISER

TAIL	A bunch of Flax-Blue Wool
BODY	Rich Gentian Blue Wool (R.H.S. Gentian Blue 42 or Prince's Blue 745/1)
RIB	Oval Silver Tinsel
BODY HACKLES	Cock Dyed Gentian Blue and Natural Black Cock (These are wound together the whole way to the Head)
SH. HACKLE	None

A first class pattern for both brown and white trout on a dark cloudy day.

CLARET BUMBLE

TAIL	Four strands G.P. Tippet
BODY	Medium Claret Seal's Fur (R.H.S. Indian Lake 826/3)
RIB	Oval Gold Tinsel
BODY HACKLES	Cock dyed Medium Claret and Natural Black Cock
SH. HACKLE	Blue Jay

An outstanding pattern for white trout and his second choice for brown trout.

MAGENTA BUMBLE

Dressing as for the Claret Bumble except that magenta (R.H.S. Magenta 27) replaces the claret, and the rib is oval silver tinsel.

FIERY BROWN BUMBLE

TAG	Golden Brown Floss (optional)
TAIL	Indian Crow
BODY	Fiery Brown Seal's Fur
RIB	Oval Gold Tinsel
BODY HACKLES	Fiery Brown and Dyed Blood Red Cock (R.H.S. Blood Red 820)
SH. HACKLE	Dark Grouse

A fly for coloured water.

GREY GHOST

TAG	Black Ostrich Herl
TAIL	G.P. Topping
BODY	Light Grey Seal's Fur (or Silver Monkey Fur)
RIB	Oval Silver Tinsel
BODY HACKLES	Dyed Irish Grey Cock (the colour of Pale Blue Dun) and Natural Black Cock
SH. HACKLE	Teal or Grey Partridge

GOLDEN OLIVE BUMBLE

TAIL	Golden Pheasant Topping
BODY	Golden Olive Seal's Fur
RIB	Oval Gold Tinsel
BODY HACKLES	Golden Olive and Natural medium Red Cock
SH. HACKLE	Blue Jay

This pattern was his first choice for brown trout but he found it less successful for white trout.

MAGENTA AND GOLD BUMBLE

TAIL	Orange Toucan
BODY	Closely wound fine Oval Gold Tinsel
BODY HACKLE	Magenta
SH. HACKLE	Pink-Cinnamon Hackle from the wing of a Landrail

SILVER BLUE BUMBLE

TAIL	G.P. Topping
BODY	Closely wound fine Oval Silver Tinsel
BODY HACKLES	Bright Medium Blue Dyed Cock (R.H.S. Butterfly Blue 645) and Natural Badger Cock – wound together rather openly
SH. HACKLE	Teal

These last two patterns for use in bright sun and/or low water.

KNOTTED MIDGE (Black)

DRY *HOOK SIZE 16*

TAIL HACKLE	Black Cock
BODY	Black Quill or Floss
HEAD HACKLE	Black Cock

KNOTTED MIDGE (Brown)

DRY *HOOK SIZE 16*

TAIL HACKLE	Brown Grizzle Cock
BODY	Quill or Dark Brown Floss
HEAD HACKLE	Fiery Red Cock

KNOTTED MIDGE (Green)

DRY *HOOK SIZE 16*

TAIL HACKLE	Green Olive Cock
BODY	Apple Green Floss
HEAD HACKLE	Dark Olive Cock

KNOTTED MIDGE (Red)

DRY *HOOK SIZE 16*

TAIL HACKLE	White Cock
BODY	Red Quill or Floss
HEAD HACKLE	White Cock

KNOTTED MIDGE (Silver)

DRY *HOOK SIZE 16*

TAIL HACKLE	Light Olive Cock
BODY	Flat Silver
HEAD HACKLE	Light Olive Cock

These are all Fore and Aft dressings and they should be tied dainty and light.

LAKE OLIVE (1)

WET *HOOK SIZE 8–12*

TAIL	Bronze Mallard fibres
BODY	$2/3$ Dark Olive Seal's Fur $1/3$ Green Olive Seal's Fur (well mixed)
RIB	Oval Gold
BODY HACKLE	Sooty Olive Cock (to shoulder)
WINGS	Bronze Mallard

An old dressing uses natural blood-red hackle and silver rib. Also known as the Large Dark Olive.

LAKE OLIVE (2)

DRY	*HOOK SIZE 14*
TAIL	Dark Olive Cock fibres
BODY	Medium Olive Seal's Fur
RIB	Gold Wire
HACKLE	Natural Red (dyed Dark Olive)

LAKE OLIVE (3)

TAIL	Golden Pheasant Tippets
BODY	Medium and Brown Olive Seal's Fur (well-mixed)
RIB	Oval Silver
HACKLE	Dark Olive
WINGS	Mallard Wing Quill Slips

LAKE OLIVE NYMPH

WET	*HOOK SIZE L.S. 14*
TAIL	Brown Olive Cock fibres
BODY	Medium Olive Floss
RIB	Gold Wire
THORAX	Hare's Ear Fur
HACKLE	Dark Olive Cock (short and sparse)

LAKE OLIVE QUILL

DRY	*HOOK SIZE 14*
TAIL	Medium Olive Cock fibres
BODY	Stripped Peacock Eye Quill
WINGS	Dark Starling (stained Medium Olive)
HACKLE	Dark Olive Cock

The wings should be double-split.

LAKE WICKHAM

DRY	*HOOK SIZE 12–14*
TAIL	Light Ginger Cock
BODY	Clipped Light Ginger Cock
RIB	Flat Gold (close-ribbed)
WINGS	Dark Starling
HACKLE	Fiery Brown Cock

LARGE DARK CLARET

WET	*HOOK SIZE 8–12*
TAG	Orange Floss or Pig's Wool
TAIL	Golden Pheasant Tippets
BODY	Darkest Claret Seal's Fur
RIB	Flat Silver
HACKLE	Black
WINGS	Hen Pheasant or Woodcock

A dressing by T. J. Hanna.

LARGE DARK OLIVE

DRY	*HOOK SIZE 14*
TAIL	Dark Grizzle Cock fibres
BODY	Hare's Ear Fur (stained olive)
RIB	Gold Wire
HACKLES	1) Natural Black
	2) Dark Honey Dun

LARGE DARK OLIVE NYMPH

WET	*HOOK SIZE L.S. 14*
TAIL	Three fibres Dark Olive
BODY	Dark Olive Floss
RIB	Clipped Brown Olive Cock
WING CASES	Cock Pheasant Tail Strands
THORAX	Dark Olive Seal's Fur
LEGS	Brown Olive Hen

Tie down wing-cases at head. A dressing by T. J. Hanna.

THE
PLATES

PLATE I

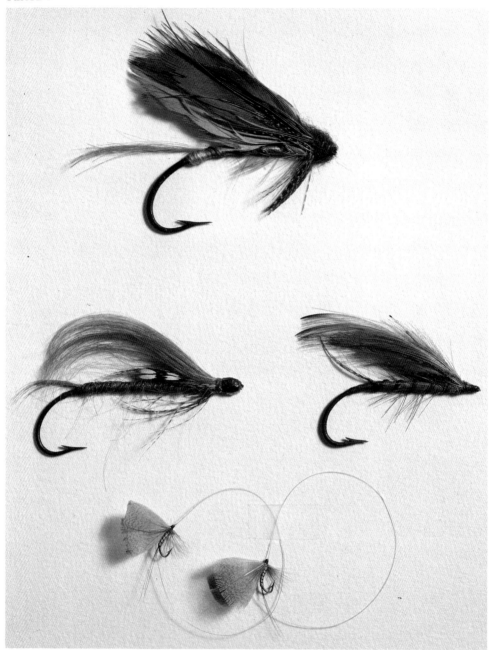

Flies of a Bygone Age

The three Salmon Flies shown are from the Lough Erne, Co. Fermanagh region, and date from 1820 to 1880. From top down: a Gaudy Fly from the Ballyshannon district, with a heavy solid wing built of vari-coloured parrot body feathers; the next fly is most remarkable in that the tail, body, and wing are composed of human hair, and must be one of the first examples of a hair-winged fly. A similar dressing is recorded by the Rev. H. Newland in *The Erne* (1851); the third, a hackle-wing fly, has hackles of brassy-dun cock dyed golden olive, and covered by Golden Pheasant crest feathers. The two Fan-winged May Flies date from 1900-1910, and are dressed on very small hooks, probably for river fishing.

PLATE II

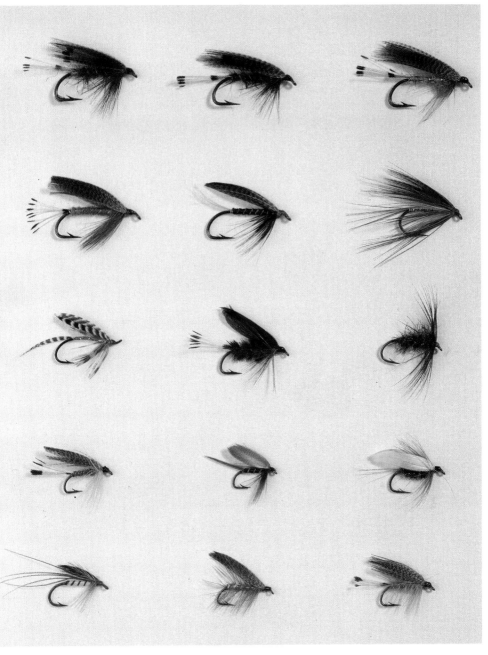

Lake Flies

Mallard & Claret	Black Claret	Ballinderry Olive
Mallard Orange & Green	Black Widow	Extractor
Teal Grouse & Silver	Bog Fly	Donegal Blue
Greer's Golden Olive	Le Fanu	Coachman
Hatching Sedge	Fenian	Melvin Olive

PLATE III

Daddy-Long-Legs
dry
wet
dapping
Rogan's Grasshopper

PLATE IV

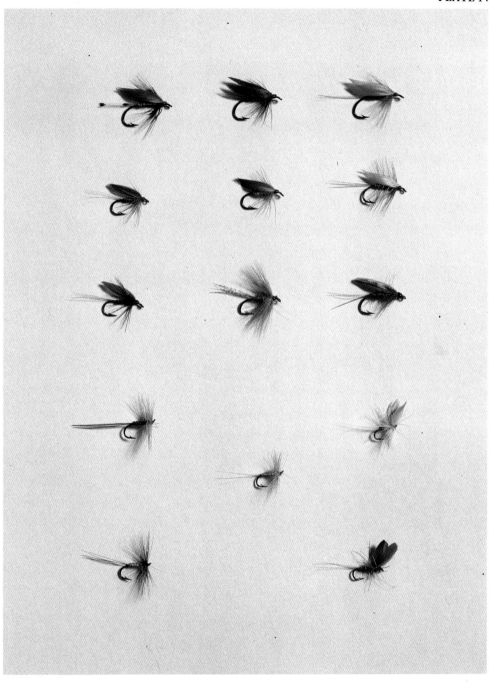

Wet and Dry River Flies
Wet

Dark Greenwell	Butcher	Red Spinner
Olive Quill	Cowdung	Wickham's Fancy
Duck Fly	Rough Olive	Bann Olive

Dry

Pheasant Tail	Tup's Indispensable	White Midge
Wire Wickham		Hare's Ear

PLATE V

Straddlebugs

Lough Arrow Green (1)
Grey Corrib (1)

Lough Arrow Green (2)
Grey Corrib (2)

Rogan's French Partridge
French Partridge Patterns

PLATE VI

Goslings

Grey Gosling	Rogan's Gosling
Mayo Gosling	Canary Gosling
Lough Erne Gosling	Sligo Straddle

PLATE VII

Mayflies and Mayfly Nymphs

Sligo May

Grey Drake (1)

Irish Mayfly

Hackled Mayfly (1)

Hackled Mayfly (2)

Hackled Mayfly (3)

Mayfly Nymphs (1) (2) (3)

Crannoge Brown (1)

PLATE VIII

Spent Gnats

Black Drake

Inny Spent

Murrough

Rogan's Vulturine Spent

Hackle Spent

Grizzle Gnat

PLATE IX

Sedges

Cinnamon Sedge   Grey Flag(1)   Green Peter   Grey Flag(2)
Hatching Sedge   Sedge Nymph

Murrough
Bann Sedges

PLATE X

Salmon Flies

Wilkinson (1)
Gold Body
Dunkeld

Wilkinson (2)
Hackley
John Robinson

PLATE XI

Salmon Shrimp Flies

Ghost Shrimp   Wye Bug
Judy of the Bogs   Quinn Shrimp

PLATE XII

Old and New Flies
Claret Dabbler

Costello Blue   Galway Butcher

Arran Blue

Spent Gnat   Daddy–Long–Legs

(both tied with a suede chenille body)

The Galway Butcher and the Costello Blue are almost-forgotten sea-trout dressings unearthed by the author.

PLATE XIII

Traditional Irish Salmon Fly Patterns
Doochary Claret
Lee Blue (1)
Fiery Brown (1)
Erne Ranger

Fully dressed salmon flies tied by Frankie McPhillips, Tempo, Co. Fermanagh, N. Ireland, on Adlington and Hutchinson Hooks by Partridge of Redditch.

PLATE XIV

Traditional Irish Salmon Fly Patterns
Thunder and Lightning (1)
Assassin
Golden Olive (5)
O'Donaghue (1)

Fully dressed salmon flies tied by Frankie McPhillips, Tempo, Co. Fermanagh, N. Ireland, on
Adlington and Hutchinson Hooks by Partridge of Redditch.

PLATE XV

Michael Rogan's Salmon Fly Patterns
Rogan's Fancy
Yellow Silk
Ballyshannon
Green Parson (1)

Fully dressed salmon flies tied by Frankie McPhillips, Tempo, Co. Fermanagh, N. Ireland, on Adlington and Hutchinson Hooks by Partridge of Redditch.

LE FANU

WET	HOOK SIZE 10–12
TAIL	Red Swan
BODY	Black Floss
RIB	Gold Wire
HACKLE	Furnace
WINGS	Starling

MAGPIE

WET	HOOK SIZE 10–12
TAIL	Green Swan or Peacock
BODY	Black Ostrich Herl
RIB	Flat Silver
HACKLE	Black
WINGS	Magpie Tail

See also Black and Silver (5).

MALLARD AND BLACK

WET	HOOK SIZE 6–12
TAG	Gold Wire
TAIL	Golden Pheasant Tippets
BODY	Black Floss or Seal's Fur
RIB	Oval Silver (or Gold)
HACKLE	Black
WINGS	Bronze Mallard

MALLARD, BLACK AND CLARET

WET	HOOK SIZE 6–12
TAG	Silver Wire and Yellow Floss
TAIL	Golden Pheasant Tippets
BODY	Black Pig's Wool or Seal's Fur
RIB	Oval Silver
HACKLE	Claret
WINGS	Bronze Mallard

MALLARD AND BLUE

WET	HOOK SIZE 6–12
TAG	Light Blue Floss
TAIL	Golden Pheasant Tippets
BODY	Medium Blue Seal's Fur
RIB	Oval Silver
HACKLE	Light Blue
WINGS	Bronze Mallard

A sea trout dressing which has, occasionally, a throat of Blue Jay.

MALLARD AND CLARET

WET	HOOK SIZE 6–12
TAG	Orange or Crimson Floss
TAIL	Golden Pheasant Tippets
BODY	Claret Pig's Wool or Seal's Fur
RIB	Flat or Oval Gold
HACKLE	Claret
WINGS	Bronze Mallard

An old dressing uses natural red hackle. This fly is probably the best used pattern in Ireland. An essential for lake fishing. Is dressed generally in two shades either light or dark. When the rich dark claret body and hackle is used, it is called the Blood Claret. This dressing I believe to be the most effective.

MALLARD, CLARET AND BLACK

WET	HOOK SIZE 6–12
TAG	Gold Wire and Red Floss
TAIL	Golden Pheasant Tippets
BODY	Claret Pig's Wool or Seal's Fur
RIB	Oval Gold
HACKLE	Black
WINGS	Bronze Mallard

In some districts is mistakenly called the Black Claret. *See under B.*

MALLARD, CLARET AND BLUE (1)

WET   *HOOK SIZE 6–12*

TAG	Silver Wire
TAIL	Golden Pheasant Tippets
BUTT	Light Blue Floss
BODY	Claret Pig's Wool
RIB	Silver
HACKLE	Natural Red
WINGS	Mallard Quill Slips

Also known as the Blue Claret.

MALLARD, CLARET AND BLUE (2)

WET   *HOOK SIZE 6-12*

TAG	Silver
TAIL	Topping
BODY	Dark Red-Claret Floss
RIB	Flat or Oval Silver
HACKLE	Light Blue
WINGS	Bronze Mallard

Sometimes called the Blue Claret.

MALLARD, CLARET AND YELLOW

WET   *HOOK SIZE 6–12*

TAG	Gold Wire
TAIL	Golden Pheasant Tippets
BUTT	Yellow Floss
BODY	Claret Floss or Pig's Wool
RIB	Oval Gold
HACKLE	Lemon Game
WINGS	Bronze Mallard

MALLARD AND GOLD

WET   *HOOK SIZE 6–12*

TAIL	Golden Pheasant Tippets and Bronze Mallard fibres
BODY	Flat Gold
RIB	Gold Wire

HACKLE	Natural Red or Black
WINGS	Bronze Mallard

Mallard, Gold and Claret as above but with claret hackle.

MALLARD AND GREEN

WET   *HOOK SIZE 6–12*

TAG	Flat Silver and Yellow Floss
TAIL	Golden Pheasant Tippets
BODY	Grass-green Seal's Fur
RIB	Oval Silver
HACKLE	Green or Black
WINGS	Bronze Mallard

An old dressing uses a ginger or red hackle.

MALLARD AND ORANGE (1)

WET   *HOOK SIZE 6–12*

TAG	Gold Wire and Yellow Floss
TAIL	Bronze Mallard fibres
BODY	Red-Orange Pig's Wool or Seal's Fur
RIB	Flat Gold
HACKLE	Natural Red Cock
WINGS	Bronze or Grey Mallard

MALLARD AND ORANGE (2)

WET   *HOOK SIZE 6–12*

TAG	Claret Floss
TAIL	Golden Pheasant Tippets
BODY	Orange Seal's Fur
RIB	Oval Gold
HACKLE	Orange
WINGS	Bronze Mallard

An old dressing used dark grouse for a hackle.

MALLARD, ORANGE AND BLACK

WET	*HOOK SIZE 6–12*
TAIL	G.P. Tippets and Topping
BODY	Rear–$^1/2$ Red-Orange Seal's Fur
	Front–$^1/2$ Black Seal's Fur
RIB	Oval Silver
HACKLE	Black
WINGS	Bronze Mallard

MALLARD, ORANGE AND GREEN

WET	*HOOK SIZE 6–12*
TAIL	Golden Pheasant Tippets
BUTT	Orange Seal's Fur
BODY	Laurel Green Seal's Fur
RIB	Fine Oval Gold (or Silver)
HACKLE	Light or Laurel Green
WINGS	Bronze Mallard

MALLARD AND RED

WET	*HOOK SIZE 6–12*
TAG	Silver Wire and Orange Floss
TAIL	Golden Pheasant Tippets
BODY	Red Floss or Seal's Fur
RIB	Flat or Oval Silver
HACKLE	Natural Red
WINGS	Bronze Mallard

MALLARD, RED AND YELLOW

WET	*HOOK SIZE 6–12*
TAG	Yellow Floss
TAIL	Golden Pheasant Tippets
BODY	Rear–$^1/2$ Red Seal's Fur
	Front–$^1/2$ Yellow Seal's Fur
RIB	Oval Gold
HACKLE	Black
WINGS	Bronze Mallard

MALLARD AND SILVER

WET	*HOOK SIZE 6–12*
TAIL	Golden Pheasant Tippets
BODY	Flat Silver
RIB	Silver Wire
HACKLE	Black
WINGS	Bronze Mallard

Occasionally the tail is bronze mallard fibres.

MALLARD, SILVER AND CLARET

WET	*HOOK SIZE 6–12*
TAIL	Tippets, Ibis, and Peacock Sword
BODY	Flat Silver
RIB	Silver Wire
HACKLE	Dark Claret
WINGS	Bronze or Grey Mallard

Known also as the Silver Claret or Claret and Silver.

MALLARD, TEAL AND CLARET

WET	*HOOK SIZE 6–12*
TAG	Silver wire and Orange Floss
TAIL	Golden Pheasant Tippets
BODY	Claret Seal's Fur
RIB	Oval Gold or Silver
BODY HACKLE	Claret Cock
SH. HACKLE	Teal Breast
WINGS	Bronze Mallard

MALLARD AND YELLOW

WET	HOOK SIZE 6–12
TAG	Silver Wire
TAIL	Golden Pheasant Tippets
BODY	Yellow Seal's Fur
RIB	Oval Gold or Silver
HACKLE	Natural Red
WINGS	Bronze Mallard

In the larger sizes it is usual to find an underwing of golden pheasant tippets and/or blue peacock. In sea trout dressings a mixed wing is used and sometimes blue jay added at the throat. When blue jay is added then the hackle usually becomes a body hackle.

MARCH BROWN (1)

DRY	HOOK SIZE 14
TAIL	Dark Partridge fibres
BODY	Hare's Ear Fur
RIB	Yellow Floss
HACKLE	Dark Speckled Partridge
WINGS	Partridge Tail

Wet version as above, Hook Size 8–12. Yellow or primrose tying silk is used in March Brown dressings.

MARCH BROWN (2)

WET	HOOK SIZE 8–12
TAIL	Three fibres of Bronze Mallard
BODY	Two parts Hare's Ear Fur One part Medium Olive Seal's Fur (well mixed)
RIB	Fine Oval Gold
HACKLE	Dark Brown Partridge
WING	Dark Partridge Rump Feather

The wing is a single rolled feather. A dressing by Michael Rogan, Ballyshannon.

MARCH BROWN (3)

DRY	HOOK SIZE 14
TAIL	Dark Speckled Partridge fibres
BODY	Hare's Ear Fur with pinch of Orange Seal's Fur added
RIB	Primrose tying silk
HACKLE	Ginger Cock
WINGS	Dark Partridge

March Brown and Claret as above but with dark claret hackle. (Claret March Brown).

MARCH BROWN NYMPH (1)

WET	HOOK SIZE L.S. 14
TAIL	Three fibres Dark Speckled Partridge
BODY	Rich Hare's Ear Fur
RIB	Orange Floss or Gold Wire
WING CASES	Cock Pheasant Tail fibres
THORAX	Rich Hare's Ear Fur (plump)
LEGS	Dark Speckled Partridge

Tie down wing cases at head.

MARCH BROWN NYMPH (2)

WET	HOOK SIZE L.S. 14
TAIL	Three fibres Dark Partridge
BODY	Orange Floss
BODY HACKLE	Dark Brown Cock (Clipped)
WING CASES	Cock Pheasant Tail fibres
THORAX	Hare's Ear Fur or Brown Olive Fur
LEGS	Dark Speckled Partridge

Tie down wing-cases at head.

These two dressings were used by T. J Hanna of Moneymore.

MARCH BROWN NYMPH (3)

WET	*HOOK SIZE L.S. 14*
TAIL	Three short fibres Dark Partridge
WING CASES	Woodcock Wing
BODY	Fiery Brown Seal's Fur
RIB	Gold Wire
THORAX	Thickened with Hare's Ear Fur
LEGS	Dark Grouse

Wing Cases tied in at tail and brought forward to head. *See also Gold March Brown, Silver March Brown, and Purple March Brown.*

MARCH BROWN SPIDER (1)

WET	*HOOK SIZE 12–14*
BODY	Dark Hare's Ear Fur (plump)
RIB	Fine Oval Gold
HACKLE	Long Dark Partridge (sparse)

MARCH BROWN SPIDER (2)

WET	*HOOK SIZE 12–14*
TAG	Flat Gold
BODY	Hare's Ear Fur (Plump)
HACKLE	From outside of Golden Plover Wing

The hackle should be gold-spangled. The March Brown is an extremely useful pattern in Spring. *See also Olive March Brown.*

MARCH BROWN SPIDER (3)

WET	*HOOK SIZE 8–12*
TAG	Flat Gold
TAIL	Rat's Whiskers
BODY	Light Oak Floss
RIB	Black or Brown Floss
HACKLE	Black Hen or Woodcock
WINGS	Starling

A very old dressing.

MATT GORMAN

WET	*HOOK SIZE 8–12*
TAIL	Bronze Mallard Fibres
BUTT	Light Blue Floss
BODY	Bronze Peacock Herl
RIB	Oval Gold
BODY HACKLE	Red or Ginger Cock (to shoulder)
WINGS	Woodcock
HORNS	Fibres Hen Pheasant Tail

The horns to be back over wings and consist of two married fibres on each side.

MELVIN OLIVE (1)

WET	*HOOK SIZE 8–12*
TAIL	Golden Pheasant Tippets
BODY	Light Greenish-Olive Seal's Fur
RIB	Oval Gold
BODY HACKLE	Golden Olive Cock (to shoulder)
WINGS	Grey Duck

See also Red Olive.

MELVIN OLIVE (2)

WET	HOOK SIZE 8–12
TAIL	Fibres Grey Mallard
BODY	Sooty Olive Seal's Fur
HACKLE	Medium Olive
WINGS	Grey Duck

Two dressings for Lough Melvin, Co. Fermanagh.

MIDGE CLUMP

DRY	HOOK SIZE L.S. 12–14
BODY	Dark Olive Floss or Seal's Fur (slim)
BODY HACKLE	from head to tail with Light or Medium Olive Cock hackles
RIB	Finest Oval Gold

It can have added slips of starling inserted between hackle turns. These do not require to be paired but look untidy as does a natural clump of midges.

MAYFLIES

(NYMPHS – STRADDLEBUGS – SPENT GNATS)

THE IRISH PATTERNS are numerous and at times seem so far removed from each other in colour as to be ludicrous. They all, however, kill their quota of fish each year but are very much a matter of personal choice.

Personal choice also comes into hooks, and whilst I prefer to use long shanked hooks – except for nymphs – many anglers prefer the normal shank. I have not,therefore, attempted to specify hook type in the dressings.

NYMPHS (1)

WET	HOOK SIZE 8
TAIL	Four short fibres Dark Partridge
BODY	Dark Olive Seal's Fur
RIB	Fine Oval Gold (close ribbed)
BODY HACKLE	Ginger Cock
SH. HACKLE	Dark Speckled Partridge

NYMPHS (2)

WET	HOOK SIZE 8
TAIL	Fibres Ginger Cock
BODY	Golden Olive Seal's Fur
RIB	Fine Oval Gold
BODY HACKLE	Orange Cock
SH. HACKLE	Grey Speckled Partridge (dyed Golden Olive)

NYMPHS (3)

WET	HOOK SIZE 8
TAIL	Few short fibres Grey Speckled Partridge
BODY	Light Olive Seal's Fur
RIB	Fine Oval Gold
BODY HACKLE	Medium Olive Cock
SH. HACKLES	1) Dark Olive Cock
	2) Grey Speckled Partridge

BISHOP'S NYMPH

WET	*HOOK SIZE 8*
TAIL	Six fibres Dark Partridge (short & well speckled)
BODY	Rear - $1/2$ Mole fur Front - $1/2$ Yellow Seal's Fur + Hare's Ear Fur
WINGS	Four, Light Red Cock hackle tips tied short and low over body — two per wing
HACKLE	Two turns Long Red Cock

CRANNOGE BROWN (1)

NYMPH	*HOOK SIZE 8*
TAIL	Fibres of Speckled Mandarin Duck
BODY	Apple Green Floss Silk
RIB	Fine Oval Gold (close-ribbed)
BODY HACKLE	Fiery Brown or Furnace Cock
SH. HACKLES	1) Dark Green Neck Feather from Golden Pheasant
	2) Speckled Mandarin Duck

CRANNOGE BROWN (2)

NYMPH	*HOOK SIZE 8*
TAIL	Short Bronze Mallard fibres
BODY	Natural Raffia
RIB	Oval Gold
BODY HACKLE	Natural Red Cock
SH. HACKLES	1) Fiery Brown Cock
	2) Dark Grouse

GRAVELLY

NYMPH	*HOOK SIZE 8*
TAG	Yellow Floss Silk
TAIL	Grey Partridge fibres
BODY	Golden Olive Seal's Fur
RIB	Oval Gold
BODY HACKLE	Ginger Cock
SH. HACKLE	Long Grey Speckled Partridge

The late Sam Anderson's pattern.

GREENDRAKE NYMPH

WET	*HOOK SIZE 8*
TAIL	Three fibres Peacock Herl
BODY	Green Peacock
RIB	Fine Oval Silver
BODY HACKLE	Olive Dun Hen
SH. HACKLE	1) Olive Dun Cock
	2) Grey Mallard (dyed dirty olive)

HACKETTS' NYMPH

WET	*HOOK SIZE 8*
TIP	Fine Oval Gold
TAIL	Bunch of badger Cock Fibres
BODY	Old Gold Floss
RIB	Black Floss
BODY HACKLE	Ginger Cock
LEGS	Three short strands of Peacock Sword projecting from each side
HEAD	Black Ostrich Herl

HANNA'S NYMPH

WET	*HOOK SIZE L.S. 10*
TAIL	Three short fibres Cock Pheasant Tail
BODY	Deep Yellow Balloon Rubber
RIB	Gold Wire
WING CASES	Cock Pheasant Tail
THORAX	Blue Hare Fur
LEGS	Dark Partridge or Grey Partridge (dyed Greenish-Olive)

HATCHING MAY

WET	*HOOK SIZE 8*
TAIL	Three fibres Cock Pheasant Tail
BODY	Yellow Floss
RIB	Scarlet Floss
HACKLE	Orange Cock (short)
WINGS	A tiny pair of grey duck breast feathers (dyed Bright Yellow) back-to-back, projecting over hook eye

LANSDALE PARTRIDGE

WET	*HOOK SIZE L.S. 10*
TAIL	Three fibres Cock Pheasant Tail
BODY	Darkest Brown Wool
HACKLES	1) Short Ginger Cock
	2) French Partridge

A killing pattern for the larger lakes.

LANSDALE SPECIAL

WET	*HOOK SIZE 8–10*
TAIL	Four fibres Cock Pheasant Tail
BODY	Thick Cock Pheasant Tail fibres
RIB	Oval Gold
HACKLES	1) Short Red Cock (from Mid-body)
	2) French Partridge

Not as well-known as the previous pattern but equally effective.

STRADDLE BUGS

THESE DRESSINGS are designed to be fished, wet-fly fashion, in the surface film. They should not be oiled or dressed to keep them afloat. The body hackles are cock but henny-cock hackles are better for shoulder hackles as they have a natural fibre curve and also absorb sufficient moisture to sink the fly into the surface.

An old Straddlebug dressing positioned the shoulder hackle with forward facing points to give greater mobility when drawn through the water. Such a method looks very rough to the fisherman but very attractive to the fish.

FRENCH PARTRIDGE (1)

STRADDLE	*HOOK SIZE 8–10*
TAIL	Three fibres Cock Pheasant Tail
BODY	Beige Seal's Fur
RIB	Fine Oval Gold
SH. HACKLES	1) Yellow Cock
	2) Brown Speckled Partridge
	3) French Partridge

An old dressing used many years ago by Major Knox-Browne on Lough Erne, Co. Fermanagh.

FRENCH PARTRIDGE (2)

STRADDLE   *HOOK SIZE 8–10*

TAIL	Three fibres Cock Pheasant Tail
BODY	Natural Raffia
RIB	Fine Oval Gold
BODY HACKLE	Medium Olive Cock
SH. HACKLES	1) Medium Olive Cock
	2) French Partridge

FRENCH PARTRIDGE (3)

STRADDLE   *HOOK SIZE 8–10*

TAIL	Three fibres Cock Pheasant Tail
BODY	Natural Raffia (dyed green-yellow)
RIB	Gold Wire
SH. HACKLES	1) Orange Cock
	2) French Partridge

FRENCH PARTRIDGE (4)

STRADDLE   *HOOK SIZE 8–10*

TAG	Flat Gold
BODY	Bronze Peacock Herl
SH. HACKLE	French Partridge

FRENCH PARTRIDGE (5)

STRADDLE   *HOOK SIZE 8–10*

TAG	Flat Gold
BODY	Dark Chestnut Mohair
RIB	Gold Wire
SH. HACKLE	French Partridge

FRENCH PARTRIDGE (6)

STRADDLE   *HOOK SIZE 8*

TAIL	Three fibres Cock Pheasant Tail
BODY	Natural Raffia
RIB	Gold Wire
BODY HACKLE	White Cock
SH. HACKLES	1) Golden Olive Cock
	2) French Partridge

LOUGH ARROW GREEN (1)

STRADDLE   *HOOK SIZE 8*

TAIL	Three fibres Cock Pheasant Tail
BODY	Natural Raffia
RIB	Fine Oval Gold or Wire
BODY HACKLE	Barred Rock Cock (dyed Medium Olive or Greendrake)
SH. HACKLES	1) Grey Partridge (dyed Golden Olive)
	2) French Partridge (dyed Greendrake)
	3) Grey Partridge (dyed Medium Olive)

LOUGH ARROW GREEN (2)

STRADDLE   *HOOK SIZE 8*

TAIL	Three fibres Cock Pheasant Tail
BODY	Natural Raffia
RIB	Finest Oval Gold
BODY HACKLE	White Cock
SH. HACKLES	1) Grey Partridge (dyed Golden Olive)
	2) French Partridge (dyed Green Olive)
	3) Grey Partridge (dyed Green Olive)

LOUGH ERNE GOSLING (1)

STRADDLE   *HOOK SIZE 8*

TAIL	Three fibres Bronze Mallard
BODY	Golden Olive Seal's Fur
RIB	Oval Gold or Wire
BODY HACKLE	Scarlet or Bright Claret Cock
SH. HACKLE	Long Grey Mallard (dyed Golden Olive)

LOUGH ERNE GOSLING (2)

STRADDLE	*HOOK SIZE 8*
TAIL	Three fibres Cock Pheasant Tail
BODY	Medium Olive Seal's Fur
RIB	Oval Gold
SH. HACKLES	1) Scarlet Cock
	2) Grey Speckled Mallard (dyed Yellow)

The Lough Erne Goslings were patterns used by Sam Anderson.

LOUGH MELVIN GOSLING

STRADDLE	*HOOK SIZE 8*
TAIL	Three fibres Bronze Mallard
BODY	Golden Olive Seal's Fur or Floss
RIB	Fine Oval Gold
SH. HACKLES	1) Orange, or Golden Olive, or Bright Yellow
	2) Grey Speckled Mallard (some dressings dyed Light Olive)

MAYO GOSLING (1)

STRADDLE	*HOOK SIZE 8*
TAIL	Six fibres Bronze Mallard
BODY	Beige Floss
RIB	Fine Oval Gold
SH. HACKLES	1) Orange
	2) Long Bronze Mallard or Grey Speckled Mallard (dyed Orange-Olive)

MAYO GOSLING (2)

STRADDLE	*HOOK SIZE 8*
TAIL	Three fibres Cock Pheasant Tail
BODY	Golden Olive Seal's Fur
RIB	Oval Gold
SH. HACKLES	1) Bright Green Cock
	2) Brown Speckled Mallard (dyed Golden Olive)

Also known as the Green Gosling.

MAYO GOSLING (3)

STRADDLE	*HOOK SIZE 8*
TAIL	Red Swan Strip
BODY	Golden Olive Seal's Fur
RIB	Flat Gold
SH. HACKLES	1) Scarlet Cock
	2) Grey Speckled Mallard (dyed Golden Olive)

ROGAN'S GOSLING

STRADDLE	*HOOK SIZE 8*
TAIL	Three fibres Cock Pheasant Tail
BODY	Golden Olive Seal's Fur
RIB	Gold Wire
SH. HACKLES	1) Brick-Orange Cock
	2) Grey Speckled Mallard

GREY GOSLING

STRADDLE	*HOOK SIZE 8*
TAIL	Three fibres Cock Pheasant Tail
BODY	Natural Raffia
RIB	Light Green Floss
BODY HACKLE	Dark Ginger Cock
SH. HACKLE	Grey Speckled Widgeon

GREY CORRIB

STRADDLE	HOOK SIZE 8
TAIL	Three fibres Cock Pheasant Tail
BODY	Natural Raffia
RIB	Fine Oval Silver
BODY HACKLE	Grey Cock
SH. HACKLES	1) Grey Partridge
	2) French Partridge (Blue-Grey)

GREEN MAY

STRADDLE	HOOK SIZE 8
TAIL	Three fibres Cock Pheasant Tail
BODY	Natural Raffia
RIB	Gold Wire
BODY HACKLE	White Cock
SH. HACKLES	1) Yellow Cock
	2) French Partridge (dyed green-olive)

CANARY GOSLING

STRADDLE	HOOK SIZE 8
TAIL	Three fibres Cock Pheasant Tail
BODY	Bright Yellow Floss
RIB	Finest Oval Gold
SH. HACKLES	1) Bright Yellow Cock
	2) Long Grey Speckled Mallard (stained Bright Yellow)

SLIGO STRADDLE

STRADDLE	HOOK SIZE 8
TAIL	Three fibres Cock Pheasant Tail
BODY	White Floss
RIB	White Cock
SH. HACKLE	Long Golden Olive Cock

CLARET STRADDLE

STRADDLE	HOOK SIZE 8–10
TAIL	Three fibres Cock Pheasant Tail
BODY	Yellow Floss
RIB	Gold Wire
BODY HACKLE	Dark Claret Cock
SH. HACKLES	1) Light Game Cock
	2) Long Brown Speckled Mallard (dyed Golden Olive)

HACKLED MAYFLIES

ERNE SPECIAL

DRY	HOOK SIZE 8–10
TAIL	Three fibres Cock Pheasant Tail
BODY	Primrose Floss
RIB	Fibre of Cock Pheasant Tail
BODY SHEATH	Clear Rubber or Plastic
HACKLES	1) Brown Olive Cock
	2) Green Olive Cock
	3) Golden Olive Cock
WINGS	Two small upright tufts of Grey Mallard (dyed Yellow) in front of hackles

HACKLED MAY (1)

DRY	*HOOK SIZE 8–10*
TAIL	Three fibres Cock Pheasant Tail
TAIL HACKLE	Short Golden Olive Cock
BODY	Yellow Floss
RIB	Bronze Peacock Quill
BODY SHEATH	Clear Rubber or Plastic
HACKLES	1) Golden Olive Cock
	2) Fiery Brown Cock
	3) Green Olive Cock
WINGS	Two tufts Grey Mallard (dyed Yellow)

Dressings of Sam Anderson.

HACKLED MAY (2)

DRY	*HOOK SIZE 8–10*
TAIL	Three fibres Cock Pheasant Tail
BODY	Natural Raffia
RIB	Fine Oval Gold
HACKLES	1) Red Game Cock
	2) Orange Cock
	3) Grey Mallard (dyed Green Olive)

HACKLED MAY (3)

DRY	*HOOK SIZE 8–10*
TAIL	Three fibres Cock Pheasant Tail
TAIL HACKLE	Short Golden Olive Cock
BODY	Yellow Floss
RIB	Brown Floss
HACKLES	1) Red Game Cock
	2) Light Olive Cock
	3) Dirty Golden Olive Cock
	4) Grey Mallard (dyed Medium Olive – one turn)

HACKLED MAY QUILL (4)

DRY	*HOOK SIZE 8–10*
TAIL	Three fibres Cock Pheasant Tail
TAIL HACKLE	Short Dirty Golden Olive
BODY	Peacock Eye Quill (dyed Golden Olive)
HACKLES	1) Fiery Brown Cock
	2) Golden Olive Cock
	3) Green Olive Cock

A dressing by Sam Anderson.

HACKLED MAY (5) (6) (7)

DRY	*HOOK SIZE 8–10*
TAIL	Three fibres Cock Pheasant Tail
TAIL HACKLE	Short Golden Olive Cock
BODY	Primrose Floss
BODY SHEATH	Clear Rubber or Plastic (varnished)
RIB	Unstripped Bronze Peacock Herl applied to wet varnish of body
HACKLES (5)	1) Golden Olive Cock
	2) Fiery Brown Cock
	3) Light Olive Cock
HACKLES (6)	1) Fiery Brown Cock
	2) Bright Yellow Cock
	3) Grey Mallard (dyed Medium Olive)
HACKLES (7)	1) Red Game Cock (dyed Yellow)
	2) Light Olive Cock
	3) Dirty Golden Olive Cock
WINGS	Two tufts of Grey Mallard (dyed Golden Olive)

These are three personal dressings by the late Sam Anderson.

GOULDEN'S FAVOURITE

DRY	*HOOK SIZE 8–10*
TAIL	Three fibres Cock Pheasant Tail
BODY	Translucent Yellow Olive Rubber
HACKLES	1) Natural Red Cock
	2) Orange Cock
	3) Grey Mallard (dyed Green Olive)

MOSELEY MAY

DRY	*HOOK SIZE 8–10*
TAIL	Three fibres Cock Pheasant Tail
BODY	Mixture of Hare's Ear and Yellow Seal's Fur
RIB	Gold Wire

HACKLES	1) Long fibred Green-Grey Olive Cock
	2) Shorter fibred Light Yellow Cock

Both hackles are bound on together and tied in half-circle position.

PLAIN MAY

DRY	*HOOK SIZE 8–10*
TAIL	Three fibres Cock Pheasant Tail
BODY	Yellow Floss
RIB	Peacock Eye Quill (dyed Red)
HACKLES	1) Two Light Straw Cock
	2) Grey Mallard (dyed Yellow)

WINGED MAYFLIES

THE CAUGHLAN

DRY FANWING	*HOOK SIZE 8–10*
TAIL	Three fibres Cock Pheasant Tail
BODY	Yellow Floss
RIB	Bronze Peacock Herl
WINGS	Brown Mallard Breast
HACKLES	Two Light Yellow Cock

THE ERNE

DRY	*HOOK SIZE 8–10*
TAIL	Three fibres Cock Pheasant Tail
TAIL HACKLE	Short Medium Olive Cock
BODY	Yellow Floss
RIB	Peacock Quill

BODY SHEATH	Clear Plastic
WINGS	Two pairs Medium Olive Cock hackle tips (tied semi-spent)
HACKLES	Two Medium Olive Cock

FURNACE MAY

DRY	*HOOK SIZE 8–10*
TAIL	Three fibres Cock Pheasant Tail
BODY	Yellow Floss
RIB	Gold Wire
BODY SHEATH	Clear Plastic
WINGS	Two pairs Furnace Cock hackle tips
HACKLES	Two Medium Olive Cock

GREENDRAKE (1)

DRY FANWING   *HOOK SIZE 8–10*

TAIL	Three fibres Cock Pheasant Tail
BODY	Natural Raffia
RIB	Claret Floss
WINGS	Grey Speckled Mallard Breast
HACKLES	1) Yellow Cock
	2) Dark Grouse

GREENDRAKE (2)

Gregory Greendrake's dressing was

BODY	Green Monkey Fur and White Dubbing
HACKLE	Cuckoo dyed Yellow
WINGS	Mallard or Widgeon Breast feathers (dyed Yellow)

The wings – well speckled.

GREY DRAKE (1)

DRY FANWING   *HOOK SIZE 8–10*

TAIL	Three fibres Cock Pheasant Tail
BODY	Natural Raffia
BODY HACKLE	Badger Cock
WINGS	Grey Speckled Mallard Breast
HACKLES	1) Badger Cock
	2) Grey Speckled Partridge (dyed Golden Olive)

Badger hackle behind wings. Partridge in front.

GREY DRAKE (2)

DRY FANWING   *HOOK SIZE 8–10*

TAIL	Three fibres Cock Pheasant Tail
BODY	Natural Raffia
RIB	Silver Wire and Scarlet Floss
BODY HACKLE	Badger Cock
WINGS	Grey Speckled Mallard Breast
HACKLES	1) Badger Cock
	2) Grey Speckled Partridge

Badger hackle behind wings. Partridge in front.

IRISH MAYFLY (1)

DRY FANWING   *HOOK SIZE 8–10*

TAIL	Three fibres Cock Pheasant Tail
BODY	Yellow Floss
RIB	Black Floss
WINGS	Speckled Mallard Breast (dyed Golden Olive)
HACKLE	Two Furnace Cock

IRISH MAYFLY (2)

DRY FANWING   *HOOK SIZE 8–10*

TAIL	Three fibres Cock Pheasant Tail
BODY	Cream Floss
RIB	Gold Wire
WINGS	Speckled Mallard Breast (dyed Golden Olive)
HACKLE	Yellow Cock

THE MONEYMORE

DRY FANWING   *HOOK SIZE 10*

TAIL	Three fibres Cock Pheasant Tail
BODY	Translucent Yellow-Olive Rubber
WINGS	Two Grey-speckled Mallard breast feathers (dyed Green-Olive) tied spent between hackles
HACKLES	1) Natural Red Cock
	2) Orange Cock

A dressing by T. J. Hanna.

SLIGO MAY (1)

DRY FANWING   *HOOK SIZE 8–10*

TAIL	Three fibres Cock Pheasant Tail
BODY	White Floss
RIB	Fine Gold Oval and Red Floss
BODY HACKLE	Ginger Cock
WINGS	Well marked Teal Breast
HACKLES	1) Ginger Cock
	2) Brown Speckled Partridge

SLIGO MAY (2)

DRY FIBREWING   *HOOK SIZE 8–10*

TAIL	Three fibres Cock Pheasant Tail
BODY	Natural Raffia
RIB	Fine Gold Wire
BODY HACKLE	Brown Grizzle Cock
WINGS	A single tuft, or paired tufts, or Golden Olive Cock Hackle Fibres
HACKLE	Brown Grizzle Cock

SLIGO MAY (3)

DRY HACKLE   *HOOK SIZE 8–10*

TAIL	Three fibres Cock Pheasant Tail
BODY	Pale Creamy-Olive Seal's Fur
RIB	Fine Gold Wire
HACKLES	1) Pale Creamy-Olive Cock
	2) Pale Green-Olive Cock

The hackles are tied in by the butt behind the wings, two turns behind the wings, and then figure eight through to the front and finish with two further turns. This was a pattern by Sam Anderson for Lough Erne, Co. Fermanagh.

WINGED MAY

DRY   *HOOK SIZE 8–10*

TAIL	Three fibres Cock Pheasant Tail
TAIL HACKLE	Golden Olive Cock
BODY	Primrose Floss
RIB	Peacock Quill (dyed Red)
BODY SHEATH	Clear Plastic
WINGS	Two pairs Brown Olive Cock hackle tips
HACKLES	1) Golden Olive Cock
	2) Light Straw Cock

YELLOW DRAKE

DRY FANWING   *HOOK SIZE 8–10*

TAIL	Three fibres Cock Pheasant Tail
BODY	Yellow Raffia
RIB	Fine Oval Gold
WINGS	Speckled Mallard Breast (dyed Golden Olive)
HACKLES	1) Yellow Cock
	2) Speckled Grey Partridge (dyed Light Olive)

YELLOW MAY

DRY FANWING   *HOOK SIZE 8–10*

TAIL	Three fibres Cock Pheasant Tail
BODY	Shaped Cork
RIB	Silver Wire
WINGS	Grey Speckled Mallard Breast (dyed Golden Olive)

HACKLES	Two Dirty Olive Cock
	or
	Two Dark Ginger Cock

Fanwing Mayflies can be difficult to use causing twisting problems to the gut cast and it is probably better modified by using two tufts of the appropriate feather fibres set upwards at a 45° angle.

SPENT GNATS

MURROUGH

DRY   *HOOK SIZE L.S. 8–10*

TAIL	Three fibres Cock Pheasant Tail
TAIL HACKLE	Short Iron Blue Cock
BODY	White Floss
RIB	Peacock Quill
BODY SHEATH	Clear Plastic
UNDERWINGS	Two Iron Blue Cock Hackle Tips
OVERWINGS	Two barred Rock Cock Hackle Tips
HACKLE	Barred Rock Cock

Hackle trimmed underneath to form half-circle.

GRIZZLE GNAT

As above but with dark grizzle over-wings and hackle.

FURNACE GNAT

As above but with Light Furnace over-wings and hackle.

GREY GNAT

As above but with bluish-grey overwings and hackle. In all dressings the Hackle is long-fibred and tied in behind the wings. Two turns behind, figure-eight to the front, and a final two turns.

The preceding dressings were S. Anderson's . He favoured the Murrough for his own fishing but did not rib the floss. After covering the floss with clear plastic he heavily varnished the plastic and ribbed it with unstripped Peacock Herl. This rib had the disadvantage of being vulnerable to the teeth of trout but as a professional fly-dresser this was no problem for him. He maintained also that the trimming of the hackle added to its floating qualities so necessary for fishing in a heavy wave. His dressing for fibre wing Spent Gnat was as follows—

TAIL	Three fibres Cock Pheasant Tail
BODY	White Floss
RIB	Peacock Quill
BODY SHEATH	Clear Plastic
WINGS	1) Long Dirty White Cock hackle
	2) Longer fibred Natural Black or Iron Blue Cock

The white hackle was tied and wound about five turns. Then the black hackle wound on in similar fashion.Both hackles are then pressed down to form spent wings and the tying silk is figure-eighted top and bottom around hackles and hook shank.

BLACK DRAKE

DRY	*HOOK SIZE 8–10*
TAIL	Three fibres Cock Pheasant Tail
BODY	White Floss
BODY SHEATH	Clear Rubber
WINGS	Two pairs White Cock hackle tips
HACKLE	Badger Cock

This was a dressing of T. J. Hanna's.

BLACK GNAT

DRY	*HOOK SIZE 8–10*
TAIL	Three fibres Cock Pheasant Tail
BODY	Gold Floss
RIB	Fine Oval Silver
WINGS	Two pairs natural Black or Iron Blue Cock hackles
HACKLE	Light Grizzle Cock tied half-circle

BROWN SPENT

DRY	*HOOK SIZE 10*
TAIL	Three fibres Cock Pheasant Tail
BODY	Natural Raffia
RIB	Silver Wire
BODY HACKLE	Clipped Barred Rock Cock
HACKLE	Two Chocolate Dun Cock tied spent fashion by figure-of-eight lashings

HACKLE SPENT (1)

DRY	*HOOK SIZE 8–10*
TAIL	Three fibres Cock Pheasant Tail
TAIL HACKLE	Short Iron Blue Cock
BODY	Hare's Ear Fur
RIB	Gold Wire
HACKLE	Long Badger Cock wound full and tied Spent wing fashion

HACKLE SPENT (2)

DRY	*HOOK SIZE 8–10*
TAIL	Three fibres Cock Pheasant Tail
BODY	White Floss
RIB	Fine Oval Gold
HACKLES	1) Short Badger Cock
	2) Long Grey Speckled Mallard tied half-circle

INNY SPENT

DRY	*HOOK SIZE 10*
TAG	Red Floss
TAIL	Six fibres Well Marked Teal Flank
BODY	White Floss
RIB	Gold Wire
BODY HACKLE	Short fibred White Cock
HACKLES	Two Smoke-Grey Cock tied half-circle

ROGAN'S SPENT

DRY	HOOK SIZE L.S. 8–10
TAG	Scarlet Floss
TAIL	Three fibres Cock Pheasant Tail
BODY	Natural Raffia
RIB	Silver Wire
BODY HACKLE	Clipped White Cock which is close wound at shoulder
WINGS	Blue Vulturine Guinea-fowl wound about six turns and tied down Spent fashion by figure-of-eight lashings

SHEELIN GNAT

DRY	HOOK SIZE 8–10
TAIL	Three fibres Cock Pheasant Tail
BODY	Natural Raffia
RIB	Gold Wire
BODY HACKLE	White Cock
HACKLE	Long Natural Black Cock wound full and tied half-circle

---

The late Sam Anderson, Maralin, Co. Down, was held in high regard as an angler and a fly-tyer, but few knew of his verses. These were his last, showing his great love for Lough Erne, and dedicated to Herby Elliot and the late Thompson Irvine – a life-long friend, at the end of the 1965 Mayfly season.

FAREWELL TO LOUGH ERNE

Farewell dearest Erne, farewell for a while,
Once more we must leave you, but we'll do it in style,
We'll sing of your praises, our time honoured Queen,
Of your bright silvery waters and islands so green.

Farewell to Hill's Island and Graham's lovely shore,
To the dear hills of Magho and Benmore.
To the Cranoges and Gravelly and Soldier between,
What raptures, what splendour, what delights we have
*   seen.*

Farewell to those anglers we meet every year,
Always waiting to greet us with good Irish cheer.
To the sweet fluting blackbird in yon thorny lair,
To the lark ever warbling in Legg's ambient air.

Farewell to those shores that your bright waters lave,
Farewell to the magic of ripple and wave.
To the long shimmering drift and blowline's proud swell,
To the 'rise' and the rapture, to all these farewell.

Farewell for a while for the days will soon speed,
And the snow of the hawthorn will call us indeed;
Call us back once again, where our hearts ever yearn,
To our first love, our last love, dear old Lough Erne.

THE OLIVES

THE OLIVES are the most important all season fly for lake and river and the dressings are many and varied.

The most common patterns are the Olive Quills and the Olive Duns but even these are varied and given a different name thus we have the Lake Olive, the Orange Olive, the Melvin Olive and very many more.

In the Quill dressings the body should have well defined rib markings and it is becoming more popular to use Teal Wing quill slips for wings in preference to the standard starling. Teal is certainly stronger and more durable.

OLIVE QUILL

DRY	*HOOK SIZE 14–16*
WET	*10–14*
TAIL	Fibres of Olive Cock
BODY	Stripped Peacock Eye Quill
WINGS	Starling
HACKLE	Olive

The tail and hackle use the colour required i.e. Light Olive, Medium Olive, Dark Olive, Sooty Olive. If the wing is dispensed with, in the dry pattern, then it becomes the Hackled Olive Quill.

OLIVE COWDUNG

WET	*HOOK SIZE 10–14*
BODY	Green Olive Seal's Fur
THORAX	Green Olive and Golden Olive Seal's Fur (mixed)
HACKLE	Dark Ginger
WINGS	Landrail

OLIVE DUN

DRY	*HOOK SIZE 14–16*
WET	*10–14*
TAG	Flat Gold
TAIL	Fibres of Olive Cock
BODY	Olive Seal's Fur
RIB	Gold Wire (optional)
WINGS	Starling
HACKLE	Olive

When tied without rib is also known as the

Rough Olive. Again the tail, body, and hackle are of the shade required. The Hackled Olive or the Hackled Rough Olive as above but without starling wing.
See also Rough Olives and Sooty Olives.

OLIVE MARCH BROWN (1)

WET	*HOOK SIZE 8–12*
TAG	Silver Wire
TAIL	Bronze Mallard Fibres
BODY	Medium Olive Seal's Fur
RIB	Oval Silver
BODY HACKLE	Medium Olive Cock
HACKLE	Furnace
WINGS	Brown Speckled Partridge

OLIVE MARCH BROWN (2)

TAIL	Dark Speckled Partridge fibres
BODY	Hare's Ear Fur
RIB	Fine Oval Silver
HACKLE	Medium Olive
WINGS	Dark Speckled Partridge

OLIVE MIDGE (1)

DRY	*HOOK SIZE 16*
TAIL	Three fibres White Cock
BODY	Beige Seal's Fur
WINGS	Light Starling
HACKLE	Light Olive Cock

OLIVE MIDGE (2)

DRY	*HOOK SIZE 16*
TAIL	Three fibres Light Ginger Cock
BODY	Clipped Honey Cock
HACKLES	1) Medium Olive Cock
	2) Light Ginger Cock (wound on together)

OLIVE MIDGE (3)

DRY	*HOOK SIZE 16*
TAIL	Three fibres Light Olive Cock
BODY	Grey Seal's Fur
RIB	Silver Wire
HACKLE	Light Olive

OLIVE NYMPH (1)

WET	*HOOK SIZE L.S. 14*
TAIL	Three fibres Olive Cock
BODY	Yellow floss
RIB	Clipped Olive Dun
WING CASES	Cock Pheasant Tail fibres
THORAX	Olive Fur
LEGS	Grey Partridge (dyed Olive)

OLIVE NYMPH (2)

WET	*HOOK SIZE L.S. 14*
TAIL	Three fibres Olive Cock
BODY	Olive Seal's Fur
RIB	Gold Wire
WING CASES	Cock Pheasant Tail fibres
THORAX	Thickened Olive Seal's Fur
LEGS	Grey or Brown Speckled partridge (dyed greenish olive)

Two dressings by Hanna. Olive shade as required.

OLIVE NYMPH (3)

WET	*HOOK SIZE L.S. 14*
TAIL	Three fibres Olive Cock
WING CASES	Mallard wing (inner flights)
BODY	Medium Olive Seal's Fur
RIB	Fine Oval Gold
THORAX	As body but thickened and unribbed
LEGS	Dark Olive Hen

Tie down wing-cases to enclose full body.

OLIVE NYMPH (4)

WET	*HOOK SIZE L.S. 14*
TAIL	Three fibres Medium Olive Cock
BODY	Green Olive Floss (tapered)
THORAX	Medium Olive Ostrich or Seal's Fur
HACKLE	Dark Olive Hen

OLIVE NYMPH (5)

WET	*HOOK SIZE L.S. 14*
TAIL	Three fibres Light Olive Cock
BODY	Grey Seal's Fur
RIB	Gold Wire
THORAX	Medium Olive Seal's Fur (unribbed)
HACKLE	Medium Olive Hen

OLIVE SNARE

WET   HOOK SIZE 10–12
TAG   Silver
TAIL   Mallard fibres
BODY   Green Monkey and Olive
           Mohair

RIB   Silver (optional)
HACKLE   Ginger or Olive Dun
WINGS   Brown Mallard

A dressing by 'Hi-Regan'.

OLD LEATHER (1)

WET   HOOK SIZE 8–12
TAIL   Golden Pheasant Tippets
BODY   Reddish Claret Seal's Fur
RIB   Oval Gold
BODY HACKLE Golden Olive
WINGS   Light Partridge

An old Co. Donegal pattern.

OLD LEATHER (2)

WET   HOOK SIZE 8–12
TAIL   Golden Pheasant Tippets
BODY   Reddish Claret Seal's Fur
RIB   Flat Gold
BODY HACKLE Claret Cock
WINGS   Teal Flank

A dressing for Connemara.

OLD LEATHER (3)

WET   HOOK SIZE 8–12
TAIL   Golden Pheasant Tippets
BODY   Rich Reddish-Brown
           Seal's Fur
RIB   Oval Gold
HACKLE   Black Cock
WINGS   Bronze Mallard.

A Co. Tyrone dressing.

ORANGE GROUSE

WET   HOOK SIZE 6–12
TAG   Silver Wire
TAIL   Golden Pheasant Topping
BODY   Orange Floss
RIB   Oval Gold
BODY HACKLE Dark Speckled Grouse
WINGS   Bronze Mallard

The sea trout dressing generally has married strips of red, yellow, and blue swan as an underwing. Body hackle is sometimes used as shoulder hackle. *See also Grouse and Orange.*

ORANGE OLIVE

WET   HOOK SIZE 8–12
TAIL   Fibres Honey Cock
BODY   Yellow-Orange Seal's Fur
RIB   Oval Silver
HACKLE   Honey Badger
WINGS   Grouse

ORANGE JAY (1)

WET   HOOK SIZE 8–12
TAIL   Bronze Mallard fibres
BODY   Orange Seal's Fur
RIB   Oval Gold or Silver
HACKLE   Blue Jay
WINGS   Jay Quill

ORANGE JAY (2)

WET   HOOK SIZE 8–12
TAG   Gold Wire
TAIL   Bronze Mallard fibres
BODY   Orange Pig's Wool
RIB   Gold
HACKLE   Black
WINGS   Blue-Barred Jay Sides

ORANGE PEGGY (1)

WET   HOOK SIZE 8–12
TAIL   Golden Pheasant Tippets
BODY   Black Floss
RIB   Oval Gold
BODY HACKLE Orange Cock from mid-
           body
HACKLE   Long Black Hen

An old Lough Erne (Co. Fermanagh) pattern.

ORANGE PEGGY (2)

WET   HOOK SIZE 8–12
TAIL   Golden Pheasant Tippets
BODY   Black Seal's Fur (slim)
RIB   Flat Gold (close ribbed)
BODY HACKLE Orange Cock from mid-
           body
HACKLE   Orange
WINGS   Mallard Speculum

An old Lough Melvin (Co. Fermanagh) pattern.

ORANGE QUILL (1)

DRY   HOOK SIZE 14–16
TAIL   Three fibres Ginger Cock
BODY   Swan Herl (dyed Orange)
RIB   Brown Olive Floss
WINGS   Dark Starling
HACKLE   Dark Ginger Cock

ORANGE QUILL (2)

DRY   HOOK SIZE 14–16
TAIL   Three fibres Furnace Cock
BODY   Stripped Peacock Eye Quill
WINGS   Starling (dyed Orange)
HACKLE   Furnace Cock

ORANGE QUILL (3)

DRY   HOOK SIZE 16
TAIL   Three fibres White Cock
BODY   Stripped Peacock Eye Quill
           (dyed Orange)
HACKLE   Barred Rock Cock

ORANGE QUILL (4)

DRY   HOOK SIZE 16
TAIL   Three fibres Badger Cock
BODY   Stripped Peacock Eye Quill
           (dyed Orange)
HACKLE   Steely-blue Cock

Dressings No. 3 and 4 are used on the Lough Neagh System.

PALE EVENING DUN

DRY   HOOK SIZE 16
TAIL   Three fibres Black Cock
BUTT   Pea-green Floss
BODY   Yellow Seal's Fur
HACKLE   Ginger Grizzle Cock

PALE WATERY DUN (1)

DRY   HOOK SIZE 16
TAIL   Three fibres Honey Cock
BODY   Claret and White Seal's
           Fur (mixed)
WINGS   Light Starling (double
           split)
HACKLE   Honey or Honey Dun
           Cock

PALE WATERY DUN (2)

DRY	*HOOK SIZE 16*
TAIL	Three fibres Light Ginger Cock
BODY	Pale Primrose Silk
RIB	Gold Wire
HACKLE	Pale Blue Dun or Cream Cock

This dressing is tied 'half-circle'.

PALE WATERY SPINNER

DRY	*HOOK SIZE 16*
TAIL	Three fibres White Cock
BODY	Palest Yellow Seal's Fur
HACKLE	Palest Blue Dun or Smoke-Grey Cock

This dressing is tied 'half-circle'.

PALE WATERY NYMPH

WET	*HOOK SIZE L.S. 14*
TAIL	Three short fibres Yellow Cock
BODY	Ivory Floss
BODY HACKLE	Clipped Pale Lemon Cock
WING CASES	Cock Pheasant Tail fibres
THORAX	Light Olive Seal's Fur with an added pinch of Hare's Ear Fur
LEGS	Grey Partridge dyed pale green

Wing Cases tied down at head.

PALMERS

BLACK PALMER

WET	*HOOK SIZE 8-12*
TAIL	Fibres Furnace Cock
BODY	Black Seal's Fur
RIB	Oval Silver
BODY HACKLE	Furnace Cock
HACKLE	Long Natural Dark Red

BLUE PALMER

WET	*HOOK SIZE 8–12*
TAIL	Fibres Dark Ginger Cock
BODY	Blue Rabbit Fur
RIB	Fine Oval Gold or Wire
BODY HACKLE	Dark Ginger Cock
HACKLE	Long Dark Ginger

BROWN PALMER

WET	*HOOK SIZE 8–12*
TAIL	Fibres Red Cock
BODY	Fiery Brown Seal's Fur
RIB	Fine Oval Gold
BODY HACKLE	Natural Red Cock
HACKLE	Long Natural Red

PINK PALMER

WET	*HOOK SIZE 8–12*
TAIL	Fibres Red Cock
BODY	Pale Pink Floss (bulky and tapered)
RIB	Fine Oval Gold or Wire
BODY HACKLE	Red or Dark Ginger Cock
HACKLE	Long Natural Red (sparse)

This wet dressing has been tried by a number of anglers over the past five years and has proved to be an extremely successful pattern for lake trout.

SOLDIER PALMER

WET	*HOOK SIZE 8–12*
Tail	Fibres Red Cock
Body	Scarlet Seal's Fur
Rib	Fine Oval Gold
Body Hackle	Natural Dark Red Cock
Hackle	Long Natural Dark Red

PARTRIDGE

WET	*HOOK SIZE 10–12*
Tag	Blue-grey Seal or Rat's Fur
Body	Lemon, or Light Green, Floss
Hackle	Grey Speckled Partridge
Wings	Grey Partridge (or Starling)

Known also as the Grey Partridge.

PARTRIDGE SPIDER

WET	*HOOK SIZE 14–16*
Body	Flat Silver (short and plump)
Hackle	Long Dark Speckled Partridge (one turn)

This spider dressing can be varied in many body colours using floss or Seal's Fur – tied plump. A claret Seal's Fur body is extremely effective.

PARTRIDGE AND BLACK

WET	*HOOK SIZE 8–12*
Body	Black Floss or Seal's Fur
Rib	Oval Gold or Wire
Hackle	Long Speckled Partridge (sparse)

There is a colour distinction in the Partridge dressings, Light or Dark. The Light is achieved by using light grey Speckled Partridge and the Dark by using dark Speckled Partridge. On occasions a tag of flat tinsel is used. Partridge and Yellow, Partridge and Claret, Partridge and Green, Partridge and Orange as above dressing but with the appropriate body colour.

PARTRIDGE AND GOLD

WET	*HOOK SIZE 8–12*
Tail	Three fibres Dark Partridge
Body	Flat Gold
Rib	Gold Wire
Hackle	Dark Speckled Partridge (sparse)
Wings	Partridge

Partridge and Silver as above but with flat silver body and silver wire.

PARTRIDGE AND ORANGE

WET	*HOOK SIZE 8–12*
Tag	Flat Gold
Body	Red-Orange Seal's Fur or Floss
Rib	Oval Gold
Hackle	From outside of Partridge Wing (elbow)

PARTRIDGE AND YELLOW (1)

WET	*HOOK SIZE 8–12*
Tag	Yellow Floss
Tail	Four fibres Dark Partridge
Body	Golden Olive Seal's Fur
Rib	Oval Gold
Body Hackle	Short Ginger Cock
Hackle	Long Dark Speckled Partridge

A very good lake pattern.

PARTRIDGE AND YELLOW (2)

WET	*HOOK SIZE 8–12*
TAG	Flat Gold
BODY	Yellow Floss
RIB	Pale Green Thread (close-ribbed)
HACKLE	From outside of Partridge Wing (elbow)

PARTRIDGE AND YELLOW (3)

WET	*HOOK SIZE 10–12*
TAG	Flat Gold
BODY	Palest Lemon Floss
WINGS	Palest Grey Partridge

PEACOCK AND CLARET

WET	*HOOK SIZE 10–12*
BODY	Bronze Peacock Herl
RIB	Oval Gold
HACKLE	Dark Claret
WINGS	Starling

See also Claret Peacock.

PETER ROSS

WET	*HOOK SIZE 8–12*
TAIL	Golden Pheasant Tippets
BODY	Flat Silver
RIB	Silver Wire
THORAX	Red Floss or Seal's Fur
RIB	Fine Oval Silver
HACKLE	Black
WINGS	Well marked Teal Flank

A well known lake and sea trout pattern.

PHEASANT TAIL (1)

DRY	*HOOK SIZE 16*
TAIL	Three fibres Honey Cock
BODY	Cock Pheasant Tail fibre
RIB	Gold Wire
WINGS	Dark Starling
HACKLES	Two Honey or Honey Dun Cock

PHEASANT TAIL (2)

DRY	*HOOK SIZE 14*
TAIL	Three fibres Barred Rock Cock
BODY	Cock Pheasant Tail fibres
RIB	Gold Wire
HACKLES	1) Barred Rock Cock
	2) Black Hen

PHEASANT TAIL (3)

WET	*HOOK SIZE 12–14*
TAIL	Three fibres Grey Partridge
BODY	Cock Pheasant Tail fibres
HACKLE	Grey Speckled Partridge (sparse)
WINGS	Landrail or Red Hen

PHEASANT TAIL (4)

SPINNER	*HOOK SIZE 14–16*
TAIL	Three fibres Blue-grey Cock
BODY	Cock Pheasant Tail fibres
RIB	Gold Wire
HACKLE	Light Blue Dun Cock

The hackle is tied down spent wing fashion by figure-of-eight lashings.

PHEASANT TAIL NYMPH

WET	HOOK SIZE L.S. 14
TAIL	Three short fibres Golden Olive Cock
BODY	Cock Pheasant Tail fibre
RIB	Gold Wire
WING CASES	Hen Pheasant Wing
THORAX	Golden Olive Seal's Fur
LEGS	Short Honey Dun

The Cock Pheasant tail used in these dressings should be from an old bird and should have a rich copper-plum colouring.

PHEASANT AND YELLOW

WET	HOOK SIZE 8–10
TAIL	Red Macaw
BODY	Yellow Seal's Fur
RIB	Oval Gold
HACKLE	Blue Jay
WINGS	Hen Pheasant

PINK LADY (1)

DRY	HOOK SIZE 10–12
TAIL	Fibres Pale Ginger Cock (or Tippets)
BODY	Pink Floss
RIB	Oval Gold
HACKLE	Pale Ginger Cock
WINGS	Starling

This is the original dressing by La Branche, an American angler and writer. He intended it to be used as a dry-fly for salmon.

PINK LADY (2)

DRY	HOOK SIZE 10–14
WET	8–12
TAIL	Fibres Natural Red Cock
BODY	Pink Floss
RIB	Fine Oval Gold
BODY HACKLE	Natural Red Cock to shoulder
WINGS	Landrail

A. Courtney Williams recounts how an Irish angler, using the Pink Lady (1) as an evening dry fly for large lake trout, was so successful that he was afraid that he would be accused of poaching them. He asked the Inspector of Fisheries to try the pattern and this resulted in a basket of 50Ibs. of trout, the largest being 8Ibs. in weight. Long hackled and dragged on the surface was the method and it may be that the fish accepted it as a Sedge.

My own, and friends' experience with the Pink Palmer leads me to believe that pink is a shade which cannot be rated too highly.

PINK SHRIMP

WET	HOOK SIZE 8–12
TAIL	Fibres Natural Light Red
BODY	Pink Floss (plump and humped)
RIB	Finest Oval Gold
BODY HACKLE	Light Red Cock to shoulder

The hackle is doubled and when tied in all the side and top fibres are clipped off close to the body.

PINK WICKHAM (1)

DRY	HOOK SIZE 14–16
WET	10–12
TAIL	Fibres Red Cock
BODY	Flat Gold
RIB	Gold Wire
BODY HACKLE	Natural Red Cock
WINGS	Landrail
HACKLE	Natural Dark Red Cock

PINK WICKHAM (2)

DRY	*HOOK SIZE 14–16*
WET	*8–12*
TAIL	Golden Pheasant Red Sword fibres
BODY	Flat Gold
RIB	Gold Wire
BODY HACKLE	Natural Red (stained Orange)
WINGS	Landrail
HACKLE	Natural Red (stained Orange)

T. J. Hanna's dressing.

PINK WICKHAM (3)

DRY	*HOOK SIZE 14–16*
WET	*10–14*
TAIL	Fibres Red Game Cock
BODY	Flat Gold
RIB	Gold Wire
BODY HACKLE	Red Game Cock
WINGS	Pale Starling (stained Pink)
HACKLE	Red Game Cock

PINK WICKHAM (4)

DRY	*HOOK SIZE 14–16*
TAIL	Fibres Ginger Cock
BODY	Clipped Red Game Cock
RIB	Fine Oval Gold
WINGS	Landrail
HACKLE	Ginger Cock

THE PRIEST

WET	*HOOK SIZE 10–12*
TAIL	Red Ibis or Red (dyed) Swan
BODY	Flat Silver Tinsel
HACKLE	Long Black Hen

An old pattern which is simply a hackled Butcher.

The hackle should be long and sparse, two turns being sufficient.

One of the early dressings included two short slips of red feather, at the sides, under the hackle – another replaced this with a very short red, or scarlet, hackle, under the black hackle. Another early dressing specified a Badger Hackle.

PURPLE BADGER (1)

DRY	*HOOK SIZE 14*
TAIL	Three fibres Badger Cock
BUTT	Flat Silver
BODY	Purple Floss
HACKLE	Badger Cock

PURPLE BADGER (2)

DRY	*HOOK SIZE 14–16*
WET	*12*
TAG	Flat Gold
TAIL	Honey Badger
BODY	Purple Floss
HACKLE	Honey Badger

T. J. Hanna's dressing.

PURPLE BADGER (3)

WET	*HOOK SIZE 10–12*
TAG	Flat Silver
BODY	Dark Purple Floss or Seal's Fur (plump)
HACKLE	Long Badger (sparse)

A spider dressing.

PURPLE BODY

WET	*HOOK SIZE 8–10*
TAIL	Golden Pheasant Tippets
BODY	Reddish-Purple Seal's Fur
RIB	Flat or Oval Silver
HACKLE	Blood Red Cock (dyed)
WINGS	Bronze Mallard

A sea trout pattern for the North-West.

PURPLE DEVIL

WET	HOOK SIZE 10–12
TAIL	G.P. Tippets
BODY	Dark Purple Floss Silk
RIB	Narrow Flat Silver
HACKLE	Black Cock
WINGS	Cinnamon Hen

Narrow slip of duck flight feather (dyed light purple) doubled over upper wing edge. A Co. Sligo pattern. *See also Black and Green Devils.*

PURPLE MARCH BROWN

WET	HOOK SIZE 10–12
TAIL	Three fibres Dark Partridge
BODY	Dark Purple Seal's Fur or Bronze Peacock (dyed Purple)
RIB	Flat Silver or Yellow Floss
HACKLE	Dark Grizzle
WINGS	Dark Speckled Partridge

PURPLE PEEWIT

WET	HOOK SIZE 8–12
TAIL	Golden Pheasant Tippets
BODY	Purple Floss
RIB	Oval Silver
HACKLE	Peewit Breast Feather
WINGS	Bronze Mallard

An old sea trout dressing for the West and North-West.

PURPLE AND BLACK

WET	HOOK SIZE 8–12
TAG	Silver Wire
TAIL	Bronze Mallard fibres
BODY	Dark Purple Seal's Fur
RIB	Oval Silver
HACKLE	Long Black

PUPAL NYMPHS

NO DOUBT THERE WILL BE MANY who disagree with the designation but I can only say that they are Pupae patterns, tied in Nymph fashion, and devised by the late Sam Anderson. Anglers will discover that they are a successful dressing. Hook Size L.S. 14.

BLACK

TAIL	Red Swan Fibres
BODY	Black Floss (slim)
RIB	Finest Oval Silver (or Wire)
THORAX	Bronze Peacock Herl
HACKLE	Short White Cock

BLOOD (1)

TAIL	Two fibres Red Swan
BODY	Crimson Floss (slim)
RIB	Finest Oval Silver
THORAX	Bronze Peacock Herl
HACKLE	Claret Cock

BLOOD (2)

TAIL	Two fibres Red Swan
BODY	Claret Floss (slim)
RIB	Black Floss
THORAX	Bronze Peacock Herl
HACKLE	Black Claret Cock

GREEN

TAIL	Three short fibres Bronze Mallard
BODY	Apple-Green Floss (slim)
RIB	Finest Oval Gold (or Wire)
THORAX	Bronze Peacock Herl
HACKLE	Light Ginger Cock

OLIVE

TAIL	Three fibres White Cock
BODY	Medium Olive Floss (slim)
RIB	Black Silk (close-ribbed)
THORAX	Green Peacock Herl
HACKLE	Cream Cock (Brassy)

YELLOW

TAIL	Three short fibres G.P. Tippets
BODY	Lemon Floss (slim)
RIB	Gold Wire
THORAX	Bronze Peacock Herl
HACKLE	Honey Badger Cock

The hackle must be short with curved fibres to form an umbrella over thorax. Two turns will be sufficient. Pupae allowed to hang motionless beneath surface. Retrieve by short jerks with long alternate pauses.

The final 'Pupal Nymph' dressing is strongly recommended by the doyen of Irish fly-tyers, Michael Rogan of Ballyshannon, Co. Donegal.

TAIL	Two turns Flat Tinsel
BODY	Hot Orange Floss
RIB	Stripped Peacock Quill (Moon) closely ribbed
THORAX	Fibres of Brown Turkey
WING-CASES	Two small Jungle Cock feathers tied on each side of the Thorax and lying down towards hook point
HACKLE	A single turn of Jungle Cock hackle (or Badger henny-cock)

RAIL FLIES

THESE ARE WET-FLY REPRESENTATIONS of sedges and are tied with bodies of many different colours. In Ireland where rough bodies are the most popular it is strange to find that in these dressings the reverse is true and shop bought flies almost invariably have floss bodies. Their name is derived from the fact that the wings are formed by the soft cinnamon landrail wing feather. A substitute for this feather might be from the jay wing or the golden pheasant wing. Hook Sizes 8–12.

Old dressings also used the landrail (corncrake) neck feather as a hackle.

BLACK RAIL (1)

TAG	Flat Silver
TAIL	Golden Pheasant Tippets
BODY	Black Floss or Seal's fur
RIB	Fine Oval Silver
HACKLE	Black
WINGS	Landrail

BLACK RAIL (2)
TAIL	Fibres Teal Flank
BODY	Black Floss
RIB	Silver
HACKLE	Black
WINGS	Well marked Guinea-fowl

BROWN RAIL
TAG	Flat Gold
TAIL	Brown Mallard fibres
BODY	Brown Floss
RIB	Fine Oval Gold
HACKLE	Natural Red or Red Grizzle
WINGS	Landrail

CAVAN BLACK RAIL
TAG	Gold
TAIL	Spine of Lapwing Topping
BODY	Black Floss
HACKLES	1) Black
	2) Guinea-fowl (sparse)
WINGS	Landrail

This is a dressing given by 'Hi-Regan'.

CINNAMON RAIL
BODY	Cinnamon Seal's Fur
RIB	Fine Oval Silver or Wire
HACKLE	Dark Ginger Cock
WINGS	Landrail

This is a dressing by T. J. Hanna which can be used wet or dry.

CLARET RAIL
TAG	Flat Gold
TAIL	Fibres Brown Mallard or Tippets
BODY	Dark Claret Floss or Seal's Fur
RIB	Fine Oval Gold
HACKLE	Dark Claret or Black
WINGS	Landrail

GREY RAIL
TAG	Silver
TAIL	Grey Duck Fibres
BODY	Grey Pig's Wool
RIB	Silver
HACKLE	Barred Rock
WINGS	Landrail

ORANGE RAIL
TAG	Flat Silver
TAIL	G.P. Tippets or Topping
BODY	Orange Pig's Wool
RIB	Flat Silver
HACKLE	Black
WINGS	Landrail

RED RAIL (1)
TAG	Flat Silver
TAIL	Fibres Brown Mallard or Tippets
BODY	Red Floss
RIB	Silver
HACKLE	Natural Red or Crimson (dyed)
WINGS	Landrail

RED RAIL (2)

TAG	Flat Gold
TAIL	Light coloured Rat's Whiskers
BODY	Cardinal Red Floss
RIB	Black Floss or Fine Gold
HACKLE	Blood Red Cock (dyed)
WINGS	Landrail

YELLOW RAIL

HOOK SIZE 10–14

TAG	Flat Gold
BODY	Lemon Floss
HACKLE	From Outside the wing of landrail
WINGS	Ruddy coloured feather of a Landrail's Pinion. Dressed long and full

These last two dressings are given by A. Courtney Williams.

RAT'S BACK

WET   *HOOK SIZE 12*

TAIL	Bronze Mallard Fibres
BODY	Fur from a Rat's back
HACKLE	Black or Natural Red Hen
WINGS	Bronze Mallard

RED ANT (1)

DRY   *HOOK SIZE 14–16*

BUTT	One turn Peacock Herl
BODY	Crimson Floss
THORAX	Two turns Peacock Herl
WINGS	Brown Grizzle Cock (tied flat)
HACKLE	Natural Red (stained Orange)

RED ANT (2)

DRY   *HOOK SIZE 14–16*

BUTT	Peacock Herl
BODY	Stripped Peacock Eye (dyed Crimson)
WINGS	Light Ginger Grizzle Cock (tied flat)
HACKLE	Red Game Cock

RED ANT (3)

DRY   *HOOK SIZE 14–16*

BUTT	Peacock Herl
BODY	Tapered Crimson Floss
WINGS	White Cock tips (tied flat)
HACKLE	Light Ginger Cock

RED BADGER

DRY   *HOOK SIZE 16*

TAG	Flat Silver
BODY	Red Floss
RIB	Silver Wire
BODY HACKLE	Badger Cock
HACKLE	Badger Cock

RED CLARET

WET   *HOOK SIZE 10–12*

TAIL	Golden Pheasant Tippets
BODY	Red Floss
RIB	Flat or Oval Gold
BODY HACKLE	Claret Cock (to shoulder)
WINGS	Bronze Mallard

A Co. Donegal sea trout pattern.

RED DRAKE

WET	*HOOK SIZE 10–12*
TAIL	Four Fibres as Hackle
BODY	Bronze Peacock herl (dyed Red)
RIB	Narrow Copper
HACKLE	Blue-green feather from the neck of a Mallard Drake

RED OLIVE (1)

WET	*HOOK SIZE 8–12*
TAG	Flat Gold
TAIL	Golden Pheasant Crest
BODY	Golden Olive Seal's Fur and Hare's Ear Fur (well mixed)
RIB	Flat or Oval Gold
HACKLE	Fiery Red Game
WINGS	Widgeon

A dressing for the large lakes.

RED OLIVE (2)

WET	*HOOK SIZE 8–12*
TAIL	Golden Pheasant Tippets
BODY	Medium Olive Seal's Fur
RIB	Fine Oval Silver or Wire
HACKLE	Natural Red
WINGS	Grey-brown Mallard

RED-TAILED OLIVE

WET	*HOOK SIZE 8–12*
TAIL	Red (dyed) hackle fibres
BODY	Yellow Seal and Hare's Ear Fur (well mixed)
RIB	Flat Gold
HACKLE	Golden Olive Cock
WINGS	Dark Partridge

RED PENNELL

WET	*HOOK SIZE 10–12*
TAIL	Dark Red Cock
BODY	Scarlet Pig's Wool or Seal's Fur
RIB	Fine Oval Gold
HACKLE	Long Dark Red Cock

RED QUILL (1)

DRY	*HOOK SIZE 14–16*
TAIL	Three fibres Ginger Cock
BODY	Peacock Eye Quill (dyed Red)
HACKLES	Two Dark Red Cock

The winged version is achieved by the addition of light starling wings tied low.

RED QUILL (2)

WET	*HOOK SIZE 12–14*
TAIL	Fibres Red Cock
BODY	Peacock Eye Quill
HACKLE	Red Cock
WINGS	Light Starling

RED SPIDER (1)

WET	*HOOK SIZE 12–14*
TAG	Flat Gold
BODY	Red Seal's Fur (short and plump)
HACKLE	From front edge of Corncrake's wing (long and sparse)

RED SPIDER (2)

WET	*HOOK SIZE 12–14*
TAG	Flat Gold
BODY	Fiery Brown and Yellow Seal's Fur (well mixed)
HACKLE	From front edge of Corncrake wing

RED SPINNER (1)

DRY	HOOK SIZE 14
Tail	Three fibres Ginger Cock
Body	Red-Orange Floss
Rib	Gold Wire
Wings	Blue Dun or Smoke-Grey hackle tips (tied spent)
Hackle	Dark Red Cock

RED SPINNER (2)

As above but with the finest oval gold rib and starling wings.

RED SPINNER (3)

As above but with flat gold rib and Landrail wings. Hackle – Dark Ginger.

RED SPINNER (4)

DRY	HOOK SIZE 14–16
Tail	Three fibres Ginger Cock
Body	Clipped Crimson Cock hackle
Rib	Gold Wire
Hackles	Two Honey Cock

RED SPINNER (5)

WET	HOOK SIZE 10–12
Tail	Fibres Ginger Cock
Body	Crimson Floss
Rib	Fine Oval Gold
Hackle	Light Ginger
Wings	Starling

RED SPINNER (6)

WET	HOOK SIZE 10–16
Tail	Fibres Red Cock
Body	Scarlet Floss
Rib	Gold Wire
Hackle	Natural Red
Wings	Light Starling

RED TURKEY

WET	HOOK SIZE 8–12
Tail	Golden Pheasant Tippets
Body	Red Floss
Rib	Flat or Oval Silver
Hackle	Yellow Cock or Grey Partridge (dyed yellow)
Wings	White-tipped Turkey

RED VIOLET (1)

WET	HOOK SIZE 8–12
Tail	Brown Mallard fibres
Body	Red-Violet Floss
Body Hackle	Dark Claret
Throat	Blue Jay
Wings	Cock Pheasant Tail fibres with Brown Mallard over

RED VIOLET (2)

WET	HOOK SIZE 8–12
Tail	Golden Pheasant Tippets
Body	Red-Violet Floss
Rib	Silver
Hackle	Claret Cock (from mid-body)
Throat	Blue Jay
Wings	Bronze Mallard

RED VIOLET (3)

Tail	None
Body	Red-Violet Floss
Rib	Flat Silver
Hackle	Red-Violet Cock
Wings	Red Swan and Blue Peacock with Bronze Mallard over

Old sea trout dressings for the West Coast.

RED WITCH

DRY	*HOOK SIZE 16*
TAIL	Fibres Natural Red Cock
BODY	Chopped Red Floss
RIB	Gold Wire
HACKLE	Steely-Blue Cock

ROGAN'S GADGET

HOOK SIZE SALMON NO5

BODY	Flat Silver Tinsel
RIB	Oval Silver
BACK & TAIL	Folded slip of Bronze Mallard tied flat on top of body
HEAD	Bronze Peacock Herl

The heavy hook is recommended by Michael Rogan. A lure for estuary fishing.

ROUGH CLARET

TAIL	Orange wool
BODY	Claret Seal's Fur
RIB	None
HACKLE	Dark Claret
WINGS	Bronze Mallard

A sea trout dressing which is also most effective for rainbow trout.

ROUGH GREEN

WET	*HOOK SIZE 8–12*
TAG	Red-Orange Floss
TAIL	Fibres Badger Cock
BODY	Light Olive Seal's Fur
RIB	Oval Gold
HACKLE	Badger
WINGS	Woodcock

A variation of the Woodcock and Green.

ROUGH OLIVE (1)

DRY	*HOOK SIZE 14*
TAIL	Olive Cock Fibres
BODY	Heron Herl (primary)
WINGS	Coot or Starling
HACKLE	Olive Cock

Although the shade is according to dressing required, for lake fishing the Dark or Sooty olive is preferred.

ROUGH OLIVE (2)

WET	*HOOK SIZE 8–12*
TAIL	Golden Pheasant Tippets
BODY	Sooty Olive Seal's Fur
RIB	Flat or Oval Silver
HACKLE	Natural Light Red
WINGS	Bronze Mallard

ROUGH LAKE OLIVE

WET	*HOOK SIZE 8–12*
TAG	Silver Wire
TAIL	Fibres Dark Olive Cock
BODY	Rear – 1/2 Flat Silver Front – 1/2 Brown Olive and Medium Olive Seal's Fur (well mixed)

The flat silver has an underbody of floss to taper the silver up to the fur.

RIB	Oval Silver
HACKLE	Medium or Dark Olive Cock
WINGS	Bronze Mallard

SEDGES

KNOWN IN IRELAND as the Flags, the Rush flies, and the Peters, the sedges are probably the most deadly of all evening flies. On a warm evening just as the light starts to fade is the most prolific period and the trout find them so appetizing that they have been known to take them in preference to the Mayfly.

The wings are long and, when at rest, fold over the body like the roof of a house. They are generally light to dark brown winged with long horns protruding forward.

On the large Irish lakes it is not unusual to find them being fished two to a cast! The tail fly is not oiled and tends to fish in the surface film whilst the bob-fly *is* oiled and scurries on the surface.

BANN SEDGE (Large)

DRY	*HOOK SIZE 8*
BODY	Tobacco Brown Seal's Fur
RIB	Fine Oval Gold
WINGS	Inner Mallard Flight Strips (dyed as body)
HACKLES	Two Ginger Cock

BANN SEDGE (Large)

Pat Curry's dressing as above but with pale grey fur from a hare's foot for the Body.

BANN SEDGE (Dark Red)

DRY	*HOOK SIZE 10*
BODY	Dark Hare's Ear Fur
RIB	Fine Oval Gold
WINGS	Woodcock
HACKLES	Two R.I. Red or Greenwell Cock

Sometimes tied with waterhen wings.

BANN SEDGE (Light Red)

DRY	*HOOK SIZE 10*
BODY	Ginger Hare's Ear Fur
RIB	Finest Oval Gold
WINGS	Woodcock
HACKLES	Two Medium Ginger Cock

BANN SEDGE (Orange)

DRY	*HOOK SIZE 12*
BODY	Ginger Hare's Ear and Orange Seal's Fur (mixed)
RIB	Gold Wire
WINGS	Woodcock
HACKLES	Two Medium Ginger Cock

BANN SEDGE (Scarlet)

DRY	*HOOK SIZE 8*
BODY	Dark Hare's Ear Fur
RIB	Fine Oval Gold
WINGS	Woodcock
HACKLES	Two Bright Scarlet Cock

All the above dressings are tied with Boat-wing (roofed).

BANN SEDGE (Claret)*

DRY	*HOOK SIZE 10*
BODY	Medium Olive Seal's Fur
RIB	Gold Wire
BODY HACKLE	Dark Claret Cock
WINGS	Dark Woodcock (double split)
SIDES	Three married fibres Hen Pheasant Tail
HACKLE	Dark Claret Cock

BANN SEDGE (Orange)*

DRY	*HOOK SIZE 10*
BODY	Hare's Ear Fur (slim) or Cock Pheasant Tail fibres
RIB	Gold Wire
WINGS	Dark Woodcock (double split)
SIDES	Three married fibres Hen Pheasant Tail
HACKLE	Red-Orange Cock (Dyed)

*These are reputed to be the old dressings by Dan O'Fee.

BLACK FLAG

DRY	*HOOK SIZE 10*
BODY	Black Seal's Fur
RIB	Silver Wire
WINGS	Rook
HACKLE	Dark Furnace Cock

BLACK SEDGE

WET	*HOOK SIZE 10*
BODY	Black Seal's Fur
RIB	Gold
HACKLE	Coch-Y-Bondhu Hen
WINGS	Rook Primary

An imitation of the Dark Caperer.

BLUE PETER

WET	*HOOK SIZE 8–10*
BODY	Dark Blue Seal's Fur
RIB	Oval Silver
HACKLE	Ginger Hen
WING	Speckled Grey Pheasant

The dry version has a body hackle of ginger cock & ginger cock shoulder hackle.

BROWN FLAG

DRY	*HOOK SIZE 10*
BODY	Fiery Brown Seal's Fur (ribbed Gold)
WINGS	Landrail or Red Hen
HACKLE	Rhode Island Red Cock

CAPERER SEDGE

DRY	*HOOK SIZE 12*
TAIL	Three short fibres Cock Pheasant Tail
BODY	Bronze Peacock Herl
RIB	Fine Crimson Floss
BODY HACKLE	Black Hen
WINGS	Dark Speckled Hen
HACKLE	Natural Red Cock

CINNAMON SEDGE (1)

DRY	*HOOK SIZE 12*
TAIL	Two short fibres Cock Pheasant Tail
BODY	Cinnamon Turkey Tail Herl
RIB	Fine Oval Gold
BODY HACKLE	Clipped Ginger Cock
WINGS	Landrail or Cinnamon Hen
HACKLE	Ginger Cock
HORNS	Two fibres Cock Pheasant Tail (projecting forward 3/4")

CINNAMON SEDGE (2)

DRY	*HOOK SIZE 12*
BODY	Rear – $^2/3$ Pea-green Seal's Fur
	Front – $^1/3$ Fiery Brown Seal's Fur
RIB	Clipped Ginger Cock
WINGS	Landrail or Light Red Hen
HACKLE	Ginger Cock
HORNS	Two fibres Cock Pheasant Tail (projecting forward $^3/4$")

CINNAMON SEDGE (3)

DRY	*HOOK SIZE 12*
BODY	Green Seal's Fur
RIB	Gold Wire
WINGS	Speckled Ginger or Red-Brown Hen
HACKLE	Light Red Cock

This is a dressing of Michael Kennedy's from *Trout Flies for Irish Waters*.

DARK PETER (1)

WET OR DRY	*HOOK SIZE 8–12*
BODY	Darkest Green Seal's Fur
RIB	Fine Oval Gold
WINGS	Dark Hen Pheasant
HACKLE	Furnace or Ginger

The Dry version has the hackle extending along the body and at shoulder.

DARK PETER (2)

BODY	Black Seal's Fur
BODY HACKLE	Coch-Y-Bondhu Cock
WINGS	Dark Speckled Pheasant
HACKLE	Coch-Y-Bondhu Cock

Another dresing of Michael Kennedy's. *See also Green Peter*

GREAT RED SEDGE (1)

DRY	*HOOK SIZE 8*
TAIL	Two short fibres Cock Pheasant Tail
BODY	Rich Dark Chestnut Seal's Fur
BODY HACKLE	Clipped Dark Red Cock
WINGS	Dark Brown Speckled Turkey
HACKLE	Two Dark Red Cock
HORNS	Two fibres Cock Pheasant Tail (projecting forward 1")

GREAT RED SEDGE (2)

DRY	*HOOK SIZE 8*
TAIL	Two short fibres Cock Pheasant Tail
BODY	Hare's Ear Fur with pinch of Orange Seal's Fur added
RIB	Clipped Red Cock
WINGS	Dark Speckled Hen
HACKLE	Two Dark Red Cock (tied full)
HORNS	Two Cock Pheasant Tail fibres (projecting forward 1")

These were two of Sam Anderson's dressings. He maintained that a Sedge *must* have the horns tied in.

165

GREEN PETER (1)

DRY	*HOOK SIZE 10*
TAIL	Two short fibres Cock Pheasant Tail
BODY	Plump Peacock Sword Herl
BODY HACKLE	Clipped Ginger Cock
WINGS	Light Brown Speckled Hen Wings Slips
HACKLE	Ginger Cock
HORNS	Fibre of Peacock Sword on each side of wings, lying back

A dressing by Sam Anderson. When tied with a dark speckled hen wing it becomes the Dark Peter.

GREEN PETER (2)

DRY	*HOOK SIZE 10*
BODY	Pea-Green Seal's Fur
RIB	Fine Oval Gold
BODY HACKLE	Light Ginger Cock (short)
WINGS	Hen Pheasant Wing
HACKLES	Two Light Ginger Cock

The wet version has a ginger hen hackle and grey pheasant wing.

GREY FLAG (1)

DRY	*HOOK SIZE 10*
BODY	Dirty White Seal's Fur
RIB	Gold Wire
BODY HACKLE	Short fibred Barred Rock
WINGS	Dirty White Turkey
HACKLE	Two Dirty Grey Cock

GREY FLAG (2)

BODY	Light Grey Seal's Fur
RIB	Gold Wire
BODY HACKLE	Short-fibred Creamy White Cock (close-ribbed)
HACKLES	Two Barred Rock Cock

LIGHT SEDGE (1)

DRY	*HOOK SIZE 12*
TAIL	Two short fibres Cock Pheasant Tail
BODY	Golden Olive Seal's Fur and Hare's Ear Fur (well mixed)
RIB	Gold Wire
BODY HACKLE	Clipped Ginger Cock
WINGS	Hen Pheasant Wing
HACKLE	Light Ginger Cock
HORNS	Two fibres Cock Pheasant Tail (projecting forward 3/4")

This is one of the day sedges.

LIGHT SEDGE (2)

WET	*HOOK SIZE 10–12*
BODY	Dark Brown Quill
HACKLE	Soft Grey Badger
WINGS	White-tipped Turkey

LITTLE RED SEDGE (1)

DRY	*HOOK SIZE 12–14*
BODY	Two turns Brown Turkey Herl
	Two turns Yellow Swan Herl
	Three turns Brown Turkey Herl
WINGS	Landrail or Cinnamon Hen
HACKLE	Rhode Island Red Cock
HORNS	Two fibres Cock Pheasant Tail (projecting forward 1/2")

LITTLE RED SEDGE (2)

DRY	*HOOK SIZE 12–14*
BODY	Dark Hare's Ear Fur
RIB	Gold Wire
BODY HACKLE	Clipped Medium Red Cock
WINGS	Landrail or Red Hen
HACKLE	Rhode Island Red Cock

MEDIUM RED SEDGE (1)

DRY	*HOOK SIZE 10*
TAIL	Two short Cock Pheasant Tail fibres
BODY	Dark Fiery Brown Seal's Fur
RIB	Fine Oval Gold
BODY HACKLE	Short fibred Ginger Cock
WINGS	Landrail or Red Hen
HACKLE	Rhode Island Red Cock
HORNS	Two fibres Cock Pheasant Tail (lying back on wings)

MEDIUM RED SEDGE (2)

DRY	*HOOK SIZE 12*
BODY	Cinnamon Floss
BODY SHEATH	Translucent Sheet Rubber
WINGS	Red Hen
HACKLE	Red Cock

T. J. Hanna's dressing.

MURROUGH SEDGE (1)

DRY	*HOOK SIZE 8*
BODY	Rich Chestnut Seal's Fur
RIB	Fine Oval Gold
WING	Dark Speckled Turkey
HACKLES	Two Red Game Cock
HORNS	Two fibres Cock Pheasant Tail (projecting forward 1")

This dressing of Sam Anderson's uses a broad piece of Turkey for the wing. It is folded in two and then tied on top of the body in ordinary wet-fly fashion. The wing extends about 1/2" behind the hook bend and has the tips trimmed flat (square). It is a most ugly wing which causes the fly to lie sideways on the water but to many anglers it is the dressing they prefer.

MURROUGH SEDGE (2)

DRY	*HOOK SIZE 8*
BODY	Rich Dark Claret Floss
RIB	Fine Oval Gold (close-ribbed)
WINGS	Oak Turkey
HACKLES	Two Red Game Cock
HORNS	Two Cock Pheasant Tail fibres

MURROUGH SEDGE (3)

DRY	*HOOK SIZE 8–10*
TAIL	Three short fibres Cock Pheasant Tail
BODY	Dark Claret Seal's Fur
RIB	Fine Oval Gold
BODY HACKLE	Clipped Dark Grizzle Cock
WINGS	Dark Speckled Turkey
HACKLES	Dark Grizzle Cock
HORNS	Two fibres Cock Pheasant Tail (projecting forward 1")

In dressings (2) and (3) the wings are roofed.

RUSH FLY (1)

TAG	Yellow Floss
BODY	Deep Brown Olive Mohair
HACKLE	Deep Brown Olive (from mid-body)
WINGS	Landrail
TOPPING	Speckled Partridge
EYES	Black or Red Beads
HORNS	Mallard Fibres

RUSH FLY (2)

BODY	Rear – $^1/_2$ Lively Green Mohair
	Front – $^1/_2$ Light Brown Mohair

Remainder as No. 1

For August and September.

These two dressings are given by O'Gorman in *The Practice of Angling* – (1845).

SILVER SEDGE (1)

DRY   *HOOK SIZE 12*

TAIL	Two short fibres Cock Pheasant Tail
BODY	White Floss
RIB	Silver Wire
BODY HACKLE	Ginger Cock
WINGS	Water Hen
HACKLE	Ginger Cock

SILVER SEDGE (2)

DRY   *HOOK SIZE 10–12*

TAIL	Two short fibres Cock Pheasant Tail
BODY	Cream Seal's Fur
RIB	Gold Wire
BODY HACKLE	Clipped Ginger Cock
WINGS	Landrail or Ginger Hen
HACKLE	Ginger Cock

SEDGE NYMPH

WET   *HOOK SIZE 10–12*

TAIL	Three short fibres Dark Grouse
BODY	Swan Herl (dyed Apple-Green)
WING CASES	Brown Turkey
THORAX	Chestnut Seal's Fur
LEGS	Dark Speckled Grouse

Wing cases tied down at head.

HATCHING SEDGE

WET   *HOOK SIZE 10–12*

TAIL	Three short fibres Cock Pheasant Tail
BODY	Pea-Green Swan Herl tapering up to thorax
THORAX	Dark Hare's Ear Fur
HACKLE	Two turns short Red Cock
WINGS	Light Red Hen (tied short)

HATCHING SEDGE (2)

                   HOOK SIZE 8–10

TAIL	None
BODY	Orange Floss
RIB	Single strand of Black Floss Silk
HORNS	Six fibres of Dark Red cock hackle (lying over body and extending as tail)
HACKLE	Light Ginger Hen
WING	Small Dark Speckled Snipe Feather (rolled and tied short)

SHERRY SPINNER

DRY	*HOOK SIZE 14–16*
TAIL	Ginger Cock fibres
BODY	Seal's Fur (Red and Light Olive and Fiery Brown) (well-mixed)
RIB	Gold Wire
HACKLE	Honey Dun or Ginger Cock

This dressing has the hackle tied half-circle.

SILVER GREY

WET	*HOOK SIZE 8–12*
TAIL	Fibres Brown Grizzle
BODY	Flat Silver
RIB	Silver Wire
HACKLE	Dark Grizzle Cock (two turns)
WINGS	Widgeon or Starling

SILVER MARCH BROWN

WET	*HOOK SIZE 8–14*
TAIL	Dark Brown Partridge fibres
BODY	Flat Silver
RIB	Silver Wire
HACKLE	Dark Speckled Partridge
WINGS	Hen Pheasant Tail

SILVER TURKEY

WET	*HOOK SIZE 8–12*
TAIL	Golden Pheasant Tippets
BODY	Flat Silver
RIB	Silver Wire
HACKLE	Dark Claret Cock
WINGS	White Tipped Turkey

SNIPE AND ORANGE

WET	*HOOK SIZE 10–14*
TAG	Flat Gold
BODY	Orange Seal's Fur (slim)
RIB	Gold Wire
HACKLE	Speckled feather from outside of a Snipe's wing

SNIPE AND PURPLE

WET	*HOOK SIZE 10–14*
TAG	Flat Gold
BODY	Dark Purple Floss or Seal's Fur
HACKLE	Dark feather from the leading edge of a Snipe's wing

A representation of the Iron Blue.

SNIPE AND YELLOW

WET	*HOOK SIZE 10–14*
TAG	Flat Gold
BODY	Yellow Floss
HACKLE	From the underside of a Snipe's wing

A representation of the Pale Watery or Light Olive.

SOLDIER

WET	*HOOK SIZE 8–12*
TAIL	Bronze Mallard fibres
BODY	Oval Gold
HACKLES	Black and Red Cock (wound together)
WINGS	Cock Pheasant Tail

SOOTY OLIVE (1)

DRY	*HOOK SIZE 14–16*
TAIL	Dark Red Cock fibres
BODY	Mole Fur
RIB	Medium Olive Floss (close ribbed)
HACKLES	Two fiery Red Cock

The winged version by adding cock blackbird wings. The wet version by adding bronze mallard wings. Hook Size 10-14.

SOOTY OLIVE (2)

DRY	*HOOK SIZE 14–16*
WET	*10–14*
TAIL	Fibres Dark Olive Cock
BODY	Sooty Olive Seal's Fur
RIB	Narrow Flat Silver
HACKLES	Two Dark Olive Cock

Winged version by adding Blackbird wings.

SOOTY OLIVE (3)

DRY	*HOOK SIZE 14–16*
TAIL	Three fibres Dark Grizzle
BODY	Hare's Ear Fur
RIB	Gold Wire
HACKLES	1) Dark Grizzle Cock
	2) Dark Honey. Both Hackles are wound on together

SOOTY OLIVE QUILL (1)

DRY	*HOOK SIZE 14–16*
TAIL	Three fibres Brown Olive Cock
BODY	Dark Peacock Quill
HACKLES	Two Sooty Olive Cock

The winged version by adding starling wings.

SOOTY OLIVE QUILL (2)

DRY	*HOOK SIZE 12–16*
TAIL	Three fibres Red Game Cock
BODY	Dark Peacock Quill
WINGS	Cock Blackbird
HACKLES	Two Red Game Cock (lightly dyed in Sooty Olive)

SOOTY OLIVE QUILL (3)

WET	*HOOK SIZE 10–14*
TAIL	Three fibres Bronze Mallard
BODY	Dark Peacock Quill
HACKLE	Chocolate Dun
WINGS	Grouse

Also known as the Grouse Quill.

SOOTY OLIVE QUILL (4)

WET	*HOOK SIZE 10–14*
TAIL	Three short fibres Bronze Mallard
BODY	Dark Peacock Quill
HACKLE	Darkest Grouse feather (sparse)

This is the spider dressing of No. 3.

SPIDER WREN

See under the Wren Series.

STONE FLY (1)

WET	*HOOK SIZE 10–12*
TAIL	Dark Grizzle Cock fibres
BODY	Hare's Ear Fur and Yellow Seal's Fur (well-mixed)
HACKLE	Dark Grizzle
WINGS	Hen Pheasant Tail

STONE FLY (2)		STONE FLY (3)	
WET	*HOOK SIZE 10–12*	*DRY*	*HOOK SIZE 14*
TAIL	Three fibres Speckled Guinea-fowl	TYING SILK	Orange
		BODY	Orange Seal's Fur and Hare's Ear Fur (well-mixed)
BODY	Hare's Ear Fur		
RIB	Yellow Floss	RIB	Gold Wire
HACKLE	Dark Grizzle	WINGS	Two Cuckoo Cock (dyed Pale Sepia, tied flat along bend)
WINGS	Hen Pheasant Tail		
		HACKLE	Cock-Y-Bondhu Cock

This dressing is by Michael Kennedy. Tied half-circle. Imitates the Early Brown Stone Fly.

SHELL-BACKS

SHRIMPS AND NYMPHS

THE SHELL-BACK DRESSINGS are probably the best remembered dressing of the late T. J. Hanna. He experimented with all colours of balloon rubber, not only in these dressings but in many other dressings of nymphs and indeed dry-flies. The bodies of the shell-back shrimps are very heavily dubbed, very rough, and the fibres below the body well picked out. The under fibres are then cut (if necessary) in a graduated fashion i.e. long at head and tapering to the tail. Some had wired under-bodies for quick-sinking. The rubber back is tied in at the tail, or thorax, and then stretched tightly to the head and tied in, Hook Size 10-12.

Nos. 1-6 are Nymphal dressings.

Nos. 7-12 are Shrimp dressings.

NYMPH (1)		NYMPH (2)	
TAIL	Fibres Blue Dun Hen	TAIL	Short fibres Red Game Cock
BODY	Cock Pheasant Tail fibres		
RIB	Gold Wire	BODY	Water Rat or Mole Fur
SHELL-CASE	Opaque Rubber	SHELL-CASE	Greenish-Olive Rubber
THORAX	Dirty White Pig's Wool	THORAX	Rabbit Fur and Dark Blue Pig's Wool

The shell-case in nymphal patterns covers the thorax only. The thorax fibres are well picked out to form legs.

171

NYMPH (3)

TAIL	Fibres Blue Dun Hen
BODY	Dirty Blue Pig's Wool (slim)
RIB	Gold Wire
SHELL-CASE	Clear Rubber
THORAX	Dirty Blue Pig's Wool (thick)

NYMPH (4)

TAIL	Fibres Iron Blue
BODY	Primrose Floss
RIB	Fine Oval Gold
SHELL-CASE	Opaque Rubber
THORAX	Inky-Blue Pig's Wool

NYMPH (5)

TAIL	Fibres Blue Dun
BODY	Brown Turkey fibres
RIB	Gold Wire
SHELL-CASE	White Rubber
THORAX	Grey Pig's Wool

NYMPH (6)

TAIL	Fibres Blue Dun
BODY	Black Floss (slim)
RIB	Silver Wire
SHELL-CASE	Clear Rubber
THORAX	Dirty Grey Pig's Wool

The shell-case in the following patterns extends from Tail to Head (Shrimps)

SHRIMP (1)

BODY	Mole Fur and Dirty Grey Pig's Wool (well-mixed)
SHELL-CASE	Clear Rubber

SHRIMP (2)

REAR BODY	Greenish Yellow Seal's Fur
FRONT BODY	Fiery Brown Seal's Fur
SHELL-CASE	Clear Rubber

SHRIMP (3)

BODY	Darkest Olive Seal's Fur with added pinch of Fiery Brown
SHELL-CASE	Opaque Rubber

SHRIMP (4)

REAR BODY	Cinnamon Pig's Wool
FRONT BODY	Black Mohair
SHELL-CASE	Opaque Rubber

SHRIMP (5)

REAR BODY	Black Seal's Fur
FRONT BODY	Crimson Pig's Wool
SHELL-CASE	Greenish Olive Rubber

SHRIMP (6)

REAR BODY	Cinnamon Pig's Wool
FRONT BODY	Creamy White Pig's Wool
SHELL-CASE	Light Green Rubber

These dressings were given to me without any appended names. I have, therefore, been content to number them rather than try to recognise what they may have been tied to represent.

TEAL SERIES

THE TEAL DRESSINGS are many and varied but have two things in common – they use teal flank for wings and they are, generally, seatrout patterns.

A great many dressings use a black hackle due, I believe, to the influence of Roger Wooley who made a great contribution to fly-fishing. His intention was to try and standardize these dressings but this is not always possible in that the fish may not agree. In Ireland you will certainly find black-hackled teals but these are generally over-shadowed by natural reds and gingers.

TEAL AND BLACK

WET	*HOOK SIZE 8–12*
TAIL	Golden Pheasant Tippets
BODY	Black Pig's Wool or Seal's Fur
RIB	Flat or Oval-Silver
HACKLE	Black
WINGS	Teal

TEAL, BLACK AND CLARET

WET	*HOOK SIZE 8–12*
TAG	Black Floss
TAIL	Fibres of Bronze Mallard or Silver Pheasant Plumage
BODY	Black Floss or Seal's Fur
RIB	Flat Silver
HACKLE	Dark Claret
WINGS	Teal

This dressing can have an underwing of blue peacock, and red and yellow swan.

TEAL, BLACK AND GREEN

WET	*HOOK SIZE 8–12*
TAIL	Golden Pheasant Tippets (and Peacock Sword)
BODY	Black Floss or Seal's Fur
RIB	Flat or Oval Silver
HACKLE	Dark Green
THROAT	Blue Jay
WINGS	Teal

A Co. Donegal pattern.

TEAL, BLACK AND ORANGE

WET	*HOOK SIZE 8–12*
TAIL	G.P. Tippets and Fibres Bronze Mallard
BODY	Rear – $1/2$ Orange Seal's Fur Front – $1/2$ Black Seal's Fur or Floss
RIB	Oval Silver
BODY HACKLE	Black Cock on Black body
THROAT	Blue Jay
WINGS	Teal

TEAL, BLACK AND SILVER

WET	*HOOK SIZE 8–12*
TAIL	Golden Pheasant Tippets
BODY	Flat Silver
RIB	Silver Wire
HACKLE	Black
WINGS	Teal

TEAL AND BLUE

WET	*HOOK SIZE 8–12*
TAIL	Fibres Black Cock
BODY	Light Blue Floss
RIB	Flat Silver
HACKLE	Black
WINGS	Teal

TEAL, BLUE AND SILVER

WET	HOOK SIZE 8–12
TAIL	Golden Pheasant Tippets
BODY	Flat Silver
RIB	Silver Wire
HACKLE	Light Blue (dyed)
WINGS	Teal

An old dressing uses blue jay in place of the light blue hackle. A dark blue hackle is used in the North-West.

TEAL AND CLARET

WET	HOOK SIZE 8–12
TAIL	Golden Pheasant Tippets
BODY	Dark Claret Seal's Fur
RIB	Oval Gold
HACKLE	Natural Red (or Claret, or Black)
WINGS	Teal

TEAL, CLARET AND SILVER

WET	HOOK SIZE 8–12
TAIL	Golden Pheasant Tippets
BODY	Flat Silver
RIB	Silver Wire
HACKLE	Claret
WINGS	Teal

TEAL AND GREEN (1)

WET	HOOK SIZE 8–12
TAIL	Golden Pheasant Tippets
BODY	Laurel Green Floss
RIB	Oval Silver
BODY HACKLE	Light Green Hen
HACKLE	Blue Jay
WINGS	Teal

An old West of Ireland dressing.

TEAL AND GREEN (2)

WET	HOOK SIZE 8–12
TAIL	Fibres Teal Plumage
BODY	Mid-Green Floss
RIB	Flat or Oval Silver
HACKLE	Ginger (or Green) (or Black)
WINGS	Blue Peacock with Teal over

TEAL AND GREEN (3)

WET	HOOK SIZE 8–12
TAIL	Golden Pheasant Tippets
BODY	Apple Green Pig's Wool
RIB	Flat Silver
HACKLE	Ginger (or Red)
WINGS	Teal

TEAL, GREEN AND SILVER

WET	HOOK SIZE 8–12
TAIL	Golden Pheasant Tippets (and Peacock Sword)
BODY	Flat Silver
RIB	Silver Wire
HACKLE	Apple Green
WINGS	Teal

TEAL AND ORANGE

WET	HOOK SIZE 8–12
TAIL	Fibres Bronze Mallard (or G.P. Tippets)
BODY	Orange Seal's Fur
RIB	Flat or Oval Gold
HACKLE	Natural Red (dyed Golden Olive)
WINGS	Teal

TEAL, ORANGE AND BLACK

WET	*HOOK SIZE 8–12*
TAIL	Golden Pheasant Tippets
BODY	Rear – $1/2$ Flat Gold Tinsel Front – $1/2$ Orange Seal's Fur
RIB	Fine Oval Gold
HACKLE	Black
WINGS	Teal

TEAL AND RED

WET	*HOOK SIZE 8–12*
TAIL	Golden Pheasant Tippets
BODY	Red Floss or Seal's Fur
RIB	Oval Silver (or Gold)
HACKLE	Natural Red (or Black)
WINGS	Teal

TEAL, RED AND BLACK

WET	*HOOK SIZE 8–12*
TAIL	Golden Pheasant Tippets
BODY	Rear – $1/2$ Red Floss Front –$1/2$ Black Seal's Fur
RIB	Oval Silver
HACKLE	Black
WINGS	Teal

TEAL, RED AND GREEN

WET	*HOOK SIZE 8–12*
TAIL	Fibres Teal Plumage
BODY	Rear – $1/3$ Red Floss Front – $2/3$ Apple Green Seal's Fur
RIB	Silver
HACKLE	Natural Red or Dark Ginger
WINGS	Teal

TEAL AND YELLOW

WET	*HOOK SIZE 8–12*
TAIL	Golden Pheasant Tippets
BODY	Yellow Seal's Fur
RIB	Flat or Oval Gold
HACKLE	Natural Red or Ginger (dyed Yellow)
WINGS	Teal

As in the Mallard Series the mixed bodies are sometimes termed Teal and Mixed, or Teal Jointers.

THUNDER AND LIGHTNING

WET	*HOOK SIZE 6–12*
TAG	Silver Wire and Orange Floss
TAIL	Golden Pheasant Crest
BODY	Black Floss
RIB	Oval Gold (or Silver)
HACKLE	Yellow or Orange
THROAT	Blue Jay
WINGS	Bronze Mallard

The old dressing used a Light Ginger hackle. Jungle Cock cheeks may be added.

TORC-LAN

WET	*HOOK SIZE 8–12*
TAG	Orange Floss
TAIL	Golden Pheasant Topping
BODY	Rear – $^1/_2$ Orange Pig's Wool
	Front –$^1/_2$ Black Pig's Wool
BODY HACKLE	Black Cock over Black Wool
HACKLE	Blood Red Cock
WINGS	Bronze Mallard

Sometimes a throat of blue jay. This sea trout dressing is given by 'Hi-Regan' for the West of Ireland.

TUP'S INDISPENSABLE (1)

DRY	*HOOK SIZE 14–16*
TAIL	Three fibres Smoke-Blue Cock
BODY	Creamy Seal's Fur tapering to thorax
THORAX	Creamy Seal's Fur with pinch of Pink or Orange added
HACKLES	Two Smoke-Blue Cock

The whole dressing must be kept light and fragile and on no account must the thorax colour be too strong. The original dressing was invented by R. S. Austin of Tiverton, Devon. This is the first variation.

(2)

T. J. Hanna's dressing was:–

TAIL	Soft Blue Whisks
BODY	Tup Mixture
HACKLE	Short Blue Dun Cock (or Hen)

TURKEY TIP

WET	*HOOK SIZE 8–12*
TAIL	Golden Pheasant Tippets
BODY	Flat Gold
RIB	Finest Oval Gold
HACKLE	Dark Ginger
WINGS	White-tipped Turkey

WALL FLY (1)

DRY   *HOOK SIZE 10*

This pattern was in use on the River Erne, Co. Donegal, prior to the river being dammed for a hydro-electric scheme.

A simple dressing:–

BODY	Brown Silk
HACKLE	Red
WING	Landrail

was recorded by Rev. Newland in 1851.

WALL FLY (2)

DRY	*HOOK SIZE 10*
TAIL	None
BODY	Cock Pheasant Tail Fibres (strong rusty-red)
RIB	Orange Floss
WINGS	Cinnamon Hen covered by shorter Woodcock slips
HACKLES	Two Ginger Cock wound on together

A Sedge pattern. Michael Rogan's dressing.

WATSON'S FANCY

WET	*HOOK SIZE 8–12*
TAIL	Golden Pheasant Crest (and Tippets)
BODY	Rear – $^1/2$ Red Floss or Seal's Fur
	Front –$^1/2$ Black Floss or Seal's Fur
RIB	Flat or Oval Silver
HACKLE	Black Hen
WINGS	Mallard Speculum, Rook, or Crow
CHEEKS	Small Jungle Cock

A well known fly. In Ireland it is a sound lake pattern for sea trout, and varies only in that the floss body is most popular in the North and the fur body in the South.

WESTMEATH FLY

O'Gorman gave the following dressings in 1845:–

TIP	Gold
TAIL	Fibres Brown Mallard
BUTT	Yellow or Green Mohair or Floss
BODIES	As below

1) Hare's Ear Fur and Yellow Mohair mixed (Hackled Red or Grey)
2) Hare's Ear Fur and Claret Mohair mixed
3) Light, Dark, or Fiery Brown Mohair
4) Cinnamon Mohair
5) Black Mohair
6) Sooty-Olive Green Mohair

RIB	Gold
BODY HACKLE	Deep Red from mid-body
WINGS	Brown Mallard
EYES	Red or Black Beads
HORNS	Speckled Mallard

He advocated a large hook. It is apparent from his writing that he copied the body colours of many of the large sedges (see also Rush Fly). It is most interesting to note his use of glass beads as eyes, which are regarded as a modern innovation – 130 years later! Until recent years the only other pattern I was aware of was Foster's Red-Eyed Beetle.

WESTMEATH LARGE (1)

WET	*HOOK SIZE 8–12*
TAIL	Golden Pheasant Tippets
BODY	Rear – $^1/3$ Yellow Seal's Fur
	Front –$^2/3$ Claret Seal's Fur
RIB	Oval Gold
HACKLE	Medium Blue (dyed) Cock
WINGS	Bronze Mallard

WESTMEATH LARGE (2)

WET	*HOOK SIZE 8–12*
TAIL	Grey Mallard Fibres
BODY	Rear - $^1/3$ Golden Olive Seal's Fur
	Front - $^2/3$ Claret Seal's Fur
RIB	Oval Gold
HACKLE	Slate
WINGS	Grey Mallard

These flies are for use on Loughs Sheelin, Ennell, Owel, Derravaragh, and indeed all the large limestone lakes.

WHITE MIDGE

DRY	*HOOK SIZE 16–18*
TAIL	Three long fibres White Cock
BODY	Palest Yellow or Palest Pink Floss
WINGS	Pale Grey Cock hackle tips
HACKLE	White Cock

The hackle is tied half-circle.

WHITE MOTH (1)

DRY	*HOOK SIZE 12*
BODY	White Seal's Fur
RIB	Oval Silver
BODY HACKLE	Short-fibred White Cock
WINGS	Light Owl
HACKLE	White Cock

WHITE MOTH (2)

DRY	*HOOK SIZE 12*
BUTT	Bronze Peacock Herl
BODY	Creamy White Seal's Fur
RIB	Black or Dark Brown Floss
BODY HACKLE	Clipped White Cock
WINGS	Mallard Satins (double split)
HACKLE	White Cock

WHITE MOTH (3)

DRY	*HOOK SIZE 12*
BODY	Lemon Floss
RIB	Silver
BODY HACKLE	Short-fibred White Cock
WINGS	White Owl
HACKLE	Barred Rock Cock

WHITE MOTH (4)

WET	*HOOK SIZE 10–12*
TAIL	Short Grey Mallard fibres
BODY	Field Mouse Fur
RIB	Gold Wire
HACKLE	Creamy White feather from Barn Owl
WINGS	Light Starling

T.J. Hanna's dressing.

WICKHAM'S FANCY (1)

DRY	*HOOK SIZE 14*
TAIL	Fibres Dark Ginger Cock
BODY	Flat Gold
RIB	Gold Wire
BODY HACKLE	Ginger or Red Cock
WINGS	Starling
HACKLE	Ginger or Red Cock

When ginger hackles are used then the wings are light starling and when red hackles are used then the wings are dark starling. Wet version as above but often tied without wings and using a long mobile neck hackle. (Hook Size 8–12)

WICKHAM'S FANCY (2)

DRY	*HOOK SIZE 14–16*
WET	*8–12*
TAIL	Fibres of Guinea-fowl (dyed Fiery Brown)
BODY	Flat Gold
RIB	Gold Wire
BODY HACKLE	Ginger Cock
HACKLE	Guinea-fowl (dyed Fiery Brown)

A dressing by Sam Anderson. *See also Blue Wickham.*

WIRE WICKHAM (1)

WET	*HOOK SIZE 10–14*

As Wickham's Fancy but with body of Gold Wire (hackled but unribbed).

WIRE WICKHAM (2)

DRY	*HOOK SIZE 16*
TAIL	Fibres Dark Ginger Cock
BODY	Gold Wire
HACKLES	1) Natural Dark Red Cock
	2) Iron Blue Cock

Alternatively may be hackled with Darkest Furnace Cock.

WICKLOW KILLER

WET HOOK SIZE 10–12
TAIL Fibres Red Cock
BODY Orange Floss
RIB Fine Oval Gold
BODY HACKLE Red Cock
WINGS Grey Mallard Flank

Peter O'Reilly informs me that the modern dressing calls for Teal Wing.

WOODCOCK AND BLACK

WET HOOK SIZE 8–12
TAIL Golden Pheasant Tippets
BODY Black Seal's Fur
RIB Oval Silver (or Wire)
HACKLE Red or Dark Ginger
WINGS Woodcock

WOODCOCK AND GREEN

WET HOOK SIZE 8–12
TAIL Golden Pheasant Tippets
BODY Mid-Green Floss or Seal's Fur
RIB Oval Silver
HACKLE Black, Green, or Natural Red
WINGS Woodcock

WOODCOCK AND HARE'S EAR (1)

WET HOOK SIZE 10–14
TAG Flat Gold
TAIL Fibres Dark Partridge
BODY Hare's Ear Fur with added pinch of Claret Seal's Fur
HACKLE Body fibres picked out
WINGS Woodcock

WOODCOCK AND HARE'S EAR (2)

WET HOOK SIZE 10–12
TAIL Fibres Dark Partridge
BUTT Yellow Floss
BODY Hare's Ear Fur
RIB Yellow Floss
HACKLE Dirty Olive
WINGS Woodcock

WOODCOCK AND ORANGE (1)

WET HOOK SIZE 8–12
TAIL Golden Pheasant Tippets
BODY Orange Seal's Fur
RIB Oval Gold
HACKLE Natural Red
WINGS Woodcock

WOODCOCK AND ORANGE (2)

WET HOOK SIZE 10–12
TAG Flat Gold
BODY Red-Orange Seal's Fur
HACKLE From Woodcock Wing

This is the spider pattern which has two dressings Light and Dark.
Light – use hackle from under the wing.
Dark – use hackle from top of wing.

WOODCOCK AND RED

WET HOOK SIZE 10–12
TAIL Golden Pheasant Tippets
BODY Red Floss or Seal's Fur
RIB Oval Gold (or Silver)
HACKLE Natural Red (or Black)
WINGS Woodcock

WOODCOCK AND YELLOW (1)

WET	*HOOK SIZE 8–12*
TAIL	Golden Pheasant Tippets
BODY	Bright Greenish Yellow Seal's Fur
RIB	Gold Wire
HACKLE	Natural Red
WINGS	Woodcock

T. J. Hanna's dressing.

WOODCOCK AND YELLOW (2)

TAG	Flat Gold or Orange Floss
BODY	Yellow Floss
HACKLE	From under Woodcock's Wing

This is the Spider dressing.

WREN FLIES

THESE PATTERNS appear to be peculiar to Ireland. Many have both the neck hackle and wings made from wren tail. Thomas Ettingsall advocated a natural red hackle with wren wing. The colours are many – red wren, green wren, black wren, etc. All are simply a change of body colour and can be dressed spider fashion. Hook Size 14–16.

BLACK WREN

TAIL	Fibres Red Cock
BODY	Black Floss
RIB	Silver Wire
HACKLE	Wren Tail fibres
WINGS	Wren Tail

GREEN WREN

TAIL	Rat's Whiskers
BODY	Light Green Floss
RIB	Gold Wire
HACKLE	Wren Tail fibres
WINGS	Wren Tail

WREN FLY

BODY	Olive or Brown-Olive or Green Olive Floss
HACKLE	Wren Tail
WINGS	Paired Wren Tail feathers

These were O'Gorman's dressings.

WREN HACKLE

TAG	Flat Gold
BODY	Cinnamon Seal's Fur
RIB	Gold Wire
HACKLE	Wren Tail

WREN SPIDER (1)

BODY	Yellow Mohair
HACKLE	Wren Tail

(2)

BODY	Brown-Olive Mohair
HACKLE	Wren Tail

These are the old dressings of Thomas Ettingsall.

WREN TAIL

TAIL	Two short fibres Bronze Mallard
BODY	Golden Olive Seal's Fur
RIB	Gold Wire
HACKLE	Wren Tail
WINGS	Grey Partridge

YELLOW EVENING DUN

DRY	*HOOK SIZE 16*
TAIL	Three fibres Ginger Cock
BODY	Primrose Floss
RIB	Gold Wire
HACKLE	Cream Cock (dyed Pale Yellow) or palest Ginger Cock

YELLOW EVENING SPINNER

DRY	*HOOK SIZE 16*
TAIL	Three fibres Ginger Cock
BODY	Amber Seal's Fur
RIB	Gold Wire
HACKLE	Palest Honey Dun or Palest Ginger Cock

YELLOW MAY DUN

DRY	*HOOK SIZE 14*
TAIL	Three fibres Ginger Cock
BODY	Primrose Silk lightly dubbed with Yellow Seal's Fur
RIB	Gold Wire
HACKLE	White or Cream Cock (dyed Yellow)

YELLOW MAY SPINNER

DRY	*HOOK SIZE 14*
TAIL	Three fibres Ginger Cock
BODY	Pale Yellow Seal's Fur
RIB	Gold Wire
HACKLE	Pale Ginger Cock

These four dressings are by Dr Michael Kennedy.

YELLOW HAWK

DRY	*HOOK SIZE 14*
TAIL	Three fibres Lemon Cock
BODY	Light Yellow Floss
BODY SHEATH	Clear Plastic

WINGS	Yellow Cock hackle tips
HACKLE	Light Yellow Cock

A dressing of the Yellow May Dun.

YELLOW PENNELL

WET	*HOOK SIZE 10–12*
TAIL	Fibres Red Cock
BODY	Gold Floss
RIB	Fine Oval Gold
HACKLE	Furnace Cock

YELLOW SALLY

DRY	*HOOK SIZE 14*
TAIL	Three fibres Yellow Cock
BODY	Light Straw Floss
RIB	Gold Wire
HACKLES	Two Yellow Cock

YELLOW WASP

WET	*HOOK SIZE 8–10*
TAG	Orange Floss
TAIL	Golden Pheasant Tippets
BUTT	Crimson Floss or Claret Seal's Fur
BODY	Golden Olive Seal's Fur
RIB	Oval Gold
HACKLE	Yellow Cock
WINGS	Well-marked Widgeon or Mallard (dyed Golden Olive)

A dressing for the Mayfly. Lough Mask.

ZULU

WET	*HOOK SIZE 8–12*
TAIL	Tuft of Red Wool
BODY	Black Seal's Fur
RIB	Fine Oval Silver or Wire
BODY HACKLE	Black Cock
HACKLE	Long Black

A well-known sea trout fly. *See also Blue Zulu.*

SALMON FLY DRESSINGS

MANY DRESSINGS of the past and present are recorded in this collection and many more could be added, but the reader will find dressings suitable for any district in Ireland. The old patterns may generally be distinguished by their use of Gold or Silver Twist for ribbing but Round or Oval Tinsel could be substituted.

Many of the well known salmon flies are also commonly used – the Silver Doctor, Blue Doctor, Black Doctor, Dusty Miller, Blue Charm, Jock Scott, etc., but as these are standard patterns I have deliberately omitted them. The Shrimp patterns are extremely popular especially Curry's Red and the Wye Bug both of which will kill fish in all waters.

In the general notes on lakes and rivers there is indicated the local preference for certain patterns but in an Irish fly-box you will also find – Clarets, Fiery Brown, Golden Olive, Lemon Grey, Lemon Blue, Orange Grouse, Hackley, John Robinson, Black Fairy, and the Thunder and Lightning.

Most of the winging materials in the very old patterns can still be obtained but some may require a substitute feather such as:

IBIS	Swan dyed Red
BUSTARD	Light Brown Speckled Turkey
SUMMER DUCK	
/WOOD DUCK	Speckled Grey Duck dyed Cinnamon
TOUCAN BREAST	Swan dyed Sulphur Yellow
BODIES	Pig's Wool-substitute-Seal's Fur

However, the patterns may be simplified by using the basic Irish Wing, i.e., a good bunch of Golden Pheasant Tippets to provide colour, bulk, and support, covered by a heavy Bronze Mallard Wing – two slips per side.

ARRAN BLUE

TAIL	None
BODY	Bright Royal Blue Seal's Fur (tied short)
RIB	Oval Silver
HACKLE	Blue Peacock neck hackle

This is the salmon version of the Donegal Blue trout fly and has been named to mark the generosity of Lord Arran who recently gave the local Donegal Town anglers a twenty-five year lease on the Eske Fishery. The Eske Angling Association has been formed and is working closely with the Northern Regional Fisheries Board to rehabilitate, enhance, and conserve, a wild sea trout lake which was beloved by the late Sidney Spenser.

ASSASSIN

TAG	Fine oval Silver and Yellow Floss
TAIL	G.P. Tippets Topping, and Kingfisher
BODY	Red or Scarlet Seal's Fur
RIB	Oval Silver
BODY HACKLE	Red (dyed) Cock
SH. HACKLE	Yellow Cock
WINGS	Golden Pheasant Tippets Red, Yellow, and Blue Swan, Teal, Bronze Mallard over
SIDES	Jungle Cock
	Golden Pheasant Topping over all

The late Pat Curry of Coleraine used only the Golden Pheasant Crest as a tail, and the body and body hackle was Orange-Scarlet.

BALLYSHANNON

TAG	Oval Silver and Blue Floss Silk
TAIL	G.P. Crest and Indian Crow
BUTT	Black Ostrich Herl
BODY	Hot Orange Floss Silk
RIB	Broad Oval Silver
BODY HACKLE	Magenta Cock
THROAT HACKLE	Torquoise-Blue Cock Hackle
WINGS	Dark Whitish Grey-tipped Turkey Tail, Bustard, G.P. Tail, Red, Yellow, and Blue Swan Bronze Mallard over
SIDES	Pintail Slips and Jungle Cock, Topping over all

Michael Rogan's dressing.

BANN OLIVE (1)

TAG	Silver
TAIL	G.P. Crest and Jungle Cock
BUTT	Black Ostrich
BODY	Oval Gold Tinsel
BODY HACKLE	Golden Olive Cock
THROAT	Blue Jay
WINGS	Ibis
	Golden Pheasant Tail
	Bronze Mallard over
HORNS	Blue Macaw

BANN OLIVE (2)

TAG	Silver
TAIL	Golden Pheasant Crest
BUTT	Black Ostrich
BODY	Golden Olive Floss
BODY HACKLE	Claret Cock
THROAT	Blue Jay
WINGS	Ibis
	Golden Pheasant Tail
	Bronze Mallard over
HORNS	Blue Macaw

Dressings for the Lower River Bann, Co. Londonderry.

BESSY BELL (Shrimp)

TAG	Silver
TAIL HACKLE	Long Purple Cock
BODY	Rear-White Floss
RIB	Oval Silver
VEILINGS	Yellow Toucan
CENTRE HACKLE	Short Dark Grizzle Cock
BODY	Front-Old Gold Floss
RIB	Oval Silver
VEILINGS	Yellow Toucan
WINGS	Jungle Cock
FRONT HACKLE	Long Grey Grizzle Cock

Also known as the Purple Tailed Shrimp.

BLACK BLOOD RED

TAG	Silver Tinsel and Orange Floss
TAIL	G.P. Topping and Tippets
BODY	Black Floss silk
RIB	Oval Silver
BODY HACKLES	Blue, ribbed from one third way up body, and followed by Dyed Blood Red hackle (or wound together)
SH. HACKLE	Dyed Amber hackle
WINGS	Strips of dyed red and yellow swan with Bronze Mallard over

BLACK CLARET

TAG	Silver and Light Blue Floss
TAIL	Golden Pheasant Topping
BODY	Black Floss
RIB	Oval Silver
BODY HACKLE	Claret Cock
THROAT	Blue Jay
WINGS	Golden Pheasant Tippets, Bronze Mallard over G. P. Topping over all
HORNS	Blue Macaw

BLACK FAIRY (1)

TAG	Gold wire and Yellow Floss
TAIL	Golden Pheasant Topping
BUTT	Black Ostrich
BODY	Black Seal's Fur
RIB	Oval Gold
HACKLE	Black Cock
WING	Bronze Mallard

This is the general dressing.

BLACK FAIRY (2)

TAG	Gold Wire and Orange Floss
TAIL	G.P. Tippets and Topping
BODY	Black Bear's Fur or Dark Purple Pig's Wool
RIB	Flat Gold
HACKLE	Black Cock from mid-body
THROAT	Blue Jay
WING	Bronze Mallard

The older dressing. Sometimes had underwing of golden pheasant tippets.

BLACK FLY

TAG	Black Mohair
TAIL	Gold Pheasant Crest
BODY	Black Floss or Pig's Wool
RIB	Silver Twist
BODY HACKLE	Black Cock (from mid-body)
THROAT	Blue Jay
WING	Gaudy
HEAD	Orange Mohair

O'Gorman's pattern.

BLACK GOLDFINCH (1)

TAG	Silver Wire and Orange Floss
TAIL	G.P. Topping and Indian Crow
BUTT	Black Ostrich Herl
BODY	Black Floss
RIB	Oval Gold
BODY HACKLE	Black or Dark Claret Cock
THROAT	Blue Jay
WINGS	Golden Pheasant Tippets, Red and Yellow Swan
	Three or Four G.P. Toppings over

BLACK GOLDFINCH (2)

TAG	Silver Wire and Red-Orange Floss
TAIL	Yellow Toucan and Indian Crow
BODY	Black Floss
RIB	Oval Silver
SH. HACKLE	Blue Jay
WINGS	Paired Jungle Cock
	Paired G.P. Toppings
	Covered by G.P. Topping
CHEEKS	Chatterer
HORNS	Blue Macaw

BLACK GOLDFINCH (3)

TAG	Silver Thread and deep Orange Floss
TAIL	G.P. Crest and Indian Crow
BUTT	Black Ostrich
BODY	Black Floss
RIB	Oval Gold
BODY HACKLE	Golden Olive Cock
TH.HACKLE	Blue Jay
WINGS	G.P. Tippets and Orange Swan Strips
	3 to 6 G.P. Crests over all
CHEEKS	Indian Crow
HORNS	Blue Macaw

BLACK JAY (1)

TAG	Silver Wire and Yellow Floss
TAIL	Golden Pheasant Topping
BUTT	Black Ostrich
BODY	Two turns Black Floss and remainder Black Seal's Fur
RIB	Silver Twist
BODY HACKLE	Black Cock over Fur
SH. HACKLE	Blue Jay
WINGS	Golden Pheasant Tippets
	Ibis
	Guinea-fowl
	Teal
	Bustard
	Green and Yellow Swan
	Bronze Mallard over
HORNS	Blue Macaw

BLACK JAY (2)

TAG	Silver Wire and Orange or Yellow Floss
TAIL	Golden Pheasant Topping
BUTT	Black Ostrich Herl
BODY	Rear – $^1/4$ Black Floss
	Front – $^3/4$ Black Seal's Fur
RIB	Oval Silver
BODY HACKLE	Black Cock (over Fur)
THROAT	Blue Jay
WINGS	Golden Pheasant Tippets
	Bustard
	Golden Pheasant Tail
	Guinea-fowl
	Red, Green, and Yellow Swan
	Bronze Mallard over
HORNS	Blue Macaw

BLACK AND CLARET (1)

TAG	Silver Twist and Orange Floss
TAIL	G.P. Topping and Chatterer
BODY	Black Floss
RIB	Flat Gold and Silver Twist
BODY HACKLE	Dark Claret Cock (from the second turn of tinsel)
SH. HACKLE	Blue Jay
WINGS	Golden Pheasant Tippets
	Golden Pheasant Tail
	Ibis
	Green Parrot
	Macaw
	Guinea-fowl
	Bronze Mallard
	Two Toppings over
HORNS	Blue Macaw

Believed to be Rogan's dressing.

BLACK AND CLARET (2)

TAG	Silver Wire and Blue Floss
TAIL	Topping and Indian Crow
BODY	Black Floss
RIB	Silver Twist
BODY HACKLE	Claret Clock
SH. HACKLE	Black Cock
THROAT	Blue Jay
WINGS	G.P. Tippets
	Bronze Mallard
	Topping over
HORNS	Blue Macaw

BLACK AND CLARET (3)

TAG	Silver Twist and Orange Floss
TAIL	G.P. Topping and Kingfisher
BUTT	Black Ostrich
BODY	Black Floss
RIB	Silver Twist
BODY HACKLE	Dark Claret Cock
SH. HACKLE	Blue Jay
WINGS	G.P. Yellow Saddle Feather
	G.P. Tail and Tippets
	Wood-duck
	Blue and Yellow Swan
	Bronze Mallard
	Topping over

A River Moy dressing.

BLACK AND CLARET (4)

Tag	Silver Wire and Yellow Floss
Tail	Topping and Indian Crow
Butt	Black Ostrich
Body	Black Floss
Rib	Oval Silver
Body Hackle	Claret Cock
Sh. Hackle	Blue Jay
Wings	G.P. Tippets
	Yellow and Red Swan
	G.P. Tail
	Teal
	Bronze Mallard over
Horns	Blue Macaw

BLACK AND CLARET (5)

Tag	Fine Oval Silver and Orange Floss
Tail	Golden Pheasant Tippets and Crest
Body	Black Floss
Rib	Silver Twist
Body Hackle	Dark Claret Cock
Sh. Hackle	Blue Jay
Wings	Golden Pheasant Tippets
	Golden Pheasant Tail
	Bronze Mallard over

BLACK AND CLARET (6)

Tag	Silver Wire and Orange floss
Tail	G.P. Topping and Guinea-fowl Fibres
Body	Black Seal's Fur
Rib	Oval Silver
Sh. Hackle	Dark Claret Cock
Wings	Paired Tippets
	Bronze Mallard over

BLACK AND MIXED

TAG	Silver Wire and Yellow Floss
TAIL	G.P. Tippets and Topping
BODY	Black Floss
RIB	Oval Silver
BODY HACKLE	Black Cock (to shoulder)
WINGS	Red, Yellow, and Blue Swan, Oak Turkey
	Bronze Mallard over

BLACK AND ORANGE

TAG	Fine Oval Gold and Yellow Floss
TAIL	G.P. Topping, Gallina, and Ibis
BODY	Black Seal's Fur
RIB	Oval Silver
BODY HACKLE	Medium Orange Cock from mid-body
SH. HACKLE	Blue Jay
WINGS	Golden Pheasant Tippets
	Golden Pheasant Tail
	Ibis
	Green Parrot
	Bronze Mallard over
HORNS	Red and Blue Macaw

Believed to be a dressing by Rogan. The general pattern had a jointed black and orange floss body with a blue jay body hackle from mid-body.

BLACKER'S SALMON FLIES

IN WM. BLACKER'S BOOK *Art of Angling,* (1842), the following dressings are recorded.
  He writes of the River Bann at Bevannachar (modern Movanagher) near Kilrea
Co. Derry, and gives the following Salmon Fly Dressings for this still notable salmon
river.

(1)

TAIL	Golden Pheasant Crest
BODY	Claret Pig-hair and Gold Tinsel
LEGS	Claret Hackle
WINGS	Mallard, Turkey light brown, and Golden
	Pheasant neck (tippets)
	Feathers mixed. Head Black

HOOK SIZE 9

(2)

BODY	Half Orange, Half Claret, Gold Tinsel
LEGS	Claret Hackle and Jay
WINGS AND TAIL	As for No. 1

(3)

TAIL	Golden Pheasant Topping and Black Ostrich Tag (butt)
BODY	Orange Pig-hair, Gold Twist
LEGS	Orange Hackle
WINGS	Golden Pheasant neck, tail, and Crest, Black Head, Macaw Smellers (horns) each side of wing

(4)

TAIL	Golden Pheasant Topping and Black Ostrich tag (butt)
BODY	Gold Colour Pig-hair (one part)
	Wine-purple (three parts). Gold and Silver Twist
LEGS	Wine-purple Hackle
WINGS	As for No. 3

HOOK SIZE 8

Whilst he advocates that body colours should be blended and the darkest portion taken to the head, in this fly (no. 4) he stresses that the body must have the gold at the head, i.e., three quarters body wine-purple, one quarter gold (at head).

(5)

TAIL	G.P. Topping
BODY	Olive Pig-hair
LEGS	Olive Hackle
WINGS	Mallard and Topping Black Head

HOOK SIZE 9

The River Bush, Bushmills, Co. Antrim, N. Ireland. A small river near the Giant's Causeway, North of the Bann, swarming with Salmon in the Spring and Summer.

(1842)

RECOMMENDED FLIES

(1)

TAIL	G.P. Toppings
BODY	Orange and Gold Twist
LEGS	Claret or Blood-Red Hackle
WINGS	Brown Mallard
	Black Head

(2)

TAIL	G.P. Topping
BODY	Orange and Gold Twist
LEGS	Orange Hackle
WINGS	Gaudy Feathers
	Black Head

(3)

BODY	Amber Mohair and Gold Twist
LEGS	Amber Hackle
WINGS	Brown Mallard

(4)

TAIL	Yellow Mohair
BODY	Dark Brown Mohair
LEGS	Black Hackle
WINGS	Brown Turkey or Mallard

(5)

TAIL	G.P. Topping
BODY	Copper coloured Peacock Herl and Gold Twist
LEGS	Black Hackle (at head)
WINGS	Sword Feather of the Peacock's Tail
HEAD	Black Ostrich

Blacker's *Art of Flymaking* published in 1855 contains 17 hand-coloured plates of flie
which in my opinion have never been surpassed for their meticulous attention t
detail; every feather fibre glistens with life as does the detailed flosses and tinsels.
consider myself extremely fortunate to own a copy of this rare and much prize
volume.

It gives much more detail of the Irish dressings than earlier recorded in 1842.

THE SPIRIT FLY NO. 1

The wings are made of six toppings with a broad strip of wood-duck on each side, a red Himalaya crest feather at the top, a cock-of-the-rock feather, blue kingfisher feather at each side, a black head and feelers of macaw. The body is made of joints of black and orange floss, with a tip of gold tinsel at the tail; tail two small toppings, a tag of puce silk and ostrich (it must be tied with very fine silk that the body may not be lumpy, but to taper gradually from the tail to the head, and the hackle to be stripped at one side to roll even) and at each joint a scarlet hackle, with a tip of gold tinsel under it to make lively looking. There is a purple hackle, or very dark blue, struck round the shoulder.

THE SPIRIT FLY NO. 2

The wings are composed of golden pheasant tail feather mixed with strips of bustard, scarlet macaw, wood-duck, mallard, yellow macaw body feather, silver pheasant, and a topping over all extending a little longer than the other feathers. Blue and yellow macaw feelers. The tail is a topping with a strip of wood-duck feather, tipped with silver twist, a tag of gold coloured floss and black ostrich. The body – puce floss to the centre and the remainder orange pig hair or mohair, ribbed with broad silver tinsel. A guinea-hen rump feather wound over the orange hair and the shoulder hackle blue jay with a head of black ostrich.

THE SPIRIT FLY NO. 3

The wings are made of the following mixtures of feathers each side to be alike:-

Brown mallard, bustard, and wood-duck; a topping, scarlet macaw, teal, golden pheasant neck feather, a strip of yellow macaw and feelers of blue and yellow macaw tail; a head of black ostrich; the tail to be a topping with green and red parrot tail; the body is composed of joints, first a tip of silver, a tag of maroon floss, a tag of black, a joint of brown, green, and brown-red hackle, puce and red, green and yellow, blue and orange, with a tip of gold tinsel at each joint, a very small red hackle and two red toucan feathers round the shoulder, and a blue kingfisher's feather on each side of the wings.

THE CLARET FLY

The wings are composed of two wood-duck feathers without the white tips and two inner strips of the same feather but showing the white tips. The head is peacock herl, and the tail is two or three fibres of hen pheasant with a short tuft of orange macaw or parrot. The tip is silver and the body of claret pig hair ribbed with gold, covered by two richly dyed claret hackles tapering from tail to shoulder.

THE BROWN FLY (FIERY BROWN?)

The wings are made of the golden pheasant tail that has the long clouded bar in the feather, rather full, and two broad strips of light brown white-tipped turkey tail at each side; a good size peacock herl head and feelers of scarlet macaw. The tip to be gold tinsel and the tail a small bright topping, and a tag of gold coloured floss silk. The body is cinnamon, or yellow-brown pig hair or mohair, ribbed with double silver twist; over the body roll a real brown-red cock hackle, and around the throttle roll on a bright red-brown small spotted grouse hackle or a brown mottled feather of the hen Argus Pheasant's neck or back.

THE SILVER GREY

The wings are made of Golden Pheasant tail feather, mixed with mallard, red macaw, blue and yellow macaw body feathers, guinea-hen, Golden Pheasant neck feathers, with feelers of blue and yellow macaw. The head is black and the tip is silver and orange floss, the tail a topping with red and blue macaw and guinea-hen. The body is of the silver dun monkey, or light dun fox, or squirrel fur, or dyed blue dun mohair mixed with yellow, (all these are good), ribbed with broad silver tinsel and a hackle of real dun cock (that has a yellowish motley shade) rolled up to the head. At the head a little orange mohair covered by a bright orange hackle. This final hackle may be varied to claret or fiery brown .

TIP	Silver Wire
TAG	Orange Floss
TAIL	G.P. Topping with red and blue macaw and Guinea-hen
BODY	Silver Dun Monkey (or Light Dun Fox, or Squirrel Fur, or Blue Dun Mohair mixed with Yellow)
RIB	Broad Silver Tinsel
BODY HACKLE	Dun Cock (with yellowish mottle)
SHOULDER	A little Orange Mohair covered by a bright Orange hackle

BLUE BLACK

TAG	Fine Oval Gold + Orange Pig's Wool
TAIL	G.P. Topping (and Tippets)
BODY	Darkest Blue Pig's Wool
RIB	Fine Gold
BODY HACKLE	Orange Cock from mid-body
SH. HACKLE	Blue Jay
WINGS	Peacock Sword with
	Bronze Mallard over

BLUE BOYNE

TAG	Silver
TAIL	Two Indian Crow Feathers
BUTT	Black Ostrich Herl
BODY	Oval Silver
VEILINGS	Chatterer or Kingfisher —above and below — dividing the body into four quarters. The throat veiling to be as long as possible
WINGS	Two or Three G.P. Toppings
HORNS	Long Blue Macaw

BLUE CHARM (1)

TAG	Silver Wire and Yellow Floss
TAIL	Golden Pheasant Crest
BUTT	Black Ostrich
BODY	Black Floss
RIB	Oval Silver
HACKLE	Rich Deep Blue
WINGS	Bronze Mallard with strips of Teal married to top edge G.P. Topping over

The butt may be omitted. The body and wings slim.

BLUE CHARM (2)

TAG	Flat Silver
TAIL	Golden Pheasant Crest
BODY	Black Floss
RIB	Silver Wire or Fine Oval
HACKLE	Rich Deep Blue
WING	Mink or Silver Fox Fur

This is a low-water dressing.

BLUE GOLDFINCH

TAG	Silver Wire and Orange Floss
TAIL	Yellow Toucan and Indian Crow
BODY	Light Blue Floss
RIB	Oval Silver
BODY HACKLE	Blue Jay (from mid-body)
WINGS	Paired Indian Crow
	Four or Five G.P. Toppings
CHEEKS	Indian Crow
HORNS	Blue Macaw

BLUE PALMER (1)

TAG	Gold Thread
TAIL	G.P. Tippets and Topping
BUTT	Black Ostrich
BODY	Deep Blue Floss
RIB	Oval Gold
BODY HACKLE	Blue Jay to throat
WINGS	Mixed. G.P. Tippets, married strips of Scarlet, Blue, Yellow and Orange Swan, strips of Bustard, G.P. Tail, Pintail and Summer Duck. Bronze Mallard over
HORNS	Blue Macaw

BLUE PALMER (2)

TAG	Fine Oval Silver and Dark Blue Floss
TAIL	Golden Pheasant Topping
BUTT	Black Ostrich Herl
BODY	Dark Blue Floss
RIB	Oval Silver
BODY HACKLE	Claret Cock
THROAT	Blue Jay
WINGS	Golden Pheasant Tippets
	Dark Mottled Turkey
	Bustard
	Golden Pheasant Tail
	Yellow, Blue, and Red Swan
	Guinea-fowl
	Bronze Mallard over

BLUE SILK

TAG	Silver Wire
TAIL	G.P. Tippets, Ibis, and Peacock Sword
BUTT	Yellow Floss
BODY	Light Blue Floss
RIB	Oval Silver
BODY HACKLE	Blood-Red Cock over Blue Floss
SH. HACKLE	Amber Cock
WINGS	Golden Pheasant Tippets
	Ibis
	Peacock Sword
	Bronze Mallard over

BLUE, GREY, AND BROWN

TAG	Silver Twist and Orange Floss
TAIL	Golden Pheasant Topping
BODY	3 turns Blue Seal's Fur
	2 turns Grey Monkey Fur
	1 turn Fiery Brown Seal's Fur
RIB	Silver Twist
BODY HACKLES	To Match Body Colour (graduated)
SH. HACKLE	Dark Claret Cock
WINGS	Golden Pheasant Tippets
	Bustard
	Wood-duck
	Blue and Yellow Swan
	Bronze Mallard over

A dressing also known as the Cork Beauty.

BOYNE

TAG	Silver and Yellow Floss
TAIL	Golden Pheasant Topping
BODY	Rear – Light Blue Pig's Wool
RIB	Silver Twist over Blue
BODY	Front – Bright Brown Pig's Wool
BODY HACKLE	Bright Brown Cock over Brown
THROAT	Blue Jay
WING	Brown Turkey or Grey Peacock
CHEEKS	Small G.P. Breast Feather
HORNS	Guinea-hen and Macaw
HEAD	Blue Mohair

A dressing by O'Gorman. This would appear to be the original of the Half Blue and Half Brown or Blue and Brown Body.

BUTCHER (1)

TAG	Silver Twist and Yellow Floss
TAIL	G.P. Topping and Blue Macaw
BUTT	Black Ostrich
BODY	Seal's Fur in equal parts:
	1. Light Cardinal Red
	2. Light Blue
	3. Dark Purplish Red
	4. Indigo Blue
RIB	Silver Twist
BODY HACKLE	Black Cock over 2, 3, and 4
SH. HACKLES	1) Golden Olive Cock
	2) Long well-speckled Guinea-fowl
WINGS	Golden Pheasant Tippets
	Golden Pheasant Breast
	Summer Duck
	Guinea-fowl
	Bustard
	Golden Pheasant Tail
	Yellow Swan
	Bronze Mallard over
SIDES	Golden Pheasant Toppings
HORNS	Long Blue Macaw
CHEEKS	Chatterer or Kingfisher

BUTCHER (2)

TAG	Silver Thread and Light Orange Floss
TAIL	G.P. Tippets, Mallard, and Blue Macaw
BUTT	Black Ostrich Herl
BODY	Dark Red Claret Mohair
RIB	Narrow Silver Tinsel
BODY HACKLE	Red Claret Cock
SH. HACKLE	Light Blue Cock
WINGS	Brown Mallard
HORNS	Blue Macaw

A Francis Francis dressing.

CANARY

TAG	Fine Oval Silver and Yellow Floss
TAIL	Golden Pheasant Crest
BUTT	Black Ostrich
BODY	Rear – Oval Silver
CENTRE HACKLE	Yellow Cock
MIDDLE JOINT	Black Ostrich
BODY	Front – Oval Silver
HACKLE	Yellow Cock
WINGS	Golden Olive Mohair
	Golden Pheasant Topping over

CLABBY

TAG	Fine Oval Gold and Red Floss
TAIL	G.P. Topping and Kingfisher
BUTT	Black Ostrich Herl
BODY	Red Floss
RIB	Oval Gold
BODY HACKLE	Dark Green Cock
SH. HACKLE	Medium Blue Cock (dyed)
THROAT	Guinea-fowl
WINGS	Golden Pheasant Tippets
	Yellow, Blue and Red Swan
	Teal
	Bronze Mallard over
SIDES	Jungle Cock
	Golden Pheasant Topping over all

A personal dressing by S. Anderson.

CLARET (1)

TAIL	G.P. Tippets and Topping
BUTT	Golden Olive Pig's Wool or Seal's Fur
BODY	Dark Claret Pig's Wool or Seal's Fur
RIB	Oval Gold
BODY HACKLE	Claret Cock (from mid-body)
THROAT	Blue Jay
WINGS	Golden Pheasant Tippets
	Ibis
	Peacock Sword
	Bronze Mallard over

On the Northern rivers a pinch of blue fur is sometimes added to the body at the throat. The Clarets are the Salmon fly dressing of the Mallard and Claret.

CLARET (2)

TAG	Orange Floss
TAIL	Golden Pheasant Tippets
BODY	Claret Floss
BODY HACKLE	Dark Claret Cock
RIB	Gold and Silver Twist
THROAT	Blue Jay
WINGS	Golden Pheasant Tippets with
	Bronze Mallard over

'Corrigeen' also noted a Rough Claret which had a rough wool claret body with three hackles, black, claret, and golden olive. Mixed wing.

CLARET (3)

TAG	Gold Twist and Golden Floss
TAIL	G.P. Topping, Blue and Red Macaw
BUTT	Black Ostrich Herl
BODY	Three turns of Orange Floss, then Medium Reddish Claret Pig's Wool
RIB	Stout Gold Thread
BODY HACKLE	Light Reddish Claret Cock
SH. HACKLE	Black Cock
WINGS	Golden Pheasant Tippets, G.P. Tail, Turkey, Bustard, Peacock, Green and Red Parrot, Bronze Mallard over
	Golden Pheasant Topping over all

The body colour may be varied from light red claret to dark purple claret.

CLARET GOLDFINCH

TAG	Silver Twist and Orange Floss
TAIL	Golden Pheasant Topping and Indian Crow
BUTT	Black Ostrich
BODY	Two turns Black Floss then Claret Floss to shoulder
RIB	Silver Twist
BODY HACKLE	Claret Cock (or Claret Fur ribbed)
THROAT	Blue Jay
WINGS	Bright Yellow Swan covered by Five G.P. Toppings
HORNS	Blue Macaw
HEAD	Black Ostrich

CLARET GREY

TAG	Silver Wire and Golden Floss
TAIL	G.P. Topping and Indian Crow
BUTT	Royal Blue Floss
BODY	Rear – Grey Seal's Fur
	Front – Claret Seal's Fur
	(in separate halves)
RIB	Silver Twist
BODY HACKLE	Claret Cock (on Claret Fur)
SH. HACKLE	Yellow Cock
THROAT	Blue Jay
WINGS	G.P. Tippets, Red, Blue and Yellow Swan, G.P. Tail, Teal, Bronze Mallard over
HORNS	Blue Macaw

CLARET OLIVE

TAG	Oval Gold
TAIL	G.P. Tippets and Crest
BODY	Golden Olive Seal's Fur
RIB	Oval Gold
BODY HACKLE	Golden Olive from mid-body
SH. HACKLE	Blood Claret Cock
WINGS	Tippets Yellow and Red Swan
	Bronze Mallard over

CLARET PALMER

TAG	Silver Tinsel and Claret Floss
TAIL	Golden Pheasant Topping
BUTT	Black Ostrich
BODY	Claret Floss
RIB	Silver
BODY HACKLE	Claret Cock
SH. HACKLE	Sky-Blue Cock
THROAT	Blue Jay
WINGS	Golden Pheasant Tippets
	Claret and Golden Yellow Swan
	Golden Pheasant Tail
	Bronze Mallard over
HORNS	Blue Macaw

CLARET PARSON

TAG	Gold Tinsel and Orange Floss
TAIL	G.P. Topping and Chatterer
BUTT	Black Ostrich Herl
BODY	Claret Floss
RIB	Oval Gold
BODY HACKLE	Claret Cock
SH. HACKLE	Blue Cock
WINGS	Golden Pheasant Tippets
	Dark Speckled Turkey
	Yellow, Red, and Blue Swan
	Blue Peacock
	Bustard
	Golden Pheasant Tail
	Wood-duck
	Teal
	Mallard
	Guinea-fowl
	G.P. Topping over all
CHEEKS	Chatterer
HORNS	Blue Macaw

CLARET AND PURPLE

TAIL	G.P. Tippets, Ibis, and Peacock Sword Tips
BODY	Rear – Claret Seal's Fur
	Front – Dark Purple Seal's Fur
RIB	Flat Silver
BODY HACKLE	Dyed Blood-Red Cock over Purple Fur
SH. HACKLE	Yellow-Orange Cock
WINGS	Golden Pheasant Tippets
	Bronze Mallard over

Also known as the Purple Claret. Claret and Blue (Blue Claret) as above but dark blue seal's fur in place of the purple.

COINER

TAG	Silver Wire and Claret Floss
TAIL	G.P. Topping and Indian Crow
BUTT	Black Ostrich Herl
BODY	Rear – One Third Yellow-Orange Floss
	Front – Grey Seal's Fur
RIB	Oval Silver
BODY HACKLES	Orange Cock on Floss
	Barred Rock Cock on Fur
SH. HACKLE	Orange (or Claret) Cock
WINGS	Golden Pheasant Tippets
	Red, Yellow, and Blue Swan
	Teal
	Guinea-fowl
	Bronze Mallard over

COMMANDER

TAG	Silver Twist and Orange Floss
TAIL	Golden Pheasant Topping
BODY	Light Brown Floss
RIB	Silver
BODY HACKLE	Blue Cock
SH. HACKLE	Yellow Cock
WINGS	Red and Yellow Swan
	Red G.P. Sword Tail feathers
HEAD	Black Ostrich

An old low water dressing for Co. Cork.

CONNEMARA BLACK

TAG	Oval Silver and Yellow Floss
TAIL	G.P. Tippets and Topping
BODY	Black Seal's Fur
RIB	Oval Silver
HACKLE	Black Henny-Cock
THROAT	Blue Jay
WINGS	Yellow, Red and Blue Swan, with Bronze Mallard over
SIDES	Pintail

CURRY'S BLUE SHRIMP

TAG	Silver Tinsel
TAIL HACKLE	Long R.I. Red Cock
BODY	Oval or Embossed Gold
CENTRE HACKLE	Deep Electric Blue Cock
FRONT HACKLE	Long R.I. Red Cock

The centre hackle is a medium dark blue but very bright and intense. A dressing favoured by Joseph Curry, brother of the late Pat Curry of Coleraine.

CURRY'S GOLD SHRIMP

TAG	Flat Silver
TAIL HACKLE	Golden Pheasant Yellow Rump Feather
BODY	Rear – Embossed Silver
RIB	Oval Silver
VEILINGS	Orange Toucan (at sides of body)
CENTRE HACKLE	Orange Cock
BODY	Front – Embossed Silver
RIB	Oval Silver
VEILINGS	Orange Toucan (at sides of body)
WINGS	Two Jungle Cock (arrow – head on top of body and roofing front section)
FRONT HACKLE	Orange Cock (or Golden Olive)
HEAD	Red Varnish

A dressing of Pat Curry's.

CURRY'S RED SHRIMP

TAG	Flat Silver
TAIL HACKLE	Golden Pheasant Red Breast
BODY	Rear – Red Floss
RIB	Fine Oval Silver
VEILINGS	Indian Crow (at sides of body)
CENTRE HACKLE	Badger Cock
BODY	Front – Black Floss
RIB	Oval Silver
VEILINGS	Indian Crow (at sides of Body)
WINGS	Two Jungle Cock (arrow – head on top of body and fully roofing Black Floss)
FRONT HACKLE	Long Grey Badger Cock
HEAD	Red Varnish

The side veilings (front) must be long enough to be clearly seen against the underside of the jungle cock wings.

A variation is to dress the rear body with red fluorescent wool. A substitute for the Indian crow may be pale cock pheasant neck feather dyed bright scarlet.

This dressing is generally recorded as having the veilings above and below but a letter written by Pat Curry, and now in the author's possession, stresses, side veilings and roofed jungle cock.

DANCER SHRIMP

TAG	Flat Silver
TAIL HACKLE	Dark Smoke Blue Cock
BODY	Rear – Claret Seal's Fur
RIB	Oval Gold
VEILINGS	Yellow Toucan
CENTRE HACKLE	Short Claret Cock
BODY	Front – Black Seal's Fur
RIB	Oval Gold
WINGS	Jungle Cock
FRONT HACKLE	Long Claret Cock

DARK ROSALEEN

TAG	Gold Wire and Yellow Floss
TAIL	Silver Pheasant Tippets
BUTT	Green Floss
BODY	Rear – Flat Gold
	Front – Black Ostrich Herl
RIB	Oval Gold
HACKLE	Dark Green Cock
WINGS	Golden Pheasant Tippets
	Blue Peacock
	Dark Speckled Turkey
SIDES	Jungle Cock

DIRTY OLIVE

TAG	Flat Silver + Yellow Floss
TAIL	G.P. Tippets and Topping
BODY	Golden Olive Seal's Fur and Hare's Ear Fur (mixed)
RIB	Flat or Oval Silver
HACKLE	Dyed Blood-Red Cock
WINGS	Golden Pheasant Tippets
	Bronze Mallard over
BODY MIXTURE	Two of Golden Olive to one of Hare's Ear

DIRTY ORANGE

TAG	Fine Oval Gold and Light Blue Floss
TAIL	G.P. Tippets and Crest
BUTT	Black Ostrich
BODY	Two turns Orange-Yellow Floss
	Remainder Dirty Orange Seal's Fur
RIB	Gold
BODY HACKLE	Dirty Orange (over Fur)
THROAT	Blue Jay
	Red Golden Pheasant Breast
WINGS	Golden Pheasant Tail
	Wood-duck
	Red, Orange, and Blue Swan
	Bronze Mallard over
HORNS	Blue Macaw

An old dressing.

DONEGAL FLY

TAIL	G.P. Crest and Tippets
BODY	Royal Blue Seal's Fur
RIB	Oval Silver
HACKLE	Black Cock
UNDER WING	Bunch of G.P. Tippets
OVER WING	Bronze Mallard

A dressing by Stephen Gwynne.

DOOCHARY CLARET

TAG	Silver Wire and Scarlet Floss
TAIL	G.P. Tippets and Crest
BODY	^{2}/3 Rich Claret Seal's Fur
	^{1}/3 Magenta Seal's Fur (well-mixed together)
RIB	Wide Flat Silver Tinsel (very closely ribbed)
SH. HACKLES	1) Rich Claret Cock
	2) Blue Jay
WINGS	Bronze Mallard
HEAD	Dark Red Varnish

The body is so closely ribbed that only very narrow bands of well-picked out fur shows between ribs. A County Donegal pattern.

DROMORE FLY

TAG	Gold or Silver Twist and Yellow or Green Mohair
TAIL	Golden Pheasant Crest
1 { BUTT	Cinnamon
BODY	Rich Dark Brown Mohair
2 { BUTT	Cinnamon
BODY	Claret Mohair
3 { BUTT	Grey
BODY	Deep Brown Floss
RIB	Five rows Gold Twist
BODY HACKLE	Natural Red Cock
WINGS	Blue Peacock
	Bronze Mallard over
HEAD	Black Ostrich or Blue Mohair

This pattern, with three alternative bodies, was given by O'Gorman almost 150 years ago for trout and salmon. Its name implies that it was used on the Dromore Lake (Co. Clare). It is very difficult to follow his dressing instructions but this is not surprising as he admits that his flies were tied by one David O'Shaughnessy.

DUNKELD (1)

TAG	Silver Wire and Gold Floss
TAIL	G.P. Crest and Jungle Cock Eye (with enamelled side resting on Crest)
BUTT	Black Ostrich
BODY	Flat Gold Tinsel
RIB	Oval Gold
BODY HACKLE	Orange-Amber Cock
THROAT	Blue Jay
WINGS	G.P. Tippets
	G.P. Tail
	Brown Speckled Turkey
	Bronze Mallard over
	G.P. Topping over all
CHEEKS	Kingfisher
HORNS	Blue Macaw (Optional)

DUNKELD (2)

TAG	Fine Oval Silver and Orange Floss
TAIL	Golden Pheasant Crest
BUTT	Black Ostrich
BODY	Flat Gold Tinsel
RIB	Gold Wire or Fine Oval
HACKLE	Orange Cock (from mid-body)
THROAT	Blue Jay
WINGS	Golden Pheasant Tippets
	Bronze Mallard over G.P. Topping over all
CHEEKS	Kingfisher
HORNS	Blue and Red Macaw

ERNE RANGER

TAG	Silver Wire
TAIL	G.P. Tippets and Crest
BODY	Rear – Scarlet Floss
	Front – Black Floss
	(In equal parts)
RIB	Oval Silver
BODY HACKLE	Scarlet Cock (over Black Floss)
SH. HACKLE	Orange Cock
WINGS	Scarlet Swan with White-Tipped Turkey over
SIDES	Jungle Cock

See also Irish Ranger.

FAUGHAN PURPLE (1)

TAIL	G.P. Tippets, Ibis, and Peacock Sword Tips
BUTT	Golden Olive Seal's Fur
BODY	Dark Purple Pig's Wool or Seal's Fur
RIB	Flat Silver
HACKLE	Dark Blood Red Cock (dyed)
WINGS	Golden Pheasant Tippets
	Ibis
	Peacock Sword
	Bronze Mallard over

A dressing for the River Faughan, Co. Londonderry, which will prove effective on all the rivers of the Foyle System.

Another dressing gives –

(2)

RIB	Oval Gold
HACKLES	1. Blood-Red Cock (dyed)
	2. Amber Cock

FENIAN (1)

TAG	Silver
TAIL	G.P. Topping, Tippets, and Blue Peacock
BODY	Rear – $1/4$ Orange Pig's Wool
	Front – $3/4$ Emerald Green Pig's Wool
RIB	Oval Gold
BODY HACKLE	Yellow Cock (over Green Pig's Wool)
THROAT	Blue Jay
WINGS	Golden Pheasant Tippets
	Golden Pheasant Tail
	Green, Yellow, and Red Swan
	Bustard
	Teal
	Bronze Mallard Over

An old dressing gave –

(2)

BODY	Orange Seal's Fur
	Violet Floss
	Black Floss
	(in equal parts)

FIERY BROWN (1)

TAG	Gold Twist and Orange Floss
TAIL	Golden Pheasant Topping
BODY	Fiery Brown Seal's Fur
RIB	Gold Twist
BODY HACKLE	Fiery Brown or Blood Red Cock
SH. HACKLE	Black Cock
WINGS	Golden Pheasant Tippets
	Bronze Mallard over
HORNS	Blue Macaw

FIERY BROWN (2)

TAG	Silver Twist and Orange Floss
TAIL	G.P. Tippets, Topping, and Green Parrot
BODY	Fiery Brown Seal's Fur
RIB	Gold Twist
BODY HACKLE	Fiery Brown Cock
THROAT	Blue Jay
WINGS	Golden Pheasant Tippets
	Bronze Mallard over
HORNS	Blue Macaw

FIERY BROWN (3)

TAG	Gold Wire
TAIL	G.P. Tippets and Topping
BUTT	Golden Olive Seal's Fur
BODY	Fiery Brown Pig's Wool
RIB	Oval Gold (or Silver)
HACKLES	Dyed Blood-Red Cock
	Orange Cock
	(Wound on together or singly)
WINGS	Golden Pheasant Tippets
	Peacock Sword
	Ibis
	Bronze Mallard over

On occasions the body colour is graduated from golden olive to fiery brown (i.e. by careful admixture of fur). The orange cock hackle is, at times, replaced by blue jay, and the windings are singly. Occasional dressings have jungle cock cheeks.

FIERY BROWN AND RED
(Co. Donegal) is as above but with -

BODY	Rear $^2/3$ – Fiery Brown Seal's Fur
	Front $^1/3$ – Dark Red Seal's Fur
BODY HACKLE	Dyed Blood-Red Cock (over Red Fur)

Fiery Brown and Blue has light blue body and hackle at front third, and fiery brown hackle at shoulder.

GARIBALDI

TAG	Silver Thread and Yellow Floss
TAIL	Golden Pheasant Topping
BUTT	Green Peacock Herl
REAR BODY	$^1/3$ Yellow-Orange Floss
JOINT	3 turns Silver Thread +
	Yellow Olive Hackle + Green Peacock Herl
CENTRE BODY	$^1/3$ Red-Orange Floss
JOINT	3 turns Silver Thread + Orange-Olive
	Hackle + Green Peacock Herl
FRONT BODY	$^1/3$ Red-Orange Floss
JOINT	3 turns Silver Thread + Light Claret Hackle
	+ Green Peacock Herl
SH. HACKLE	Blue Jay
WINGS	Paired Tippet Feathers
SIDES	Slips of Brown Jay
	G.P. Topping over
HORNS	Red & Blue Macaw
HEAD	Green Peacock Herl

An old pattern for the lower River Bann, Co. Derry. Dressing recorded by Francis Francis.

GHOST SHRIMP

TAG	Flat Silver
TAIL HACKLE	Furnace Cock
BODY	Rear – Old Gold Floss
RIB	Oval Silver
VEILINGS	Red Toucan
CENTRE HACKLE	Short White Cock
BODY	Front – Black Floss
RIB	Oval Silver
VEILINGS	Red Toucan
WINGS	Jungle Cock
FRONT HACKLE	Long White Cock

GILL FLY (1)

TAG	Gold Twist
TAIL	Mallard, Gallina, and Pheasant Tail
BODY	Rear 3/4 – Black Seal's Fur
	Front 1/4 – Honey Pig's Wool
HACKLE	Natural Red Cock (dyed Olive)
THROAT	Blue Jay
WINGS	Golden Pheasant Tippets
	Gallina
	Golden Pheasant Tail
	Peacock Sword
	Ibis
	Teal
	Brown Mallard
HORNS	Blue Macaw

Believed to be Rogan's dressing.

GILL FLY (2)

TAG	Silver Twist and Orange Floss
TAIL	G.P. Topping and Brown Mallard Fibres
BODY	Black Mohair with a broad ring of Dark Dirty Red Mohair in the centre
SH. HACKLE	Twist of Long Dirty Red Mohair
THROAT	Blue Jay
WINGS	Golden Pheasant Tippets
	Brown Mallard over

Given by Francis Francis for Lough Gill, Co. Sligo.

THE GOAT (1)

TAG	Oval Silver
TAIL	G.P. Tippets and Crest
BODY	Bright Yellow Seal's Fur
RIB	Oval Silver
HACKLE	Bright Yellow Cock
WING	Goat's Hair (dyed Bright Yellow)

The wing is very heavy and solid in this dressing and the ends cut square at correct length. An ugly looking wing. A North of Ireland dressing.

THE GOAT (2)

TAG	Silver and Yellow Floss
TAIL	Golden Pheasant Topping
BUTT	Black Ostrich Herl
BODY	Grey Seal's Fur
RIB	Oval Silver
HACKLE	Yellow Cock
WINGS	Goat's Beard dyed Yellow

A West of Ireland dressing.

GOAT'S TOE

TAIL	Red Wool
BODY	Red Seal's Fur
RIB	Bronze Peacock Herl (close-ribbed)
HACKLE	Long Blue Peacock

A dressing for Connemara and the West of Ireland.

GOLD BODY

TAIL	G.P. Tippets and Topping
BODY	Oval or Flat Gold
RIB	Fine Oval Gold
BODY HACKLE	Dyed Blood-Red Cock
SH. HACKLE	Orange Cock (Orange Crottle, or Brick Orange)
WINGS	Golden Pheasant Tippets Ibis Blue Peacock Bronze Mallard over

GOLDFINCH (1)

TAG	Gold Twist and Orange Mohair
TAIL	Crest and Orange and Yellow Mohair
BODY	Yellow (or Black) Pig's Wool
RIB	Gold Twist
BODY HACKLE	Yellow Cock
WINGS	Golden Pheasant Yellow Body Feather, Paired Golden Pheasant Toppings (tied in so that tips incline inward and cross each other)
THROAT	Blue Jay
HEAD	Blue Ostrich Herl

A dressing given by O'Gorman in 1845; the use of a black body gave the Black Goldfinch.

GOLDFINCH (2)

TAG	Silver Twist and Pale Blue Floss
TAIL	Golden Pheasant Crest
BUTT	Black Ostrich
BODY	Yellow Floss
RIB	Oval Silver
BODY HACKLE	Golden Olive Cock
THROAT	Blue Jay
WINGS	Six Golden Pheasant Toppings
HEAD	Black Ostrich

A dressing from Co. Galway.

GOLDFINCH (3)

TAG	Gold Tinsel and Black Floss
TAIL	G.P. Topping
BODY	Golden Floss
RIB	Gold
BODY HACKLE	Ginger Cock
THROAT	Blue Jay
WINGS	Eight or Nine G.P. Toppings
HORNS	Long Red Macaw
CHEEKS	Kingfisher
HEAD	Black Ostrich

A dressing given by 'Ephemera' in 1853. Attributed to the Shannon.

GOLDEN OLIVE (1)

TAG	Silver Wire and Orange Floss
TAIL	G.P. Tippets and Topping
BODY	Golden Olive Seal's Fur
RIB	Oval Silver (or Gold)
HACKLE	Blood-Red Cock (Natural)
WINGS	Golden Pheasant Tippets
	Bronze Mallard over

Optional throat – Blue Jay.

GOLDEN OLIVE (2)

TAG	Fine Oval Silver and Orange Floss
TAIL	G.P. Crest and Indian Crow
BUTT	Black Ostrich
BODY	Golden Olive Seal's Fur
RIB	Gold Twist
BODY HACKLE	Golden Olive Cock
THROAT	Blue Jay
WINGS	Golden Pheasant Tail
	Bustard
	Green Parrot
	Bronze Mallard over

GOLDEN OLIVE (3)

TAG	Silver Wire and Violet Floss
TAIL	G.P. Tippets and Toucan
BUTT	Violet Chenille
BODY	Yellow-Orange Floss
RIB	Silver Twist
BODY HACKLE	Golden Olive Cock
THROAT	Blue Jay
WINGS	Golden Pheasant Tippets
	Bronze Mallard over

Topping over all. Also known as the Violet Olive.

GREY OLIVE
as above but with –

TAG	Silver Wire and Grey Floss
BUTT	Grey Chenille
BODY	Palest Orange

GOLDEN OLIVE (4)

TAG	Silver Wire and Orange Floss
TAIL	Golden Pheasant Topping
BODY	Seal's Fur graduating from Golden Olive at tail to Brown Olive at the shoulder
BODY HACKLE	Golden Olive Cock
THROAT	Blue Jay
WINGS	Golden Pheasant Tippets
	Blue Peacock
	Red and Yellow Swan
	Guinea-fowl
	Bronze Mallard over

The golden olive fur is darkened by the admixture of brown olive until the final turn is wholly Brown Olive.

GOLDEN OLIVE (5)

TAG	Silver Twist and Claret Floss
TAIL	G.P. Topping and Indian Crow
BODY	Rich Golden Olive Seal's Fur
RIB	Gold Twist or Flat Gold
BODY HACKLE	Rich Golden Olive Cock
SH. HACKLE	Claret Cock
WINGS	Golden Pheasant Tippets
	Bustard
	Wood-duck
	Blue and Yellow Swan
	Bronze Mallard over

This is an old Co. Cork dressing which was known as the Butterman.

GOLDEN OLIVE (6)

TAG	Silver Wire
BODY	Golden Olive Seal's Fur
RIB	Oval Silver
BODY HACKLE	Natural Red Cock
THROAT	Blue Jay
WINGS	Ibis
	Teal
	Bronze Mallard over

GOLDEN OLIVE (7)

TAG	Gold Wire and Blue Floss
TAIL	Golden Pheasant Crest
BUTT	Black Ostrich
BODY	Golden Olive Seal's Fur
RIB	Oval Gold
BODY HACKLE	Golden Olive Cock (from mid-body)
THROAT	Blue Jay
WINGS	Golden Pheasant Tippets
	Peacock Sword
	Bronze Mallard over

GOLDEN OLIVE (8)

TAG	Silver Twist and Ruby Floss
TAIL	G.P. Tippets and Topping
BODY	Golden Olive Seal's Fur
RIB	Flat Gold (or Silver Twist)
BODY HACKLE	Golden Olive Cock (from second turn of tinsel)
THROAT	Blue Jay
WINGS	Golden Pheasant Tippets
	Guinea-fowl
	Ibis and Green Parrot
	Golden Pheasant Tail
	Bronze Mallard over

Two G.P. Toppings over all.

GOLD SHRIMP (1)

TAG	Flat Gold
TAIL HACKLE	Long Furnace Cock
BODY	Rear – Oval Gold
CENTRE HACKLE	Orange Cock
BODY	Front – Oval Gold
WINGS	Jungle Cock
FRONT HACKLE	Long Grey Badger Cock

GOLD SHRIMP (2)

TAG	Gold Wire
TAIL HACKLE	Long Badger Cock (dyed Orange-Red)
BODY	Rear $2/3$ – Flat Gold
JOINT	Black Ostrich Herl
BODY	Front – Flat Gold
RIB	Fine Oval Gold (over Front Body)
SH. HACKLE	Red-Orange Cock
FRONT HACKLE	Long Badger Cock

GOSHAWK

TAG	Gold Wire and Orange Floss
TAIL	G.P. Topping, Ibis, and Green Peacock
BUTT	Black Ostrich Herl
BODY	Black Floss
RIB	Gold Twist (or Silver)
BODY HACKLE	Claret Cock
THROAT	Blue Jay
WINGS	1. Paired Yellow Toucan
	Four G.P. Toppings over
	or
	2. Yellow Mohair
	Two G.P. Toppings over
	or
	3. Paired Golden Pheasant Yellow Rump
	Two G.P. Toppings over
HORNS	Red Macaw

The difference between Goshawk, Goldfinch, and Parson, are to my mind only variations in the local dressing and probably all commenced life as a humble Parson.

GREEN FLY

TAG	Silver and Orange Mohair
TAIL	G.P. Breast Fibres and Parrot and Guinea-hen
BODY	Rear – 3/4 Green Peacock Herl Front – Orange Mohair or Pig's Wool
RIB	Gold Tinsel
BODY HACKLE	Natural Red and Orange
THROAT	Blue Jay
WINGS	Green Peacock Sword
SIDES	Pheasant, Macaw, and Guinea-hen Fibres
HEAD	Black Ostrich Herl

Another of O'Gorman's patterns.

GREEN GROUSE (1)

TAG	Silver and Orange Floss
TAIL	Golden Pheasant Tippets
BODY	Light Green Floss
RIB	Oval Silver
BODY HACKLE	Dark Speckled Grouse
THROAT	Blue Jay
WINGS	Golden Pheasant Tippets Red Macaw Bronze Mallard over

GREEN GROUSE (2)

TAG	Gold Thread and Reddish-Orange Floss
TAIL	Golden Pheasant Topping
BUTT	Brown Ostrich Herl
BODY	Pea-green Floss
RIB	Narrow Gold
BODY HACKLE	Grouse
SH. HACKLE	Yellow-Olive Cock
WINGS	Golden Pheasant Tippets Bustard Grey Mallard, Golden Pheasant Topping over
HORNS	Blue Macaw
HEAD	Black Ostrich Herl

GREEN PARSON (1)

TAG	Oval Silver and Red Floss
TAIL	G.P. Crest, G.P. Tippets, Teal, Red, Yellow, and Blue Swan
BUTT	Black Ostrich
BODY	Rear $1/3$ – Orange Floss
	Front $2/3$ – Green Peacock
RIB	Oval Silver and fine Oval Gold
HACKLES	1. Yellow Cock
	2. Orange Cock
THROAT	Blue Jay
WINGS	G.P. Tippets, Golden Pheasant Tail, Red, White, Blue, and Green Swan, Pintail, Bronze Mallard, G.P. Topping over all

Michael Rogan's Dressing.

GREEN PARSON (2)

TAG	Fine Oval Gold and Red Floss
TAIL	G.P. Topping, Tippets, and Wood-duck
BUTT	Black Ostrich Herl
BODY	Rear – $1/3$ Orange Floss, Front – $2/3$ Peacock Sword
RIB	Gold Twist (or Flat Gold)
BODY HACKLE	Yellow Cock (over Peacock Sword)
THROAT	Blue Jay
WING	Mixed
SIDES	Chatterer or Kingfisher
HORNS	Blue Macaw

GREEN PARSON (3)

TAG	Silver Wire and Dark Red Floss
TAIL	G.P. Crest and Summer-Duck
BUTT	Black Ostrich
BODY	Orange Floss
RIB	Gold Twist and Green Peacock Herl
SH. HACKLE	Golden Olive Cock
THROAT	Blue Jay
WINGS	Golden Pheasant Tail
	Green Parrot
	Bronze Mallard over

GREEN SILK (1)

TAG	G.P. Tippets and Crest
BODY	Green Floss
RIB	Oval Gold
BODY HACKLE	Lemon Cock (on front third)
SH. HACKLE	Orange Cock
WINGS	Golden Pheasant Tippets
	Green Peacock
	Bronze Mallard over

GREEN SILK (2)

TAIL	G.P. Tippets and Crest
BODY	Green-Olive Floss
RIB	Oval Gold
SH. HACKLES	1. Yellow Cock
	2. Orange Cock
WINGS	Golden Pheasants Tippets
	Green Peacock
	Bronze Mallard over

A pattern for the West and North-West.

GREEN STOAT (Tube Fly)

BODY	Black Floss
RIB	Fine Oval Silver
HACKLE	Mid-Green Cock
	Stoat tail at quarters

GREY CLARET

TAG	Silver and Orange Floss
TAIL	G.P. Topping and Indian Crow
BUTT	Light Blue Floss
BODY	Rear – Grey Monkey Fur
	Front – Claret Seal's Fur
BODY	Irish Grey Cock over
HACKLES	Grey Fur, Claret Cock over Claret Fur
SH. HACKLE	Lemon Cock
THROAT	Blue Jay
WINGS	Golden Pheasant Tippets
	Red, Blue, and Yellow Swan
	Bustard
	Golden Pheasant Tail
	Wood-duck
	Bronze Mallard over

GREY FLY

TAIL	Gaudy
BODY	Rear – $^3/4$ Light Donkey Fur with added pinch of Light Brown Pig's Wool
RIB	Silver or Gold over Donkey Fur
BODY	Front – Bright Brown or Claret Pig's Wool
BODY HACKLE	Deep Red Cock over Pig's Wool
THROAT	Blue Jay
WINGS	1. Brown Turkey
	Pheasant Tail
	Guinea-hen
	or
	2. Green Peacock Sword
	Brown Turkey or Mallard over
CHEEKS	Macaw
HEAD	Dark Blue Mohair

Another O'Gorman pattern which he also referred to as the Donkey Fly.

GREY MONKEY

TAG	Silver and Yellow Floss
TAIL	Golden Pheasant Topping
BUTT	Black Ostrich Herl
BODY	Grey Monkey Fur
RIB	Silver Twist
BODY HACKLE	Green Olive Cock
SH. HACKLE	Lemon Cock
WINGS	Golden Pheasant Tippets
	Red and Blue Swan
	Bustard
	Golden Pheasant Tail
	Bronze Mallard over

GREY THUNDER

TAG	Flat Gold tinsel
TAIL	G.P. Crest (dyed Orange)
REAR BODY	Black Floss Silk
RIB	Flat Gold Tinsel
CENTRE HACKLE	Red-Orange Cock
FRONT BODY	Darkest Claret Seal's Fur
SH. HACKLE	Black Cock (dyed Claret)
THROAT	Grey Duck Fibres
WINGS	G.P. Tippets with
	Grey Duck Flank over

The Seal's Fur is well picked out – no rib on fur

GREY THUNDER SHRIMP

TAG	Flat Gold tinsel
TAIL	G.P. Red Body Feather (dyed Orange)
REAR BODY	Black Floss Silk
RIB	Flat Gold Tinsel
CENTRE HACKLE	Red-Orange Cock
FRONT BODY	Darkest Claret Seal's Fur
SH. HACKLE	Long Black Cock (dyed Claret)
FRONT HACKLE	Long Grey Duck Flank

In each dressing the Fur body is bulky. Personal dressings of the Author.

225

GROUSE HACKLEY

TAG	Silver Tinsel and Orange Floss
TAIL	G.P. Topping and Tippet Strands
BODY	Crottle, Purple, Crottle,
	Blue and Blood Red (dyed) hackles
RIB	Oval Silver
SH. HACKLE	Dark Grouse
WINGS	Strands of Red and Yellow Swan with
	Bronze Mallard over

A dressing from the Mourne system, Co. Tyrone.
See also Hackley.

GROUSE LOCHABER

TAIL	Golden Pheasant Crest
ALTERNATIVE BODIES	Mohair or Seal's Fur –
	1. Yellow
	2. Orange
	3. Green
	4. Purple
RIB	Five Rows Gold Twist
BODY HACKLE	From an old Cock Grouse (very dark)
THROAT	Old Cock Grouse

The above is the hackle pattern For a winged pattern the following is added –

WING	Golden Pheasant Red Breast
	Macaw
	Guinea-hen
	Pheasant Tail over
HEAD	Black Ostrich or Blue Mohair

This dressing was given by O'Gorman and he writes that the body hackle is to be cut under the body so as not to project below hook-point.

An alternative dressing was the Partridge Lochaber – with green mohair body and dark partridge replacing grouse.

GUINEA HEN

TAG	Silver Wire and Orange Floss
TAIL	Golden Pheasant Crest
BUTT	Black Ostrich
BODY	Black Floss
RIB	Silver Twist
BODY HACKLE	Guinea-hen
THROAT	Blue Jay
WINGS	Toucan
	Golden Pheasant Tail
	Bronze Mallard over
CHEEKS	Jungle Cock
	or
WINGS	Toucan
	Bustard
	Bronze Mallard over
HORNS	Blue Macaw
HEAD	Black Ostrich

This is an old low-water dressing for Co. Mayo. The high-water pattern varied as follows—

BODY	Deep Orange Floss
BODY HACKLE	Guinea-hen dyed in Turmeric or Saffron
SIDES	Jungle Cock

Topping over wings.

GENERAL FLIES

O'GORMAN (1)

TAG	Orange Mohair
TAIL	Golden Pheasant Topping
BODY	Black Pig's Wool
RIB	Silver Twist
BODY HACKLE	Yellow Cock (from mid-body)
THROAT	Blue Jay
WING	Gaudy

(2)

TAG	Green Mohair
TAIL	Golden Pheasant Topping
BODY	Orange Pig's Wool
RIB	Silver Twist
BODY HACKLE	Black Cock (from mid-body)
THROAT	Blue Jay
WING	Gaudy

(3)

TAIL	Golden Pheasant Topping
BODY	Rear – Green Pig's Wool
	Front – Orange Pig's Wool
RIBS	Gold Twist on Orange
	Silver Twist on Green
BODY HACKLE	Black Cock (or Crow) on Orange
THROAT	Blue Jay
WING	Gaudy

O'Gorman wrote that his general flies all had a Gaudy (or Butterfly) Wing, composed of mixed coloured feathers, usually parrot feathers.

(4)

For a more orthodox wing he gave –

WINGS	Paired G.P. Breast Feathers (stripped on one side)
	Pheasant Tail
	Guinea-hen
	Brown Turkey over
HORNS	Long Blue Macaw
HEAD	Blue Mohair

(5)

For sea trout he gave the following–

TAIL	G.P. Breast Fibres
BODY	Yellow Pig's Wool
BODY HACKLE	Deep Red
WINGS	White Satins
CHEEKS	Kingfisher

Rev. Newland *(The Erne – Its Legends and its Fishing)* writing in 1851 stated–

"The Butterfly is distinguished from all others by its underwings, which, being made of the tippet feather of the Golden Pheasant tied on whole, gives it the appearance of a Copper-coloured butterfly".

HACKLEY (1)

TAG	Silver Wire and Gold Floss
TAIL	G.P. Tippets and Topping
BODY	Purple, Fiery Brown, Blue, Blood-Red (dyed) and Amber Cock Hackles
RIB	Oval Silver spearating hackle colours
WINGS	G.P. Tippets, Red, Blue and Yellow Swan with Bronze Mallard over

HACKLEY (2)

TAG	Silver Wire and Brown Olive Floss
TAIL	G.P. Tippets and Topping
BODY	Green or Bronze Peacock Herl
BODY HACKLES	From Tail to Shoulder in close turns
	1. Purple Cock
	2. Fiery Brown Cock
	3. Light Blue Cock
	4. Red (dyed) Cock
THROAT	Guinea-fowl
WINGS	Golden Pheasant Tippets
	Married Red and Blue Swan
	Bronze Mallard over

Grouse Hackley – the guinea-fowl throat is replaced by a dark speckled grouse hackle.

HACKLEY (3)

TAG	Silver Tinsel and Orange Floss
TAIL	G.P. Topping and Tippets
BODY	Orange, Black, Amber, Blue, Blood Red (dyed), and Amber Cock hackles wound from tail to throat
RIB	Oval Silver separating hackle colours
WINGS	Married Red, Blue, and Yellow Swan
	Bronze Mallard over

A dressing for the River Mourne, Co. Tyrone. (The oval silver rib is sometimes omitted.)

HALF GREY AND BROWN

TAG	Silver Wire and Orange Floss
TAIL	G.P. Crest and G.P. Red Breast Feather
BODY	Rear $1/2$– Grey Monkey or Seal's Fur
	Front $1/2$– Fiery Brown Seal's Fur
RIB	Oval Silver
BODY HACKLES	1. Light Grizzle Cock over Grey Fur
	2. Fiery Brown Cock over Brown Fur
SH. HACKLE	Lemon Cock
WINGS	G.P. Tippets. Married strands of Orange, Yellow and Red Swan. Strips of G.P. Tail and Pintail
	Bronze Mallard over

HALF YELLOW AND BLACK

TAG	Silver Thread
TAIL	G.P. Crest and Indian Crow
BUTT	Black Ostrich
BODY	Rear $1/2$– Gold Floss
	Front $1/2$– Black Floss
RIB	Oval Gold
BODY HACKLE	Dark Blood-Red Cock over Black Floss
SH. HACKLE	Blue Jay
WINGS	G.P. Tippets, married strands of Scarlet, Yellow and Orange Swan. Bustard, G.P. Tail. Bronze Mallard over.

INCHIQUIN

TAG	Gold Thread
TAIL	Brown Mallard and Purple Peacock Breast
BODY	Fiery Red Pig's Wool
RIB	Gold Thread
BODY HACKLE	Natural Red Cock
WINGS	Blue Peacock
	Brown Mallard over

A dressing for the Midland lakes given by Francis Francis. This pattern was given earlier by O'Gorman and its origin was probably on Inchiquin Lake, Co. Clare. Tied also in smaller size for lake trout.

IRISH RANGER

TAG	Fine Oval Silver and Light Blue Floss
TAIL	G.P. Topping and Indian Crow
BODY	Rear – $1/3$ Reddish Orange Floss
	Front – $2/3$ Black Seal's Fur
RIB	Oval Silver
BODY HACKLE	Claret or Purple Cock (on Fur)
THROAT	Blue Jay
WINGS	Paired G.P. Tippets
	Paired Jungle Cock
	Summer Duck (or Teal) over
	G.P. Topping over all
	Yellow Macaw Horns optional

See also Erne Ranger.

JAY CLARET

TAG	Silver Wire and Orange Floss
TAIL	G.P. Topping and Tippets
BODY	Rear – $3/4$ Dark Claret Seal's Fur
	Front – Reddish-Purple Seal's Fur
RIB	Oval Gold
BODY HACKLE	Dark Claret Cock (over Purple Fur)
THROAT	Blue Jay
WINGS	Golden Pheasant Tippets
	Blue Peacock
	Bronze Mallard over

Known also as the Claret Jay. *See Also Doochary Claret.*

JOCK SCOTT SHRIMP

TAG	Silver Tinsel
TAIL HACKLE	Golden Pheasant Red Breast
BODY	Rear – Yellow Floss
RIB	Silver Thread
VEILINGS	Scarlet Swan
CENTRE HACKLE	Badger Cock
BODY	Front – Black Floss
RIB	Silver Thread
VEILINGS	Scarlet Swan
WINGS	Two Jungle Cock (back-to-back)
FRONT HACKLE	Long Badger Cock

A useful pattern for all waters.

A variation is the Colonel Christie Shrimp which is as above except that the veilings are Bright Yellow Swan and fully veil the body sections. Both dressings were given by a well-known fly-dresser and angler whose opinion is that the use of Fluorescent Yellow Wool for rear bodies improves their efficiency.

It is interesting to note that the Jock Scott Shrimp is almost identical to the dressing of E. C. Heaney's Secret Weapon.

JOHN ROBINSON (1)

TAG	Oval Silver and Orange Floss
TAIL	G.P. Crest and Tippets
BODY	Bronze Peacock Herl
RIB	Oval Silver
BODY HACKLE	Purple and Red (dyed) Cock wound up length of body
SH. HACKLE	Amber (dyed) Cock
WINGS	Strips of Red and Yellow Swan Tippets Bronze Mallard over

A killing pattern for the North-West.

JOHN ROBINSON (2)

TAG	Fine Oval Silver and Orange Floss
TAIL	G.P. Crest and Tippets
BODY	Green Peacock Herl
RIB	Oval Silver
BODY HACKLES	Rear – Dark Blue Violet Cock
	Front – Crimson Cock
SH. HACKLE	Dark Ginger (dyed Yellow)
WINGS	Long Paired Jungle Cock
	Golden Pheasant Tippets
	Crimson, Green and Yellow Swan
	Bronze Mallard over

Golden Pheasant Topping over all in large sizes.

The inner Jungle Cock may be replaced by long paired strips of Woodcock Tail (longer than remainder of wing) and showing white tip at wing point.

JUDGE

TAG	Silver Thread and Light Orange
TAIL	Golden Pheasant Topping
BUTT	Peacock Herl
BODY	Silver Tinsel
BODY HACKLE	Golden Olive or Yellow-Orange Cock
SH. HACKLE	Red Orange Cock
THROAT	Blue Jay
WINGS	Peacock
	Golden Pheasant Tippets
	Bustard
	Two Toppings over
HORNS	Blue Macaw
HEAD	Peacock Herl

A Francis Francis dressing for the River Bush. Another dressing gives the body as being of gold tinsel.

JUDY OF THE BOGS (1)

TAG	Flat Gold
TAIL	Golden Pheasant Topping (dyed Orange)
TAIL HACKLE	Grey Heron Feather
BODY	Black Floss
CENTRE VEILING	G.P. Crests (dyed Orange)
RIB	Oval Gold
WINGS	Jungle Cock
FRONT HACKLE	Long Black Henny-cock or Black Heron

This is the shrimp dressing. The veilings should protrude from the sides (*not* top and bottom) of the body. The wings are not placed back-to-back, but are roofed over the body.

JUDY OF THE BOGS (2)

TAG	Gold Wire
TAIL	Golden Pheasant Crest (dyed Orange)
BODY	Black Floss
RIB	Oval Gold
HACKLE	Black Cock
WINGS	Grey Heron Wing Slips

Tied this way for low water. A personal pattern.

KATE KEARNEY

TAG	Silver Wire and Orange Floss
BUTT	None
TAIL	G.P. Crest
BODY	1/3 Cardinal Red, 1/3 Pale Green, 1/3 Dark Orange, (All Floss Silk)
RIB	Five Turns Flat Silver Tinsel
HACKLE	Medium Claret, Blue Jay Throat
WINGS	Tippets; Yellow, Blue, Orange Swan; G.P. Tail and Mallard

KILLARNEY PET

TAG	Gold Wire and Crimson Floss
TAIL	G.P. Crest, Tippets, and Bronze Mallard Fibres
BUTT	Black Ostrich
BODY	Rear $1/2$ – Yellow Floss
	Front $1/2$– Orange Floss
RIB	Oval Gold
BODY HACKLE	Orange Cock over Orange Floss
HACKLE	Orange Cock
THROAT	Blue Jay
WINGS	Tippets, G.P. Tail, Red, Yellow, and Blue Swan, Summer Duck, Bronze Mallard over

KINGFISHER SHRIMP

TAG	Flat Gold
TAIL HACKLE	Long Red Game Cock
BODY	Rear – Yellow Floss
RIB	Flat Copper
CENTRE HACKLE	Orange Cock
BODY	Front – Claret Floss
RIB	Oval Gold
WINGS	Jungle Cock
SH. HACKLE	1. Light Blue Cock
	2. Long Crow
SIDES	Kingfisher Neck Feather

LEE BLUE (1)

TAG	Silver Wire and Yellow Floss
TAIL	G.P. Tippets and Topping
BODY	Light Blue Floss
RIB	Oval Silver
BODY HACKLE	Light Blue Cock
SH. HACKLE	Yellow Cock
WINGS	Golden Pheasant Tippets
	Yellow, Blue, and Red Swan
	Golden Pheasant Tail
	Teal
	Bronze Mallard over
HEAD	Black Ostrich

LEE BLUE (2)

TAG	Silver and Golden Floss
TAIL	G.P. Topping and Tippets
BUTT	Black Ostrich
BODY	Sky-Blue Bear or Seal's Fur, Golden Yellow Fur at Shoulder
RIB	Silver
HACKLE	Yellow Fur picked out or Yellow Cock
WINGS	Claret, Orange, Green, and Blue Swan
	Golden Pheasant Tail
	Bronze Mallard over

Hi-Regan's dressing.

LEE BLUE (3)

TAG	Silver Twist and Yellow Floss
TAIL	G.P. Topping and Indian Crow
BODY	Light Blue Pig's Wool, Mohair, or Seal's Fur
RIB	Silver Twist
BODY HACKLE	Blue Cock
SH. HACKLE	Bright Yellow Cock
WINGS	Golden Pheasant Tippets
	Golden Pheasant Tail
	Wood-duck
	Yellow and Red Swan
	Bronze Mallard over
HORNS	Blue Macaw

A Co. Cork and Co. Kerry pattern. The wing to be dressed sparse and low on body.

LEE BLUE AND GREY

TAG	Silver Wire and Yellow Seal's Fur
TAIL	G.P. Crest and Indian Crow
BUTT	Black Ostrich
BODY	Rear $^1/_2$ – Light Blue Seal's Fur
	Front $^1/_2$ – Grey Donkey Fur
RIB	Oval Silver
BODY HACKLES	1. Natural Blue Cock over Blue Fur
	2. Speckled Grey over Donkey Fur
SH. HACKLE	Yellow Cock
WINGS	Mixed. Bronze Mallard over.
	Topping over all

LEMON BLUE

TAG	Fine Oval Silver and Orange Floss
TAIL	G.P. Tippets and Topping
BUTT	Black Ostrich Herl
BODY	Medium Dark Blue Seal's Fur
RIB	Oval Silver
BODY HACKLE	Medium, or Light Blue Cock
SH. HACKLE	Lemon Cock
WINGS	Golden Pheasant Tippets
	Guinea-fowl
	Teal
	Bronze Mallard over

LEMON GREY (1)

TAG	Fine Oval Silver and Yellow Floss
TAIL	G.P. Topping and Indian Crow
BUTT	Black Ostrich Herl
BODY	Silver Monkey Fur or Grey Seal's Fur
RIB	Oval Silver
BODY HACKLE	Speckled Irish Grey Cock
SH. HACKLE	Lemon Cock
WINGS 1.	Golden Pheasant Tippets
	Guinea-fowl
	Teal
	Bronze Mallard over
	G.P. Topping over all
	or
WINGS 2.	Golden Pheasant Tippets
	Blue Peacock
	Red and Yellow Swan
	Guinea-fowl
	Bronze Mallard over

LEMON GREY (2)

TAG	Silver Wire and Yellow Floss
TAIL	G.P. Crest
BUTT	Black Ostrich
BODY	Grey Donkey Fur
RIB	Oval Silver
BODY HACKLE	Grey-Blue Dun Cock (from mid-body)
SH. HACKLES	1. Claret Cock
	2. Lemon Cock
WINGS	G.P. Tippets, Guinea-fowl, Teal, and Bronze Mallard. Topping over all

LEMON GREY (3)

TAG	Silver Wire and Yellow Floss
TAIL	G.P. Crest with a shorter cut Crest (dyed Red) on top
BUTT	Black Ostrich
BODY	Grey Seal's Fur
RIB	Oval Silver
BODY HACKLE	Plymouth Rock Cock
SH. HACKLE	Lemon Cock
WINGS	G.P. Tippets, Dark Speckled Turkey, married strips of Green, Yellow, and Orange Swan, Teal, Bronze Mallard over

This is a modern dressing.

MAGPIE

TAIL	Golden Pheasant Crest
BODY	Rear – Black Floss or Pig's Wool
	Front – Orange Floss or Pig's Wool
RIB	Silver Twist over Black
BODY HACKLE	Black Cock over Orange
THROAT	Blue Jay
WING	Gaudy (or Butterfly)
HORNS	Long Blue Macaw
HEAD	Dark Blue Mohair

Another of O'Gorman's patterns.

MAJOR'S RED

TAIL	G.P. Tippets and Topping
BUTT	Golden Olive Pig's Wool or Seal's Fur
BODY	Golden Red Pig's Wool or Seal's Fur
RIB	Oval Gold
HACKLE	Golden Red (dyed) Cock
WINGS	Golden Pheasant Tippets
	Bronze Mallard over

This pattern is given by E. C. Heaney who stated that it was tied by a Major McConachie who found it a killing pattern on the River Faughan, Co. Londonderry.

MALLARD AND CINNAMON

TAG	Silver Twist and Orange Floss
TAIL	G.P Topping and Guinea-fowl fibres
BODY	Dark Cinnamon Seal's Fur
RIB	Oval Gold (or Silver)
BODY HACKLE	Light Cinnamon Cock
SH. HACKLE	Fiery Brown Cock
WINGS	Golden Pheasant Tippets
	Bronze Mallard over

MASTER FLY

TAG	Silver Wire and Magenta Floss
TAIL	G.P. Tippets and Topping
BODY	Rear – Grey Seal's Fur
	Front – Yellow Seal's Fur
RIB	Oval Silver
BODY HACKLES	Grey Cock on Grey Fur
	Light Amber Cock on Yellow Fur
SH. HACKLE	Blood-Red Cock (dyed)
THROAT	Blue Jay
WINGS	Golden Pheasant Tippets
	Peacock Sword
	Blue, Red, Yellow, and Green Swan
	Bronze Mallard over

A dressing by E. C. Heaney for the River Faughan, Co. Londonderry. Also used as a sea trout dressing.

McGILDOWNEY

TAG	Silver Thread and Light Orange Floss
TAIL	Blue Macaw, Mallard, and G.P. Tippets
BUTT	Peacock Herl
BODY	Two turns Light Orange Floss then Yellow Mohair
RIB	Narrow Silver
BODY HACKLE	Dirty Medium Brick Red Cock (on two-thirds body)
THROAT	Blue Jay
WINGS	Golden Pheasant Tippets Peacock Bustard Mallard
HEAD	Peacock Herl

A Francis Francis dressing for the River Bush, Co. Antrim.

MIXED OLIVE

TAIL	G.P. Tippets and Topping
BODY	Mixed Seal's Fur (equal parts of Green, Golden Olive, Fiery Brown, with a mixed pinch of Blue, Purple, and Red)
RIB	Oval Gold (or Silver)
HACKLE	Blood-Red Cock (Natural)
THROAT	Blue Jay
WINGS	Golden Pheasant Tippets Green Peacock Red, Blue, and Yellow Swan Teal Bronze Mallard over

NORA CRIENA

TAG	Silver Twist and Yellow Floss
TAIL	G.P. Topping and Tippets
BUTT	Black Ostrich
BODY	Three turns Yellow Floss then Golden Yellow Seal's Fur
RIB	Silver
BODY HACKLE	Light Furnace (over Fur)
SH. HACKLE	Golden Olive Cock
WING	Golden Olive Mohair
	G.P. Topping over

A variation of the Parson genus.

O'DONAGHUE (1)

TAG	Oval Silver and Yellow Floss Silk
TAIL	G.P. Crest and Indian Crow
BODY	Rear Third – Yellow Seal's Fur
	Centre Third – Black Seal's Fur
	Front Third – Claret Seal's Fur
RIB	Oval Gold Tinsel
SH. HACKLE	Claret Cock
THROAT	Blue Jay
WING	G.P. Tippets, G.P. Tail, Red, White, Blue,
and	Green Swan, Bronze Mallard over
SIDES	Pintail Slips
	Topping over all

Michael Rogan's dressing.

A variation used in Co. Sligo and known as the Dark O'Donaghue is dressed as follows—

TAG	Gold Wire
TAIL	G.P. Tippets
BODY	Rear Half – Orange Seal's Fur
	Front Half – Black Seal's Fur
RIB	Fine Oval Gold
SH. HACKLES	1. R.I. Red Cock (stained Claret)
	2. R.I. Red Cock
WING	G.P. Tippets, Bronze Mallard over

O'DONAGHUE (2)

TAG	Silver Twist and Yellow Floss
TAIL	Golden Pheasant Topping
JOINTED BODY	Pig's Wool or Seal's Fur:
	Rear – Yellow
	Centre – Black
	Front – Claret
RIB	Silver or Gold Twist
BODY HACKLE	Medium Claret (over Black and Claret)
THROAT	Blue Jay
WINGS	Golden Pheasant Tippets
	Bronze Mallard over
HORNS	Blue Macaw

This was Hi-Regan's dressing.

O'DONAGHUE (3)

TAG	Gold Tinsel and Orange Floss
TAIL	Golden Pheasant Topping
BUTT	Black Ostrich Herl
BODY	Rear – Olive Yellow Pig's Wool
	Centre – Fiery Claret Pig's Wool
	Front – Black Pig's Wool (blended together
	at joints)
RIB	Gold Twist
BODY HACKLE	Dark Claret Cock (from centre)
THROAT	Blue Jay
WINGS	Golden Pheasant Tippets
	Brown Mallard over
HORNS	Blue Macaw

Francis Francis gave this dressing for Lough Melvin, Co. Fermanagh.

OLIVE FIERY BROWN

TAG	Silver Twist and Orange Floss
TAIL	G. P. Tippets, Topping, and Mallard
BODY	Rear – Golden Olive Seal's Fur
	Front – Fiery Brown Pig's Wool
RIB	Oval Gold
BODY HACKLE	Fiery Brown Cock (over Wool)
THROAT	Blue Jay
WINGS	Golden Pheasant Tippets
	Golden Pheasant Tail
	Bronze Mallard over
HORNS	Blue Macaw

Believed to be Rogan's dressing.

ORANGE GOSHAWK

TAG	Silver and Blue Floss
TAIL	Golden Pheasant Crest
BUTT	Black Ostrich
BODY	Orange Floss
RIB	Silver Twist
BODY HACKLE	Golden Olive Cock
THROAT	Blue Jay
WINGS	Six Golden Pheasant Toppings
HORNS	Macaw

A yellow body used for high-water and a pale lemon for low-water flies. A Co. Mayo dressing.

ORANGE GROUSE (1)

TAG	Silver Wire and Orange Floss
TAIL	G. P. Tippets and Topping
BODY	Medium Orange Floss
RIB	Oval Gold
BODY HACKLE	Speckled Grouse
THROAT	Blue Jay
WINGS	Golden Pheasant Tippets
	Golden Pheasant Tail
	Bronze Mallard over
HORNS	Red Macaw

This was Rogan's dressing.

243

ORANGE GROUSE (2)

TAG	Silver and Orange Floss
TAIL	G.P. Tippets and Topping
BUTT	Black Ostrich
BODY	Three turns Royal Blue Floss then Orange Floss to shoulder
RIB	Gold Oval
BODY HACKLE	Dark Grouse
SH. HACKLE	Dark Grouse
WINGS	Golden Pheasant Tippets
	Golden Pheasant Tail
	Guinea-hen
	Bronze Mallard over

ORANGE GROUSE (3)

TAG	Silver Twist and Claret Floss
TAIL	G.P. Topping and Kingfisher
BUTT	Black Ostrich
BODY	Orange-Yellow Floss
RIB	Silver Twist
BODY HACKLE	Dark Speckled Grouse (from mid-body)
SH. HACKLE	Well speckled Teal or Blue Jay
WINGS	Golden Pheasant Tippets
	Golden Pheasant Tail
	Bustard
	G.P. Topping over
HORNS	Blue Macaw
HEAD	Black Ostrich

A dressing for Connemara and Galway. Was a favourite River Moy dressing.

ORANGE SILK

TAG	Silver Wire and Orange Floss
TAIL	G.P. Crest and Tippets
BODY	Yellow-Orange Floss
RIB	Oval Gold
BODY HACKLE	Amber Cock (or Blood-Red)
SH. HACKLE	Dark Grouse
WINGS	Golden Pheasant Tippets
	Bronze Mallard over

Sometimes with a throat of blue jay. A similar dressing uses amber cock hackle for the body and a blood-red cock replacing the grouse throat.

ORANGE AND GREY

TAG	Silver Thread and Golden Yellow Floss
TAIL	G.P. Topping, Indian Crow and Chatterer
BODY	Rear – $1/3$ Bright Orange Floss
	Front – $2/3$ Grey Monkey or Seal's Fur
RIB	Oval Gold over Orange Floss
	Oval Silver over Grey Fur
BODY HACKLES	1. Orange Cock over Orange Floss
	2. Grey Grizzle over Grey Fur
SH. HACKLE	Lemon Cock
WINGS	Mixed. G.P. Tippets, married strands of Scarlet, Blue, Yellow and Orange Swan, slips of G.P. Tail, Bustard, Pintail and Summer Duck, Bronze Mallard over

ORANGE AND SILVER

TAG	Silver
TAIL	Golden Pheasant Tippets
BODY	Rear – Flat Silver
	Front – Orange Seal's Fur
RIB	Oval Silver
BODY HACKLE	Golden Olive Cock (over Fur)
SH. HACKLE	Guinea-fowl
WINGS	Golden Pheasant Tippets Red, Yellow, and Blue Swan Peacock Breast Bronze Mallard over

ORANGEMAN (1)

TAG	Silver Twist and Dark Orange Floss
TAIL	G.P. Topping and Indian Crow
JOINTED BODY	Seal's Fur:
	Blue
	Orange
	Green
	Grey
RIB	Silver
BODY HACKLES	To match body colours
	(graduated in length)
SH. HACKLE	Orange Cock
WINGS	Golden Pheasant Tippets
	Golden Pheasant Tail
	Wood-duck
	Yellow and Red Swan (wide)
	Bronze Mallard over
HORNS	Blue Macaw

A dressing for Co. Kerry, and Connemara.

ORANGEMAN (2)

TAG	Fine Oval Silver and Orange Floss
TAIL	Golden Pheasant Crest
JOINTED BODY	Mohair:
	Light Blue
	Dark Blue
	Orange
	Dark Red
	Grass Green
	Grey (picked out under as Hackles)
RIB	Silver – closely ribbed to separate the joints
HACKLE	Orange Cock
WINGS	Golden Pheasant Tippets
	Golden Pheasant Tail
	Red and Blue Swan
	Summer Duck
	Bronze Mallard over

An old Co. Cork pattern.

THE O'SHAUGHNESSY

Gold tip; a turn of bright blue silk, another of crimson; topping, kingfisher feather and a roll of black ostrich form the tag.

The body is made of rich yellow floss, gold tinsel and a hackle of the same hue. The wings consist of four or five toppings, six or eight orange feathers from the Toucan, a few strands from the Cock-of-the-Rock, four fibres from the tail of the Golden Pheasant, and two long crimson horns. A black head to finish.

From *A Year of Liberty* (Salmon Angling in Ireland by Peard).

PADDY

TAG	Oval Silver
TAIL	G.P. Topping and Indian Crow
BUTT	Black Ostrich Herl
BODY	Rear – Silver Embossed Tinsel ribbed with Silver Oval and Veiled with Toucan, Centre – Black Ostrich Herl
	Front – Blue Floss Silk ribbed with Blood-Red Hackle (dyed) and Oval Silver
HACKLE	Lemon Cock
WINGS	Strips of Red, Blue and Yellow dyed Swan Bronze Mallard over Two strands of Green Peacock Herl and G.P. Topping over all
SIDES	Jungle Cock

A dressing for the River Mourne system, Co. Tyrone.

PARSON (1)

TAG	Silver Twist and Ruby Floss
TAIL	G.P. Topping, Indian Crow, and Chatterer
BODY	Golden Olive Pig's Wool with Fiery Brown Pig's Wool at shoulder
RIB	Gold and Silver Twist
BODY HACKLE	Pale Yellow Cock
SH. HACKLE	Dark Claret Cock
WINGS	Cock-of-the-Rock (covered by Five or Six Toppings)
HORNS	Blue and Red Macaw
CHEEKS	Chatterer

Believed to be Rogan's original dressing. The 'Cock-of-the-Rock' is a fruit-eating bird of the Amazon and the tropical forests of South America. There are two types – one with a Bright Orange colouring in the male, the other a soft red. Each has a full fan-shaped head crest extending from the back of the skull to the tip of the beak. It would seem probable that the orange crest was the Cock-of-the-Rock feather used by Rogan in this wing. A pair of bright brick-orange cock hackles could be substituted.

PARSON (2)

TAG	Yellow Floss
TAIL	Golden Pheasant Crest
BODY	Yellow Floss
RIB	Gold Tinsel
WINGS	Six or Eight G.P. Toppings
HACKLE	Blue Jay (over wings)
SIDES	Kingfisher
HEAD	Black Ostrich Herl

This was Newlands's description of the fly created for the Erne in 1836. Three variations he gave were:–

Jack the Giant-Killer. As Parson but with a green body and hackle and crimson or green sides, horns – red macaw. For bright weather.

Kill-Many. As Parson but with claret body and hackles, horns – yellow Macaw. For dull weather.

Kill-More. As Parson but with deep yellow body, a bright crimson underwing and bright crimson sides, horns – yellow macaw. For dull weather.

PARSON SHRIMP

TAG	Oval Gold
TAIL HACKLE	Long Yellow Hen
BODY	Yellow Floss
RIB	Oval Gold
WINGS	Jungle Cock
FRONT HACKLE	Golden Olive Cock
CHEEKS	Kingfisher

PINK AND ORANGE

TAG	Silver Twist and Ruby Floss
TAIL	G.P. Tippets, Topping, and Green Parrot
BODY	Rear – $1/3$ Orange Floss
	Front – $2/3$ Light Claret Seal's Fur
RIB	Gold and Silver Twist
BODY HACKLE	Claret Cock (on Fur)
THROAT	Blue Jay
WINGS	Golden Pheasant Tippets
	Gallina
	Ibis
	Golden Pheasant Tail
	Green Parrot
	Bronze Mallard over
	Two G.P. Toppings over all

For the Ballyshannon District, Co. Donegal and Co. Fermanagh. Believed to be Rogan's dressing.

PONSONBY

TAG	Silver and Orange Floss
TAIL	G.P. Topping and Indian Crow
BUTT	Black Ostrich Herl
BODY	Rear – Grey Seal's Fur
	Front – Light Blue Seal's Fur
RIB	Silver twist
BODY HACKLES	1. Black Cock (over Grey Fur)
	2. Black Cock and Blood-Red Cock (over Blue Fur)
THROAT	Blue Jay
WINGS	Golden Pheasant Tippets
	Brown Mallard
	Bustard
	White-Tipped Turkey
SIDES	Jungle Cock
CHEEKS	G.P. Toppings
HORNS	Blue Macaw

In Hi-Regan's dressing he gives the blue fur as being dyed bear fur.

PURPLE BODY

TAG	Silver Wire
TAIL	G.P. Tippets and Crest
BUTT	Golden Olive Seal's Fur
BODY	Purple Seal's Fur
RIB	Oval Silver
SH. HACKLE	Dark Purple Cock
WINGS	Golden Pheasant Tippets
	Blue Peacock Breast (or Blue Swan)
	Bronze Mallard over

A dressing for the North and North West.

PURPLE GUINEA FOWL

TAG	Silver Tinsel and Orange Floss
TAIL	G.P. Topping and Tippets
BODY	Purple Floss Silk
RIB	Oval Silver
BODY HACKLE	Purple ribbed from $^1/_3$ way up body
SH. HACKLES	1. Blood-Red hackle (dyed)
	2. Guinea-fowl
WINGS	Strands of dyed Red and Yellow Swan with Bronze Mallard over

A dressing for the Mourne system, Co. Tyrone.

PURPLE PEE-WIT (1)

TAG	Silver Tinsel and Orange Floss
TAIL	G.P. Topping and Tippets
BODY	Purple Floss ribbed with Black Crest feather from a Green Plover
RIB	Oval Silver
HACKLES	Purple and Blood-Red (dyed) ribbed up body from $^1/_2$ way
THROAT	Dyed Amber hackle
WINGS	Strands of Dyed Red and Yellow Swan with Bronze Mallard over

A dressing for the Mourne System.

PURPLE PEE-WIT (2)

TAG	Oval Silver and Orange Floss
TAIL	Golden Pheasant Crest
BODY	Light Purple or Violet Floss
RIB	Fine Oval Silver and Pee-wit Crest
BODY HACKLE	Dark Ginger (dyed Yellow) to shoulder
THROAT	Blue Jay
WINGS	Red, Green, and Purple Swan
	Bronze Mallard over

PURPLE PEE-WIT (3)

TAG	Fine Oval Silver and Orange Floss
TAIL	Golden Pheasant Crest
BODY	Purple Floss
RIB	Silver Twist
BODY HACKLE	Black Cock
SH. HACKLES	1. Blood-Red Cock (dyed)
	2. Pee-wit Breast Feather
WINGS	Mixed
	Bronze Mallard over
HORNS	Blue and Red Macaw

An old river Mourne dressing.

These body colours – purple – appear to have been the original Pee-wit fly, but it is also dressed with – 1. Navy-blue body (blue Pee-wit). 2. Orange body (Orange Pee-wit), and finally a black body with a bustard wing (Black Pee-wit).

PURPLE RED AND WHITE

TAG	Silver Tinsel and Orange Floss
TAIL	G.P. Topping and Tippets
BODY	Purple, Red , and White Seal's Fur mixed together (1 part each Red and Purple and 2 parts White)
RIB	Oval Silver
SH. HACKLES	Dyed Blood-Red and Amber Cock
WINGS	Red and Yellow dyed Swan strips, Tippet strands with Bronze Mallard over

The sea trout dressing –

TAIL	Golden Pheasant tippets
BODY	As above
RIB	Oval Silver
SH. HACKLE	Natural Black Cock (dyed Yellow)
WINGS	Woodcock

Both patterns for the North-West.

QUINN CLARET AND SILVER RIB

TAG	Fine Silver Thread and Yellow Fluorescent Wool
TAIL	Golden Pheasant Crest (and Indian Crow)
BODY	Black Floss
RIB	Flat Silver followed by Oval or Round Silver
BODY HACKLE	Darkest Claret Cock from second turn of tinsel
SH. HACKLE	Darkest Claret Cock (slightly *shorter* than the body hackle)
	Long White-Tipped Woodcock Tail
WINGS	Golden Pheasant Tippets
	Golden Pheasant Tail
	Four Strands Blue Peacock
	Married strips of Medium and Dark Speckled Hen. Dark at bottom and longer
	Bronze Mallard over
SIDES	Jungle Cock

The white tips of the woodcock tail *must* show at the extreme point of the mallard wing. An exceptionally good pattern.

QUINN SHRIMP

TAG	Silver Tinsel
TAIL HACKLE	Golden Pheasant Red Breast
BODY	Rear – Flat Silver
RIB	Silver Wire
VEILINGS	Bright Blue Hen Hackle Fibres
CENTRE HACKLE	Pale Magenta Cock
BODY	Front – Flat Silver
RIB	Silver Wire
VEILINGS	As before
WINGS	Two Jungle Cock (back-to-back)
SH. HACKLE	Magenta Cock
FRONT HACKLE	Grey Badger Henny-cock

The veilings are to the sides of the body.

RED EYE

TAG	Crimson Wool
TAIL	G.P. Crest, Tippet and Blue Macaw in strands
BODY	Black Floss
RIB	Fine Oval Silver Tinsel
HACKLE	Dark Claret, Throat Dark Grey
WINGS	Tippet, Red and Yellow Swan, Bustard, G.P. Tail, Mallard, Macaw Horns
HEAD	Black Ostrich

Note: Tag is tied in a ball.

RED VIOLET

TAG	Silver Tinsel and Orange Floss
TAIL	Golden Pheasant Crest
BUTT	Black Ostrich Herl
BODY	Red-Violet Floss
RIB	Silver Twist
BODY HACKLE	Claret Cock
THROAT	Blue Jay

Alternative wings as below –

(1)	(2)
Toucan Breast	G.P. Tippets
G.P. Tail	Bustard
Brown Mallard	or Brown Mallard
Blue Macaw	Red Macaw

On occasions the body hackle was natural blood-red cock.

ROBBER

TAG	Fine Oval Silver and Yellow Floss
TAIL	Golden Pheasant Topping
BODY	Rear – 3/4 Honey Pig's Wool
	Front – 1/4 Dark Claret Pig's Wool
RIB	Oval Silver
SH. HACKLE	Coch-Y-Bondhu Cock (dyed Olive)
THROAT	Blue Jay
WINGS	Golden Pheasant Tippets
	Bronze Mallard over
HORNS	Blue Macaw

ROE PURPLE

TAG	Oval Silver
TAIL	Golden Pheasant Crest and Red Swan
BUTT	Golden Olive Seal's Fur
BODY	Purple Seal's Fur
RIB	Oval Gold
HACKLE	Crimson or Medium Claret Cock
WINGS	Golden Pheasant Tippets
	Yellow, Red, and Blue Swan
	Bronze Mallard over

Roe Blue as above but with darkest blue body and greenish-olive hackle. Both dressings for the River Roe, Co. Londonderry.

ROGAN'S FANCY

TAG	Oval Silver and Orange Floss
TAIL	G.P. Crest and Tippets
BUTT	Black Ostrich
BODY	1. Orange Floss
	2. Orange Seal's Fur
	3. Claret Seal's Fur
	(Three Sections)
RIB	Broad Flat Gold and Medium Oval Silver
HACKLE	Dark Claret Cock
THROAT	Blue Jay
WINGS	G.P. Tippets, G.P. Tail, Married strips of Red, White, Blue and Green Swan, Pintail, Bronze Mallard over
SIDES	Jungle Cock
CHEEKS	Kingfisher

From the doyen of fly-tyers, Michael Rogan of Ballyshannon.

ROGAN'S FAVOURITE

TAG	Silver Tinsel and Orange Floss
TAIL	G.P. Topping, Tippets, and Bronze Mallard
BODY	Rear – Golden Olive Seal's Fur
	Front – Orange Pig's Wool
RIB	Silver and Gold Twist
BODY HACKLE	Golden Olive Cock (on Orange body)
THROAT	Blue Jay
	Red Pheasant Breast
WINGS	Golden Pheasant Tippets
	Gallina
	G.P. Tail
	Green and Red Parrot
	Teal
	Peacock
	Bronze Mallard
HORNS	Blue Macaw

ROUGH CLARET (1)

TAG	Silver Wire and Orange Floss
TAIL	G.P. Crest and Tippets
BUTT	Black Ostrich Herl
BODY	Dark Claret Seal's Fur
BODY HACKLE	Claret Cock
THROAT	Blue Jay
WINGS	Toucan Breast
	G.P. Tippets
	G.P. Tail
	Teal
	Bronze Mallard over
HORNS	Blue Macaw

ROUGH CLARET (2)

TAG	Silver Wire
TAIL	G.P. Crest and Tippets
BODY	Claret Pig's Wool
HACKLES	1. Black Cock
	2. Claret Cock (wound together from mid-body)
SH. HACKLE	Golden Olive Cock
WINGS	Mixed
	Bronze Mallard over

SCARLET FLY

TAG	Silver Twist and Golden Floss
TAIL	G.P. Topping, Bustard, Mallard, and Tippets
BODY	Bright Scarlet Pig's Wool with Golden Olive Pig's Wool at the shoulder
RIB	Silver Twist
BODY HACKLE	Scarlet Cock
THROAT	Blue Jay
	Golden Pheasant Tippets
WINGS	Paired Jungle Cock, Topping over all
HORNS	Crimson Macaw

An old Co. Kerry pattern.

SECRET WEAPON

TAG	Silver Wire
TAIL HACKLE	Long Red G.P. Breast Feather
BODY	Rear – Yellow Floss Silk Ribbed with fine Oval Silver
VEILING	Cock-of-the-Rock, or Scarlet Ibis, above and below
CENTRE HACKLE	Badger Henny-cock (medium length)
BODY	Front – Black Floss Silk ribbed with medium Oval Silver
VEILING	As before
WINGS	Two Jungle Cock feathers back-to-back
FRONT HACKLE	Long Badger Henny-cock

A dressing by E. C. Heaney, a shrimp pattern for the North West.

SILVER BLUE

TAG	Silver Tinsel
TAIL	Golden Pheasant Topping
BODY	Flat Silver Tinsel
RIB	Oval Silver
HACKLE	Light Blue Cock
WINGS	Blue Peacock
	Teal over

SILVER CANARY

TAG	Silver Twist and Yellow Floss
TAIL	G.P. Crest, Tippets, Widgeon, and Chatterer
BUTT	Black Ostrich
BODY	Flat Silver
RIB	Oval Silver
BODY HACKLE	Canary Yellow Cock
SH. HACKLE	Indigo Blue Cock
WINGS	Golden Olive Mohair with G.P Topping over
SIDES	Jungle Cock
CHEEKS	Chatterer or Kingfisher

Also known as the Canary Silver.

SILVER CLARET

TAG	Silver Wire and Claret Floss
TAIL	G.P. Tippets, Teal, and Ibis
BODY	Flat Silver
RIB	Oval Silver
HACKLE	Dark Claret Cock
WINGS	Golden Pheasant Tippets Ibis (or Red Swan) Peacock Sword Teal Bronze Mallard over

Also known as the Silver Body.

SILVER DOCTOR (Hairwing)

TAG	Silver Wire
TAIL	Peacock Sword and G.P. Crest
BUTT	Bright Red Floss
BODY	Flat Silver
RIB	Fine Oval Silver
SH. HACKLES	1. Light Blue Cock 2. Guinea-fowl
WINGS	Brown Squirrel with fibres of Red, Yellow, and Blue Squirrel over

SKIN-THE-GOAT

TAG	Silver Wire and Yellow Floss
BUTT	Black Ostrich
BODY	Lilac Floss
RIB	Oval Silver Tinsel
HACKLE	Dirty Golden Olive and Dirty Teal (or Light Brown Mallard)
WINGS	Tippets, Teal and Mallard, G.P. Crest over
HORNS	Macaw (Green and Yellow)

SPADE GUINEA

TAG	Gold Tinsel and Blue Floss
TAIL	Golden Pheasant Topping
BUTT	Black Ostrich
BODY	Deep Plum-Red Mohair
RIB	Fine Gold Twist
BODY HACKLES	Rear – Blood-Red Cock
	Centre – Claret Cock
	Front – Golden Yellow Cock
THROAT	Blue Jay
WINGS	Golden Pheasant Tippets
	Peacock Sword
	Brown Turkey
	Blue, Green and Red Swan
	Bronze Mallard
	Topping over all
HORNS	Blue Macaw

An old Shannon pattern.

SPRING BLUE

TAG	Silver Wire and Yellow Floss
TAIL	G.P. Tippets and Crest
BUTT	Black Ostrich
BODY	Light Blue Pig's Wool or Seal's Fur
RIB	Oval Silver
BODY HACKLE	Light Blue Cock (from mid-body)
SH. HACKLE	Yellow Cock
WINGS	Golden Pheasant Tippets
	Golden Pheasant Tail
	Red and Yellow Swan
	Teal
	Bronze Mallard over
	Topping over all

TANDY

TAG	Silver and Claret Floss
TAIL	Golden Pheasant Tippets
JOINTED BODY	Rear – Yellow Floss
	Centre – Sky-Blue Seal's Fur
	Front – Silver Grey Seal's Fur
RIB	Silver Twist
BODY HACKLES	Yellow Cock (on Yellow Floss)
	Light Blue Cock (on Blue Fur)
	Grey Cock (on Grey Fur)
SH. HACKLE	Claret Cock
WINGS	Golden Pheasant Tippets
	Green Parrot
	Red and Blue Swan
	Golden Pheasant Tail
	Summer Duck
	Bronze Mallard over

THUNDER AND LIGHTNING (1)

TAG	Gold Wire and Yellow Floss
TAIL	Golden Pheasant Topping
BUTT	Black Ostrich Herl
BODY	Black Floss
RIB	Oval Gold
BODY HACKLE	Orange Cock (from mid-body)
THROAT	Blue Jay
WINGS	Bronze Mallard
SIDES	Jungle Cock

Golden Pheasant Topping over all

This is the present day dressing.

THUNDER AND LIGHTNING (2)

TAG	Silver Twist and Blue Floss
TAIL	Golden Pheasant Crest
BUTT	Black Ostrich
BODY	Black Floss
RIB	Silver Twist
BODY HACKLE	Blood-Red Cock
THROAT	Blue Jay
WINGS	Red Swan
	Golden Pheasant Tail
	Bronze Mallard over

An old dressing.

THUNDER AND LIGHTNING (3)

TAG	Silver Twist
TAIL	Golden Pheasant Crest
BUTT	Black Ostrich
BODY	Black Floss
RIB	Broad Silver Twist
BODY HACKLE	Canary Yellow Cock
THROAT	Blue Jay
WINGS	Toucan Breast
	Golden Pheasant Tail
	Bustard
	Bronze Mallard over
HEAD	Black Ostrich

Another dressing gives –

TAG	Gold Twist and Yellow Floss
REMAINDER	As above
WINGS	Bronze Mallard
SIDES	Jungle Cock
HORNS	Blue Macaw
	Topping over all.

WILKINSON

TAG	Finest Oval Silver and Fiery Brown Seal's Fur
TAIL	G.P. Tippets and/or Topping
BUTT	Scarlet Floss (or Fluorescent Wool)
BODY	Flat Silver
RIB	Oval Silver
HACKLES	1. Light Magenta Cock
	2. Light Blue Cock
	or
	1. Dark Magenta Cock
	2. Dark Rich Blue Cock
WINGS	Golden Pheasant Tippets
	Red, Blue, and Yellow Swan
	Golden Pheasant Tail
	Teal over
	Golden Pheasant Topping over all
SIDES	Jungle Cock
CHEEKS	Blue Chatterer or Kingfisher

Jay Wilkinson by substituting Blue Jay for the Light Blue Hackle.
Light Hackle Colour – Black Head
Dark Hackle Colour – Bright Red Head

WYE BUG (1)

TAG	Oval Silver
TAIL HACKLE	Long Red G.P. Breast
BODY	Rear – Orange Seal's Fur
RIB	Finest Oval Silver
VEILINGS	Indian Crow or Orange Swan
CENTRE HACKLE	Orange Cock
BODY	Front – Black Seal's Fur
RIB	Oval Silver
WINGS	Jungle Cock
SH. HACKLE	Orange Cock
FRONT HACKLE	Long Red Game Cock

A very popular Shrimp pattern.

WYE BUG (2)

Another dressing leaves the Orange Fur unribbed and has a Flat Silver Rib on the Black Fur. The centre hackle here is Orange or Furnace Cock (and if Orange may omit the Orange Shoulder Hackle).

WYE BUG (3)

As (1) but with Floss bodies and Orange ribbed Silver Wire, Black ribbed Oval silver.

YELLOW ANTHONY (1)

TAG	Silver Twist
TAIL	Golden Pheasant Topping
BUTT	Yellow Mohair
BODY	Bluish Silver-Grey Pig's Wool or Seal's Fur
RIB	Fine Silver Twist
BODY HACKLE	Silver Grey Dun Hackle
SH. HACKLE	Dirty Yellow Cock
WINGS	Peacock
	Brown Mallard
HORNS	Blue Macaw

A Francis Francis dressing for Co. Cork.

YELLOW ANTHONY (2)

TAG	Silver Twist and Yellow Floss
TAIL	G.P. Topping and Indian Crow
BODY	Grey Monkey Fur
RIB	Silver
BODY HACKLE	Grey Cock
SH. HACKLE	Bright Yellow
WINGS	Golden Pheasant Tippets
	Yellow and Red Swan
	Golden Pheasant Tail
	Wood-duck
	Bronze Mallard over
HORNS	Blue Macaw
	Optional – G.P. Topping over all

YELLOW ANTHONY (3)

TAG	Silver and Yellow Floss
TAIL	Golden Pheasant Crest
BUTT	Black Ostrich Herl
BODY	Light Grey Seal's Fur with Rich Gold Seal's Fur at shoulder
RIB	Silver
BODY HACKLE	Golden Yellow (over Gold Fur) to shoulder
WINGS	Golden Pheasant Tippets
	Red G.P. Tail Sword
	Red and Magenta Swan
	Golden Pheasant Tail
	Bustard
	Brown Mallard over

YELLOW GOLDFINCH (1)

TAG	Gold Twist and Yellow Floss
TAIL	G.P. Crest and Orange or Yellow Mohair
BODY	Yellow Mohair
RIB	Gold Twist
BODY HACKLE	Yellow Cock
SH. HACKLE	Yellow Cock
THROAT	Blue Jay
WINGS	Golden Pheasant Yellow Rump. Six G.P. Crests tied in so that the tips incline inward and cross each other
HEAD	Black Mohair

O'Gorman's old dressing

YELLOW GOLDFINCH (2)

TAG	Blue Floss
TAIL	Golden Pheasant Crest
BODY	Yellow Floss
RIB	Silver Twist
BODY HACKLE	Golden Olive Cock
THROAT	Blue Jay
WINGS	Six Golden Pheasant Crests
HORNS	Long Blue Macaw

YELLOW GOLDFINCH (3)

TAG	Gold Wire and Yellow Floss
TAIL	Golden Pheasant Topping
BODY	Yellow Floss
RIB	Oval Gold
BODY HACKLE	Yellow Cock
THROAT	Blue Jay
WINGS	Six G.P. Toppings
HORNS	Red Macaw

YELLOW GOSHAWK

TAG	Three turns Silver Twist and Claret Floss
TAIL	G.P. Topping and Kingfisher
BUTT	Black Ostrich
BODY	Orange-Yellow Floss
RIB	Silver
BODY HACKLE	Natural Red Cock
THROAT	Blue Jay
WING	Four or Five G.P. Toppings
CHEEKS	Wood-duck
HEAD	Black Ostrich

YELLOW PARSON

TAG	Oval Silver and Red and Floss
TAIL	G.P. Crest and Paired Jungle Cock
BUTT	Black Ostrich
BODY	Rear $^1/_3$ – Yellow Floss
	Front $^2/_3$– Green Peacock Sword Herl
RIB	Oval Silver
SH. HACKLE	Yellow Cock
THROAT	Long G.P. Topping lying back to cover hook point
WINGS	G.P. Toppings
SIDES	Jungle Cock

The present-day dressing by Michael Rogan.

YELLOW SILK

TAG	Oval Silver and Red Floss Silk
TAIL	G.P. Crest and Tippets, Teal, Red, Yellow and Blue Swan
BUTT	Black Ostrich Herl
BODY	Yellow Floss Silk
RIB	Gold & Silver Oval Tinsel
BODY HACKLE	Yellow Cock
TH. HACKLE	1. Yellow Cock
	2. Blue Jay
WINGS	Two Red Golden Pheasant Feathers with Jungle Cock Feather each side
	Bronze Mallard over
	Topping over all

RECOMMENDED BOOKS
FOR ALL FLY-TYERS

A. Courtney Williams, *A Dictionary of Trout Flies*, London (A. & C. Black), 1949.

John Veniard, *The Fly-dresser's Guide*, London (A. & C. Black), 1952

The above two works are most comprehensive and essential to the serious fly-dresser.

Joseph Adams, *The Angler's Guide to the Irish Fisheries*, London (Hutchinson), 1924.

William Blacker, *Blacker's Art of Flymaking* etc. London (privately printed) 1855.

C. John Goddard, *Trout Flies of Still Waters*, London (A. & C. Black), 1969.

C. John Goddard, *Trout Fly Recognition*, London (A. & C. Black), 1966.

Gregory Greendrake, *Angling Excursions*, 4th edition, London (Grant & Bolton), 1832.

T. J. Hanna, *Fly-fishing in Ireland*, London (H. F. & G. Witherby), 1933.

J. R. Harris, *An Angler's Entomology*, London (Collins), 1952; revised 1956, last reprint 1977.

E. C. Heaney, *Fly-fishing for Trout & Salmon on the Faughan*, Londonderry (privately printed), 1947.

T. R. Henn, *Practical Fly-tying*, London (A. & C. Black), 1950.

Michael Kennedy, *Trout Flies for Irish Waters*, Dublin (Inland Fisheries Trust), n.d. [c. 1961].

T. C. Kingsmill Moore, *A Man May Fish*, London (Herbert Jenkins) 1960; revised and enlarged Gerrards Cross (Colin Smythe), 1979.

Rev. H. Newland, *The Erne, its Legends and its Fly-fishing*, London (Chapman & Hall), 1851.

O'Gorman, *The Practice of Angling*, Dublin (Wm. Curry & Co.), 1845.

Overfield, Donald, *Famous Flies and their Originators*, London (A. & C. Black), 1972.

Frank Sawyer, *Nymphs and the Trout*, London (A. & C. Black), 1958

John Veniard, *A Further Guide to Fly-dressing*, London (A. & C. Black), 1964.

John Veniard, *Reservoir and Lake Flies*, London (A. & C. Black), 1970.

AN IRISH BLESSING

May the road rise to meet you,
the wind be always at your back,
and the sun shine warm upon your face.
May the rain fall soft upon your fields,
and until we meet again,
May God hold you in the palm of His hand.

INDEX TO FLY DRESSINGS

Patterns may be found in both TROUT *and* SALMON *sections*

TROUT

SALMON

THE BEGGAR'S BLESSING

May God bless you and
Send you plenty.
And may your giving hand
Never want.